Gift of
W. H. Smith

MY MEMORIES OF
EIGHTY YEARS

From a photograph, copyrighted by Underwood and Underwood

Chauncey M. Depew.

ON HIS 86TH BIRTHDAY

MY MEMORIES OF EIGHTY YEARS

BY
CHAUNCEY M. DEPEW

NEW YORK
CHARLES SCRIBNER'S SONS
1922

COPYRIGHT, 1921, 1922, BY
CHARLES SCRIBNER'S SONS

Printed in the United States of America

Published March, 1922

TO MY WIFE
MAY PALMER DEPEW
THIS BOOK GREW FROM HER
ENCOURAGEMENT

FOREWORD

For many years my friends have insisted upon my putting in permanent form the incidents in my life which have interested them. It has been my good fortune to take part in history-making meetings and to know more or less intimately people prominent in world affairs in many countries. Every one so situated has a flood of recollections which pour out when occasion stirs the memory. Often the listeners wish these transcribed for their own use.

My classmate at Yale in the class of 1856, John D. Champlin, a man of letters and an accomplished editor, rescued from my own scattered records and newspaper files material for eight volumes. My secretary has selected and compiled for publication two volumes since. These are principally speeches, addresses, and contributions which have appeared in public. Several writers, without my knowledge, have selected special matter from these volumes and made books.

Andrew D. White, Senator Hoar, and Senator Foraker, with whom I was associated for years, have published full and valuable autobiographies. I do not attempt anything so elaborate or complete. Never having kept a diary, I am dependent upon a good memory. I have discarded the stories which could not well be published until long after I have joined the majority.

I trust and earnestly hope there is nothing in these recollections which can offend anybody. It has been my object so to picture events and narrate stories as to illumine the periods through which I have passed for eighty-eight years, and the people whom I have known and mightily enjoyed.

C. M. D.

CONTENTS

		PAGE
I.	CHILDHOOD AND YOUTH	3
II.	IN PUBLIC LIFE	17
III.	ABRAHAM LINCOLN	52
IV.	GENERAL GRANT	67
V.	ROSCOE CONKLING	75
VI.	HORACE GREELEY	87
VII.	RUTHERFORD B. HAYES AND WILLIAM M. EVARTS	99
VIII.	GENERAL GARFIELD	107
IX.	CHESTER A. ARTHUR	116
X.	GROVER CLEVELAND	124
XI.	BENJAMIN HARRISON	129
XII.	JAMES G. BLAINE	141
XIII.	WILLIAM MCKINLEY	147
XIV.	THEODORE ROOSEVELT	158
XV.	UNITED STATES SENATE	175
XVI.	AMBASSADORS AND MINISTERS	191
XVII.	GOVERNORS OF NEW YORK STATE	209

CONTENTS

		PAGE
XVIII.	FIFTY-SIX YEARS WITH THE NEW YORK CENTRAL RAILROAD COMPANY	225
XIX.	RECOLLECTIONS FROM ABROAD	256
XX.	ORATORS AND CAMPAIGN SPEAKERS	313
XXI.	NATIONAL REPUBLICAN CONVENTIONS	339
XXII.	JOURNALISTS AND FINANCIERS	344
XXIII.	ACTORS AND MEN OF LETTERS	358
XXIV.	SOCIETIES AND PUBLIC BANQUETS	374
	INDEX	411

MY MEMORIES OF
EIGHTY YEARS

I
CHILDHOOD AND YOUTH

It has occurred to me that some reminiscences of a long life would be of interest to my family and friends.

My memory goes back for more than eighty years. I recall distinctly when about five years old my mother took me to the school of Mrs. Westbrook, wife of the well-known pastor of the Dutch Reformed church, who had a school in her house, within a few doors. The lady was a highly educated woman, and her husband, Doctor Westbrook, a man of letters as well as a preacher. He specialized in ancient history, and the interest he aroused in Roman and Greek culture and achievements has continued with me ever since.

The village of Peekskill at that time had between two and three thousand inhabitants. Its people were nearly all Revolutionary families who had settled there in colonial times. There had been very little immigration either from other States or abroad; acquaintance was universal, and in the activities of the churches there was general co-operation among the members. Church attendance was so unanimous that people, young or old, who failed to be in their accustomed places on Sunday felt the disapproval of the community.

Social activities of the village were very simple, but very delightful and healthful. There were no very rich nor very poor. Nearly every family owned its own house or was on the way to acquire one. Misfortune of any kind aroused common interest and sympathy. A helping hand of neighborliness was always extended to those in trouble or distress. Peekskill was a happy community and presented conditions of life and living of common interest, endeavor, and sympathy not possible in these days of restless crowds and fierce competition.

The Peekskill Academy was the dominant educational institution, and drew students not only from the village but from a distance. It fitted them for college, and I was a student there for about twelve years. The academy was a character-making institution, though it lacked the thoroughness of the New England preparatory schools. Its graduates entering into the professions or business had an unusual record of success in life. I do not mean that they accumulated great fortunes, but they acquired independence and were prominent and useful citizens in all localities where they settled.

I graduated from the Peekskill Academy in 1852. I find on the programme of the exercises of that day, which some old student preserved, that I was down for several original speeches, while the other boys had mainly recitations. Apparently my teachers had decided to develop any oratorical talent I might possess.

I entered Yale in 1852 and graduated in 1856. The college of that period was very primitive compared with the university to which it has grown. Our class of ninety-seven was regarded as unusually large. The classics and mathematics, Greek and Latin, were the dominant features of instruction. Athletics had not yet appeared, though rowing and boat-racing came in during my term. The outstanding feature of the institution was the literary societies: the Linonia and the Brothers of Unity. The debates at the weekly meetings were kept up and maintained upon a high and efficient plane. Both societies were practically deliberative bodies and discussed with vigor the current questions of the day. Under this training Yale sent out an unusual number of men who became eloquent preachers, distinguished physicians, and famous lawyers. While the majority of students now on leaving college enter business or professions like engineering, which is allied to business, at that time nearly every young man was destined for the ministry, law, or medicine. My own class furnished two of the nine judges of the Supreme Court of the United States, and a large majority of those who were admitted to the bar attained judicial honors. It is a singular commentary on the education of that time that the students who won the highest honors and carried off the college prizes, which could only be done by excelling in Latin, Greek, and mathematics, were far outstripped in after-life by their classmates who fell below their high standard of collegiate scholarship but were distinguished for an all-around interest in subjects not featured in the college curriculum.

My classmates, Justice David J. Brewer and Justice Henry Billings Brown, were both eminent members of the Supreme Court of the United States. Brewer was distinguished for the wide range of his learning and illuminating addresses on public occasions. He was bicentennial orator of the college and a most acceptable one. Wayne McVeagh, afterwards attorney-general of the United States, one of the leaders of the bar, also one of the most brilliant orators of his time, was in college with me, though not a classmate. Andrew D. White, whose genius, scholarship, and organization enabled Ezra Cornell to found Cornell University, was another of my classmates. He became one of the most famous of our diplomats and the author of many books of permanent value. My friendship with MacVeagh and White continued during their lives, that is, for nearly sixty years. MacVeagh was one of the readiest and most attractive of speakers I ever knew. He had a very sharp and caustic wit, which made him exceedingly popular as an after-dinner speaker and as a host in his own house. He made every evening when he entertained, for those who were fortunate enough to be his guests, an occasion memorable in their experience.

John Mason Brown, of Kentucky, became afterwards the leader of the bar in his State, and was about to receive from President Harrison an appointment as justice of the Supreme Court when he died suddenly. If he had been appointed it would have been a remarkable circumstance that three out of nine judges of the greatest of courts, an honor which is sought by every one of the hundreds of thousands of lawyers in the United States, should have been from the same college and the same class.

The faculty lingers in my memory, and I have the same reverence and affection for its members, though sixty-five years out of college, that I had the day I graduated. Our president, Theodore D. Woolsey, was a wonderful scholar and a most inspiring teacher. Yale has always been fortunate in her presidents, and peculiarly so in Professor Woolsey. He had personal distinction, and there was about him an air of authority and reserved power which awed the most radical and rebellious student, and at the same time he had the respect and affection of all. In his historical lectures he had a standard joke on the Chinese, the narration of which amused him the more with each repetition. It was that when a Chinese army was beleaguered and besieged in a fortress their provisions gave out and they decided to escape. They selected a very dark night, threw open the gates, and as they marched out each soldier carried a lighted lantern.

In the faculty were several professors of remarkable force and originality. The professor of Greek, Mr. Hadley, father of the distinguished ex-president of Yale, was more than his colleagues in the thought and talk of the undergraduates. His learning and pre-eminence in his department were universally admitted. He had a caustic wit and his sayings were the current talk of the campus. He maintained discipline, which was quite lax in those days, by the exercise of this ability. Some of the boys once drove a calf into the recitation-room. Professor Hadley quietly remarked: "You will take out that animal. We will get along to-day with our usual number." It is needless to say that no such experiment was ever repeated.

At one time there was brought up in the faculty meeting a report that one of the secret societies was about to bore an artesian well in the cellar of their club house. It was suggested that such an extraordinary expense should be prohibited. Professor Hadley closed the discussion and laughed out the subject by saying from what he knew of the society, if it would hold a few sessions over the place where the artesian well was projected, the boring would be accomplished without cost. The professor was a sympathetic and very wise adviser to the students. If any one was in trouble he would always go to him and give most helpful relief.

Professor Larned inspired among the students a discriminating taste for the best English literature and an ardent love for its classics. Professor Thacher was one of the most robust and vigorous thinkers and teachers of his period. He was a born leader of men, and generation after generation of students who graduated carried into after-life the effects of his teaching and personality. We all loved Professor Olmstead, though we were not vitally interested in his department of physics and biology. He was a purist in his department, and so confident of his principles that he thought it unnecessary to submit them to practical tests. One of the students, whose room was immediately over that of the professor, took up a plank from the flooring, and by boring a very small hole in the ceiling found that he could read the examination papers on the professor's desk. The information of this reaching the faculty, the professor was asked if he had examined the ceiling. He said that was unnecessary, because he had measured the distance between the ceiling and the surface of his desk and found that the line of vision connected so far above that nothing could be read on the desk.

Timothy Dwight, afterwards president, was then a tutor. Learning, common sense, magnetism, and all-around good-fellowship were wonderfully united in President Dwight. He was the most popular instructor and best loved by the boys. He had a remarkable talent for organization, which made him an ideal president. He possessed the rare faculty of commanding and convincing not only the students but his associates in the faculty and the members of the corporation when discussing and deciding upon business propositions and questions of policy.

The final examinations over, commencement day arrived. The literary exercises and the conferring of degrees took place in the old Center Church. I was one of the speakers and selected for my subject "The Hudson River and Its Traditions." I was saturated from early association and close investigation and reading with the crises of the Revolutionary War, which were successfully decided on the patriots' side on the banks of the Hudson. I lived near Washington Irving, and his works I knew by heart, especially the tales which gave to the Hudson a romance like the Rhine's. The subject was new for an academic stage, and the speech made a hit. Nevertheless, it was the saddest and most regretful day of my life when I left Yale.

My education, according to the standard of the time, was completed, and my diploma was its evidence. It has been a very interesting question with me how much the academy and the college contributed to that education. Their discipline was necessary and their training essential. Four years of association with the faculty, learned, finely equipped, and sympathetic, was a wonderful help. The free associations of the secret and debating societies, the campus, and the sports were invaluable, and the friendships formed with congenial spirits added immensely to the pleasures and compensations of a long life.

In connection with this I may add that, as it has been my lot in the peculiar position which I have occupied for more than half a century as counsel and adviser for a great corporation and its creators and the many successful men of business who have surrounded them, I have learned to know how men who have been denied in their youth the opportunities for education feel when they are in possession of fortunes, and the world seems at their feet. Then they painfully recognize their limitations, then they know their weakness, then they understand that there are things which money cannot buy, and that there are gratifications and triumphs which no fortune can secure. The one lament of all those men has been: "Oh, if I had been educated! I would sacrifice all that I have to obtain the opportunities of the college, to be able to sustain not only conversation and discussion with the educated men with whom I come in contact, but competent also to enjoy what I see is a delight to them beyond anything which I know."

But I recall gratefully other influences quite as important to one's education. My father was a typical business man, one of the pioneers of river transportation between our village and New York, and also a farmer and a merchant. He was a stern man devoted to his family, and, while a strict disciplinarian, very fond of his children.

My mother was a woman of unusual intellect bordering upon genius. There were no means of higher education at that period, but her father, who was an eminent lawyer, and her grandfather, a judge, finding her so receptive, educated her with the care that was given to boys who were intended for a professional life. She was well versed in the literature of the time of Queen Elizabeth and Queen Anne, and, with a retentive memory, knew by heart many of the English classics. She wrote well, but never for publication. Added to these accomplishments were rare good sense and prophetic vision. The foundation and much of the superstructure of all that I have and all that I am were her work. She was a rigid Calvinist, and one of her many lessons has been of inestimable comfort to me. Several times in my life I have met with heavy misfortunes and what seemed irreparable losses. I have returned home to find my mother with wise advice and suggestions ready to devote herself to the reconstruction of my fortune, and to brace me up. She always said what she thoroughly believed: "My son, this which you think so great a calamity is really divine discipline. The Lord has sent it to you for your own good, because in His infinite wisdom He saw that you needed it. I am absolutely certain that if you submit instead of repining and protesting, if you will ask with faith and proper spirit for guidance and help, they both will come to you and with greater blessings than you ever had before." That faith of my mother inspired and intensified my efforts and in every instance her predictions proved true.

Every community has a public-spirited citizen who unselfishly devotes himself or herself to the public good. That citizen of Peekskill in those early days was Doctor James Brewer. He had accumulated a modest competence sufficient for his simple needs as bachelor. He was either the promoter or among the leaders of all the movements for betterment of the town. He established a circulating library upon most liberal terms, and it became an educational institution of benefit. The books were admirably selected, and the doctor's advice to readers was always available. His taste ran to the English classics, and he had all the standard authors in poetry, history, fiction, and essay.

No pleasure derived in reading in after-years gave me such delight as the Waverley Novels. I think I read through that library and some of it several times over.

The excitement as the novels of Dickens and Thackeray began to appear equalled almost the enthusiasm of a political campaign. Each one of those authors had ardent admirers and partisans. The characters of Dickens became household companions. Every one was looking for the counterpart of Micawber or Sam Weller, Pecksniff or David Copperfield, and had little trouble in finding them either in the family circle or among the neighbors.

Dickens's lectures in New York, which consisted of readings from his novels, were an event which has rarely been duplicated for interest. With high dramatic ability he brought out before the audience the characters from his novels with whom all were familiar. Every one in the crowd had an idealistic picture in his mind of the actors of the story. It was curious to note that the presentation which the author gave coincided with the idea of the majority of his audience. I was fresh from the country but had with me that evening a rather ultra-fashionable young lady. She said she was not interested in the lecture because it represented the sort of people she did not know and never expected to meet; they were a very common lot. In her subsequent career in this country and abroad she had to her credit three matrimonial adventures and two divorces, but none of her husbands were of the common lot.

Speaking of Dickens, one picture remains indelibly pressed upon my memory. It was the banquet given him at which Horace Greeley presided. Everybody was as familiar with Mr. Pickwick and his portrait by Cruikshank in Dickens's works as with one's father. When Mr. Greeley arose to make the opening speech and introduce the guest of the evening, his likeness to this portrait of Pickwick was so remarkable that the whole audience, including Mr. Dickens, shouted their delight in greeting an old and well-beloved friend.

Another educational opportunity came in my way because one of my uncles was postmaster of the village. Through his post-office came several high-class magazines and foreign reviews. There was no rural delivery in those days, and the mail could only be had on personal application, and the result was that the subscribers of these periodicals frequently left them a long time before they were called for. I was an omnivorous reader of everything available, and as a result these publications, especially the foreign reviews, became a fascinating source of information and culture. They gave from the first minds of the century criticisms of current literature and expositions of political movements and public men which became of infinite value in after-years.

Another unincorporated and yet valuable school was the frequent sessions at the drug store of the elder statesmen of the village. On certain evenings these men, representing most of the activities of the village, would avail themselves of the hospitable chairs about the stove and discuss not only local matters but the general conditions of the country, some of them revolving about the constitutionality of various measures which had been proposed and enacted into laws. They nearly all related to slavery, the compromise measures, the introduction of slaves into new territories, the fugitive slave law, and were discussed with much intelligence and information. The boys heard them talked about in their homes and were eager listeners on the outskirts of this village congress. Such institutions are not possible except in the universal acquaintance, fellowship, and confidences of village and country life. They were the most important factors in forming that public opinion, especially among the young, which supported Mr. Lincoln in his successful efforts to save the Union at whatever cost.

A few days after returning home from Yale I entered the office of Edward Wells, a lawyer of the village, as a student. Mr. Wells had attained high rank in his profession, was a profound student of the law, and had a number of young men, fitting them for the bar under his direction.

I was admitted to the bar in 1858, and immediately opened an office in the village. My first client was a prosperous farmer who wanted an opinion on a rather complicated question. I prepared the case with great care. He asked me what my fee was, and I told him five dollars. He said: "A dollar and seventy-five is enough for a young lawyer like you." Subsequently he submitted the case to one of the most eminent lawyers in New York, who came to the same conclusion and charged him five hundred dollars. On account of this gentleman's national reputation the farmer thought that fee was very reasonable. In subsequent years I have received several very large retainers, but none of them gave so much satisfaction as that dollar and seventy-five cents, which I had actually earned after having been so long dependent on my father.

After some years of private practice Commodore Vanderbilt sent for me and offered the attorneyship for the New York and Harlem Railroad. I had just been nominated and confirmed United States minister to Japan. The appointment was a complete surprise to me, as I was not an applicant for any federal position. The salary was seven thousand five hundred dollars and an outfit of nine thousand. The commodore's offer of the attorneyship for the Harlem Railroad, which was his first venture in railroading, was far less than the salary as minister. When I said this to the commodore, he remarked: "Railroads are the career for a young man; there is nothing in politics. Don't be a damned fool." That decided me, and on the 1st of January, 1921, I rounded out fifty-five years in the railway service of this corporation and its allied lines.

Nothing has impressed me more than little things, and apparently immaterial ones, which have influenced the careers of many people. My father and his brothers, all active business men, were also deeply interested in politics, not on the practical side but in policies and governmental measures. They were uncompromising Democrats of the most conservative type; they believed that interference with slavery of any kind imperilled the union of the States, and that the union of the States was the sole salvation of the perpetuity of the republic and its liberties. I went to Yale saturated with these ideas. Yale was a favorite college for Southern people. There was a large element from the slaveholding States among the students. It was so considerable that these Southerners withdrew from the great debating societies of the college and formed a society of their own, which they called the Calliopean. Outside of these Southerners there were very few Democrats among the students, and I came very near being drawn into the Calliopean, but happily escaped.

The slavery question in all its phases of fugitive slave law and its enforcement, the extension of slavery into the new territories, or its prohibition, and of the abolition of the institution by purchase or confiscation were subjects of discussion on the campus, in the literary societies, and in frequent lectures in the halls in New

Haven by the most prominent and gifted speakers and advocates.

That was a period when even in the most liberal churches the pulpit was not permitted to preach politics, and slavery was pre-eminently politics. But according to an old New England custom, the pastor was given a free hand on Thanksgiving Day to unburden his mind of everything which had been bubbling and seething there for a year. One of the most eminent and eloquent of New England preachers was the Reverend Doctor Bacon, of Center Church, New Haven. His Thanksgiving sermon was an event eagerly anticipated by the whole college community. He was violently anti-slavery. His sermons were not only intently listened to but widely read, and their effect in promoting anti-slavery sentiment was very great.

The result of several years of these associations and discussions converted me, and I became a Republican on the principles enunciated in the first platform of the party in 1856. When I came home from Yale the situation in the family became very painful, because my father was an intense partisan. He had for his party both faith and love, and was shocked and grieved at his son's change of principles. He could not avoid constantly discussing the question, and was equally hurt either by opposition or silence.

II

IN PUBLIC LIFE

The campaign of 1856 created an excitement in our village which had never been known since the Revolutionary War. The old families who had been settled there since colonial days were mainly pro-slavery and Democratic, while the Republican party was recruited very largely from New England men and in a minority.

Several times in our national political campaigns there has been one orator who drew audiences and received public attention and reports in the newspapers beyond all other speakers. On the Democratic side during that period Horatio Seymour was pre-eminent. On the Republican side in the State of New York the attractive figure was George William Curtis. His books were very popular, his charming personality, the culture and the elevation of his speeches put him in a class by himself.

The Republicans of the village were highly elated when they had secured the promise of Mr. Curtis to speak at their most important mass meeting. The occasion drew together the largest audience the village had known, composed not only of residents but many from a distance. The committee of arrangements finally reported to the waiting audience that the last train had arrived, but Mr. Curtis had not come.

It suddenly occurred to the committee that it would be a good thing to call a young recruit from a well-known Democratic family and publicly commit him. First came the invitation, then the shouting, and when I arose they cried "platform," and I was escorted to the platform, but had no idea of making a speech. My experience for years at college and at home had saturated me with the questions at issue in all their aspects. From a full heart, and a sore one, I poured out a confession of faith. I thought I had spoken only a few minutes, but found afterwards that it was over an hour. The local committee wrote to the State committee about the meeting, and in a few days I received a letter from the chairman of the State committee inviting me to fill a series of engagements covering the whole State of New York.

The campaign of 1856 differed from all others in memory of men then living. The issues between the parties appealed on the Republican side to the young. There had grown up among the young voters an intense hostility to slavery. The moral force of the arguments against the institution captured them. They had no hostility to the South, nor to the Southern slaveholders; they regarded their position as an inheritance, and were willing to help on the lines of Mr. Lincoln's original idea of purchasing the slaves and freeing them. But the suggestion had no friends among the slaveholders. These young men believed that any extension or strengthening of the institution would be disastrous to the country. The threatened dissolution of the Union, secession, or rebellion did not frighten them.

Political conventions are the most interesting of popular gatherings. The members have been delegated by their fellow citizens to represent them, and they are above the average in intelligence, political information of conditions in the State and nation, as the convention represents the State or the republic. The belief that they are generally boss-governed is a mistake. The party leader, sometimes designated as boss, invariably consults with the strongest men there are in the convention before he arrives at a decision. He is generally successful, because he has so well prepared the way, and his own judgment is always modified and frequently changed in these conferences.

In 1858 I had the first sensation of the responsibility of public office. I was not an applicant for the place; in fact, knew nothing about it until I was elected a delegate to the Republican State convention from the third assembly district of Westchester County. The convention was held at Syracuse. The Westchester delegates arrived late at night or, rather, early in the morning, and we came to the hotel with large numbers of other delegates from different sections who had arrived on the same train. It was two o'clock, but the State leader, Thurlow Weed, was in the lobby of the hotel to greet the delegates. He said to me: "You are from Peekskill. With whom are you studying law?" I answered: "With Judge William Nelson." "Oh," he remarked, "I remember Judge Nelson well. He was very active in the campaign of 1828." It was a feat of memory to thus recall the usefulness of a local politician thirty years before. I noticed, as each delegate was introduced, that Mr. Weed had some neighborhood recollections of the man which put a tag on him.

The next day, as we met the leader, he recalled us by name, the places where we lived, and the districts represented. Mr. Blaine was the only other man I ever met or knew who possessed this extraordinary gift for party leadership.

There was a revolt in the convention among the young members, who had a candidate of their own. Mr.

Weed's candidate for governor was Edwin D. Morgan, a successful New York merchant, who had made a good record as a State senator. I remember one of Mr. Weed's arguments was that the Democrats were in power everywhere and could assess their office-holders, while the Republicans would have to rely for campaign funds upon voluntary contributions, which would come nowhere so freely as from Mr. Morgan and his friends. When the convention met Mr. Weed had won over a large majority of the delegates for his candidate. It was a triumph not only of his skill but of his magnetism, which were always successfully exerted upon a doubtful member.

I was elected to the assembly, the popular branch of the New York Legislature, in 1861. I was nominated during an absence from the State, without being a candidate or knowing of it until my return. Of course, I could expect nothing from my father, and my own earnings were not large, so I had to rely upon a personal canvass of a district which had been largely spoiled by rich candidates running against each other and spending large amounts of money. I made a hot canvass, speaking every day, and with an investment of less than one hundred dollars for travel and other expenses I was triumphantly elected.

By far the most interesting member of the legislature was the speaker, Henry J. Raymond. He was one of the most remarkable men I ever met. During the session I became intimate with him, and the better I knew him the more I became impressed with his genius, the variety of his attainments, the perfection of his equipment, and his ready command of all his powers and resources. Raymond was then editor of the *New York*

Times and contributed a leading article every day. He was the best debater we had and the most convincing. I have seen him often, when some other member was in the chair of the committee of the whole, and we were discussing a critical question, take his seat on the floor and commence writing an editorial. As the debate progressed, he would rise and participate. When he had made his point, which he always did with directness and lucidity, he would resume writing his editorial. The debate would usually end with Mr. Raymond carrying his point and also finishing his editorial, an example which seems to refute the statement of metaphysicians that two parts of the mind cannot work at the same time.

Two years afterwards, when I was secretary of state, I passed much of my time at Saratoga, because it was so near Albany. Mr. Raymond was also there writing the "Life of Abraham Lincoln." I breakfasted with him frequently and found that he had written for an hour or more before breakfast. He said to me in explanation that if one would take an hour before breakfast every morning and concentrate his mind upon his subject, he would soon fill a library.

Mr. Raymond had been as a young man a reporter in the United States Senate. He told me that, while at that time there was no system of shorthand or stenography, he had devised a crude one for himself, by which he could take down accurately any address of a deliberate speaker.

Daniel Webster, the most famous orator our country has ever produced, was very deliberate in his utterances. He soon discovered Raymond's ability, and for several years he always had Raymond with him, and once said to him: "Except for you, the world would have very few of my speeches. Your reports have preserved them."

Mr. Raymond told me this story of Mr. Webster's remarkable memory. Once he said to Mr. Webster: "You never use notes and apparently have made no preparation, yet you are the only speaker I report whose speeches are perfect in structure, language, and rhetoric. How is this possible?" Webster replied: "It is my memory. I can prepare a speech, revise and correct it in my memory, and then deliver the corrected speech exactly as finished." I have known most of the great orators of the world, but none had any approach to a faculty like this, though several could repeat after second reading the speech which they had prepared.

In 1862 I was candidate for re-election to the assembly. Political conditions had so changed that they were almost reversed. The enthusiasm of the war which had carried the Republicans into power the year before had been succeeded by general unrest. Our armies had been defeated, and industrial and commercial depression was general.

The leader of the Democratic party in the State was Dean Richmond. He was one of those original men of great brain-power, force, and character, knowledge of men, and executive ability, of which that period had a number. From the humblest beginning he had worked his way in politics to the leadership of his party, to the presidency of the greatest corporation in the State, the New York Central Railroad Company, and in his many and successful adventures had accumulated a fortune. His foresight was almost a gift of prophecy, and his judgment was rarely wrong. He believed that the disasters in the field and the bad times at home could be charged up to the Lincoln administration and lead to a Democratic victory. He also believed that there was only one man in the party whose leadership would surely win, and that man was Horatio Seymour. But Seymour had higher ambitions than the governorship of New York and was very reluctant to run. Nevertheless, he could not resist Richmond's insistence that he must sacrifice himself, if necessary, to save the party.

The Republicans nominated General James W. Wadsworth for governor. Wadsworth had enlisted at the beginning of the war and made a most brilliant record, both as a fighting soldier and administrator. The Republican party was sharply divided between radicals who insisted on immediate emancipation of the slaves, and conservatives who thought the time had not yet arrived for such a revolution. The radicals were led by Horace Greeley, and the conservatives by Thurlow Weed and Henry J. Raymond.

Horatio Seymour made a brilliant canvass. He had no equal in the State in either party in charm of personality and attractive oratory. He united his party and brought to its ranks all the elements of unrest and dissatisfaction with conditions, military and financial. While General Wadsworth was an ideal candidate, he failed to get the cordial and united support of his party. He represented its progressive tendencies as expressed and believed by President Lincoln, and was hostile to reaction. Under these conditions Governor Seymour carried the State.

The election had reversed the overwhelming Republican majority in the legislature of the year before by making the assembly a tie. I was re-elected, but by reduced majority. The assembly being a tie, it was several weeks before it could organize. I was the candidate in the caucus of the Republican members for speaker, but after the nomination one of the members, named Bemus, threatened to bolt and vote for the Democratic candidate unless his candidate, Sherwood, was made the nominee. So many believed that Bemus would carry out his threat, which would give the organization of the House to the Democrats by one majority, that I withdrew in favor of Sherwood. After voting hopelessly in a deadlock, day after day for a long period, a caucus of the Republican members was called, at which Sherwood withdrew, and on his motion I was nominated as the party candidate for speaker.

During the night a Democratic member, T. C. Callicot, of Kings County, came to my bedroom and said: "My ambition in life is to be speaker of the assembly. Under the law the legislature cannot elect the United States senator unless each House has first made a nomination, then the Senate and the House can go into joint convention, and a majority of that convention elect a senator. You Republicans have a majority in the Senate, so that if the House nominates, the legislature can go into joint convention and elect a Republican senator. As long as the House remains a tie this cannot be done. Now, what I propose is just this: Before we meet tomorrow morning, if you will call your members together and nominate me for speaker, the vote of your party and I voting for myself will elect me. Then I will agree to name General Dix, a Democrat, for United States senator, and if your people will all vote with me for him he will be the assembly nominee. The Senate has already nominated Governor Morgan. So the next day the legislature can go into joint convention and, having a Republican majority, elect Governor Morgan United States senator." I told Mr. Callicot that I would present the matter to my party associates.

In the early morning Saxton Smith and Colonel John Van Buren, two of the most eminent Democrats in the State and members of the legislature, came to me and said: "We know what Callicot has proposed. Now, if you will reject that proposition we will elect you speaker practically unanimously."

This assured my election for the speakership. I had a great ambition to be on that roll of honor, and as I would have been the youngest man ever elected to the position, my youth added to the distinction. On the other hand, the government at Washington needed an experienced senator of its own party, like Edwin D. Morgan, who had been one of the ablest and most efficient of war governors, both in furnishing troops and helping the credit of the country. I finally decided to surrender the speakership for myself to gain the senatorship for my party. I had difficulty in persuading my associates, but they finally agreed. Callicot was elected speaker and Edwin D. Morgan United States senator.

The event was so important and excited so much interest, both in the State and in the country, that representative men came to Albany in great numbers. The rejoicing and enthusiasm were intense at having secured so unexpectedly a United States Senator for the support of Mr. Lincoln's administration.

That night they all united in giving me a reception in the ballroom of the hotel. There was a flood of eulogistic and prophetic oratory. I was overwhelmed with every form of flattery and applause, for distinguished service to the party. By midnight I had been nominated and elected Governor of the State, and an hour later I was already a United States senator. Before the morning hour the presidency of the United States was impatiently waiting for the time when I would be old enough to be eligible. All this was soon forgotten. It is a common experience of the instability of promises and hopes which come from gratified and happy enthusiasts, and how soon they are dissipated like a dream! I have seen many such instances, and from this early experience deeply sympathize with the disillusioned hero.

The Democrats of the assembly and also of the State were determined that Mr. Callicot should not enjoy the speakership. They started investigations in the House and movements in the courts to prevent him from taking his seat. The result was that I became acting speaker and continued as such until Mr. Callicot had defeated his enemies and taken his place as speaker in the latter part of the session.

I was also chairman of the committee of ways and means and the leader of the House. The budget of my committee was larger than usual on account of the expenses of the war. It was about seven million dollars. It created much more excitement and general discussion than does the present budget of one hundred and forty millions. The reason is the difference in conditions and public necessities of the State of New York in the winter of 1863 and now. It is also partly accounted for by the fact that the expenses of the State had then to be met by a real-estate tax which affected everybody, while now an income tax has been adopted which is capable of unlimited expansion and invites limitless extravagance because of the comparatively few interested.

Eighteen hundred and sixty-three was an eventful year; the early part was full of gloom and unrest. Horatio Seymour, as governor, violently antagonized President Lincoln and his policies. Seymour was patriotic and very able, but he was so saturated with State rights and strict construction of the Constitution that it marred his judgment and clouded his usually clear vision. In the critical situation of the country Mr. Lincoln saw the necessity of support of the State of New York. The president said: "The governor has greater power just now for good than any other man in the country. He can wheel the Democratic party into line, put down the rebellion and preserve the government. Tell him from me that if he will render this service to his country, I shall cheerfully make way for him as my successor." To this message, sent through Thurlow Weed, Governor Seymour made no reply. He did not believe that the South could be defeated and the Union preserved.

Later President Lincoln sent a personal letter to the governor. It was a very human epistle. The president wrote: "You and I are substantially strangers, and I write this that we may become better acquainted. In the performance of duty the co-operation of your State is needed and is indispensable. This alone is sufficient reason why I should wish to be on a good understanding with you. Please write me at least as long a letter as this, of course saying in it just what you think fit."

Governor Seymour made no reply. He and the other Democratic leaders thought the president uncouth, unlettered, and very weak. The phrase "please write me at least as long a letter as this" produced an impression upon the scholarly, cultured, cautious, and diplomatic

Seymour which was most unfavorable to its author. Seymour acknowledged the receipt of the letter and promised to make a reply, but never did.

Seymour's resentment was raised to fever heat when General Burnside, in May, 1863, arrested Clement L. Vallandigham. The enemies of the war and peace at any price people, and those who were discouraged, called mass meetings all over the country to protest this arrest as an outrage. A mass meeting was called in Albany on the 16th of May. Erastus Corning, one of the most eminent Democrats in the State, presided.

I was in Albany at the time and learned this incident. One of Governor Seymour's intimate friends, his adviser and confidant in personal business affairs was Charles Cook, who had been comptroller of the State and a State senator. Cook was an active Republican, a very shrewd and able man. He called on the governor and tried to persuade him not to write a letter to the Vallandigham meeting, but if he felt he must say something, attend the meeting and make a speech. Cook said: "Governor, the country is going to sustain ultimately the arrest of Vallandigham. It will be proved that he is a traitor to the government and a very dangerous man to be at large. Whatever is said at the meeting will seriously injure the political future of the authors. If you write a letter it will be on record, so I beg you, if you must participate, attend the meeting and make a speech. A letter cannot be denied; it can always be claimed that a speech has been misreported."

The Governor wrote the letter, one of the most violent of his utterances, and it was used against him with fatal effect when he ran for governor, and also when a candidate for president.

On July 11th the draft began in New York City. It had been denounced as unconstitutional by every shade of opposition to Mr. Lincoln's administration and to the prosecution of the war. The attempt to enforce it led to one of the most serious riots in the history of the city, and the rage of the rioters was against the officers of the law, the headquarters of the draft authorities, and principally against the negroes. Every negro who was caught was hung or burned, and the negro orphan asylum was destroyed by fire. The governor did his best to stop the rioting. He issued a proclamation declaring the city in a state of insurrection, and commanded obedience to the law and the authorities.

In this incident again the governor permitted his opposition to the war to lead him into political indiscretion. He made a speech from the steps of the City Hall to the rioters. He began by addressing them as "My friends." The governor's object was to quiet the mob and send them to their homes. So instead of saying "fellow citizens" he used the fatal words "my friends." No two words were ever used against a public man with such fatal effect. Every newspaper opposed to the governor and every orator would describe the horrors, murders, and destruction of property by the mob and then say: "These are the people whom Governor Seymour in his speech from the steps of the City Hall addressed as 'my friends.'"

The Vallandigham letter and this single utterance did more harm to Governor Seymour's future ambitions than all his many eloquent speeches against Lincoln's administration and the conduct of the war.

The political situation, which had been so desperate for the national administration, changed rapidly for the better with the victory at Gettysburg, which forced General Lee out of Pennsylvania and back into Virginia, and also by General Grant's wonderful series of victories at Vicksburg and other places which liberated the Mississippi River.

Under these favorable conditions the Republicans entered upon the canvass in the fall of 1863 to reverse, if possible, the Democratic victory the year before. The Republican State ticket was:

Secretary of State	Chauncey M. Depew.
Comptroller	Lucius Robinson.
Canal Commissioner	Benjamin F. Bruce.
Treasurer	George W. Schuyler.
State Engineer	William B. Taylor.
Prison Inspector	James K. Bates.
Judge of the Court of Appeals	Henry S. Selden.
Attorney-General	John Cochran.

The canvass was one of the most interesting of political campaigns. The president was unusually active, and his series of letters were remarkable documents. He had the ear of the public; he commanded the front page of the press, and he defended his administration and its acts and replied to his enemies with skill, tact, and extreme moderation.

Public opinion was peculiar. Military disasters and increasing taxation had made the position of the administration very critical, but the victories which came during the summer changed the situation. I have never known in any canvass any one incident which had greater effect than Sheridan's victory in the Shenandoah Valley, and never an adventure which so captured the popular imagination as his ride from Washington to the front; his rallying the retreating and routed troops,

IN PUBLIC LIFE 31

reforming them and turning defeat into victory. The poem, "Sheridan's Ride," was recited in every audience, from every platform, and from the stage in many theatres and created the wildest enthusiasm.

My friend, Wayne MacVeagh, who was at Yale College with me, had succeeded as a radical leader in defeating his brother-in-law, Don Cameron, and getting control for the first time in a generation against the Cameron dynasty of the Republican State organization of Pennsylvania. He had nominated a radical ticket, with Andrew G. Curtin as a candidate for governor.

MacVeagh wrote to me, saying: "You are running at the head of the Republican ticket in New York. Your battle is to be won in Pennsylvania, and unless we succeed you cannot. Come over and help us."

I accepted the invitation and spent several most exciting and delightful weeks campaigning with Governor Curtin and his party. The meetings were phenomenal in the multitudes which attended and their interest in the speeches. I remember one dramatic occasion at the city of Reading. This was a Democratic stronghold; there was not a single Republican office-holder in the county. The only compensation for a Republican accepting a nomination and conducting a canvass, with its large expenses and certain defeat, was that for the rest of his life he was given as an evidence of honor the title of the office for which he ran, and so the county was full of "judges, Mr. District Attorneys, State Senators, and Congressmen" who had never been elected.

We arrived at Reading after midday. The leading street, a very broad one, was also on certain days the market-place. A friend of the governor, who had a handsome house on this street, had the whole party for luncheon. The luncheon was an elaborate banquet. Governor Curtin came to me and said: "You go out and entertain the crowd, which is getting very impatient, and in about twenty minutes I will send some one to relieve you." It was raining in torrents; the crowd shouted to me encouragingly: "Never mind the rain; we are used to that, but we never heard you." As I would try to stop they would shout: "Go ahead!" In the meantime the banquet had turned into a festive occasion, with toasts and speeches. I had been speaking over two hours before the governor and his party appeared. They had been dining, and the Eighteenth Amendment had not been dreamed of. I was drenched to the skin, but waited until the governor had delivered his twenty-minute speech; then, without stopping for the other orators, I went over to the house, stripped, dried myself, and went to bed.

Utterly exhausted with successive days and nights of this experience, I did not wake until about eight o'clock in the evening. Then I wandered out in the street, found the crowd still there, and the famous John W. Forney making a speech. They told me that he had been speaking for four hours, delivering an historical address, but had only reached the administration of General Jackson. I never knew how long he kept at it, but there was a tradition with our party that he was still speaking when the train left the next morning.

Governor Curtin was an ideal party leader and candidate. He was one of the handsomest men of his time, six feet four inches in height, perfectly proportioned and a superb figure. He never spoke over twenty minutes, but it was the talk in the familiar way of an expert to his neighbors. He had a cordial and captivating manner, which speedily made him the idol of the crowd and a most agreeable companion in social circles. When he was minister to Russia, the Czar, who was of the same height and build, was at once attracted to him, and he took a first place among the diplomats in influence.

When I returned to New York to enter upon my own canvass, the State and national committees imposed upon me a heavy burden. Speakers of State reputation were few, while the people were clamoring for meetings. Fortunately I had learned how to protect my voice. In the course of the campaign every one who spoke with me lost his voice and had to return home for treatment. When I was a student at Yale the professor in elocution was an eccentric old gentleman named North. The boys paid little attention to him and were disposed to ridicule his peculiarities. He saw that I was specially anxious to learn and said: "The principal thing about oratory is to use your diaphragm instead of your throat." His lesson on that subject has been of infinite benefit to me all my life.

The programme laid out called upon me to speak on an average between six and seven hours a day. The speeches were from ten to thirty minutes at different railway stations, and wound up with at least two meetings at some important towns in the evening, and each meeting demanded about an hour. These meetings were so arranged that they covered the whole State. It took about four weeks, but the result of the campaign, due to the efforts of the orators and other favorable conditions, ended in the reversal of the Democratic victory of the year before, a Republican majority of thirty thousand and the control of the legislature.

In 1864 the political conditions were very unfavorable for the Republican party, owing to the bitter hostility between the conservative and radical elements. Led by such distinguished men as Thurlow Weed and Henry J. Raymond, on the one side, and Horace Greeley, with an exceedingly capable body of earnest lieutenants on the other, the question of success or defeat depended upon the harmonizing of the two factions.

Without having been recognized by the politicians or press of the State, Reuben E. Fenton, who had been for ten years a congressman from the Chatauqua district, had developed in Congress remarkable ability as an organizer. He had succeeded in making Galusha A. Grow speaker of the House of Representatives, and had become a power in that body. He had behind him the earnest friendship and support of the New York delegation in the House of Representatives and had not incurred the enmity of either faction in his own State. His nomination saved the party in that campaign.

As an illustration how dangerous was the situation, though the soldiers' vote in the field was over one hundred thousand and almost unanimously for the Republican ticket, the presidential and gubernatorial candidates received less than eight thousand majority, the governor leading the president.

The re-election of Mr. Lincoln and the election of Reuben E. Fenton over Governor Seymour made our State solidly Republican, and Governor Fenton became at once both chief executive and party leader. He had every quality for political leadership, was a shrewd judge of character, and rarely made mistakes in the selection of his lieutenants. He was a master of all current political questions and in close touch with public opinion. My official relations with him as secretary of state became at once intimate and gratifying. It required in after-years all the masterful genius of Roscoe Conkling and the control of federal patronage granted to him by President Grant to break Fenton's hold upon his party.

Governor Fenton was blessed with a daughter of wonderful executive ability, singular charm, and knowledge of public affairs. She made the Executive Mansion in Albany one of the most charming and hospitable homes in the State. Its influence radiated everywhere, captured visitors, legislators, and judges, and was a powerful factor in the growing popularity and influence of the governor.

One of the most interesting of political gatherings was the Democratic convention, which met at Tredwell Hall in Albany in the fall of 1864, to select a successor to Governor Seymour. The governor had declared publicly that he was not a candidate, and that under no conditions would he accept a renomination. He said that his health was seriously impaired, and his private affairs had been neglected so long by his absorption in public duties that they were in an embarrassing condition and needed attention.

The leaders of the convention met in Dean Richmond's office and selected a candidate for governor and a full State ticket. When the convention met the next day I was invited to be present as a spectator. It was supposed by everybody that the proceedings would be very formal and brief, as the candidates and the platform had been agreed upon. The day was intensely hot, and most of the delegates discarded their coats, vests, and collars, especially those from New York City.

When the time came for the nomination, the platform was taken by one of the most plausible and smooth talkers I ever heard. He delivered a eulogy upon Governor Seymour and described in glowing terms the debt the party owed him for his wonderful public services, and the deep regret all must have that he felt it necessary to retire to private life. He continued by saying that he acquiesced in that decision, but felt it was due to a great patriot and the benefactor of the party that he should be tendered a renomination. Of course, they all knew it would be merely a compliment, as the governor's position had been emphatically stated by himself. So he moved that the governor be nominated by acclamation and a committee appointed to wait upon him at the Executive Mansion and ascertain his wishes.

When Mr. Richmond was informed of this action, he said it was all right but unnecessary, because the situation was too serious to indulge in compliments.

In an hour the delegation returned, and the chairman, who was the same gentleman who made the speech and the motion, stepped to the front of the platform to report. He said that the governor was very grateful for the confidence reposed in him by the convention, and especially for its approval of his official actions as governor of the State and the representative of his party at the national convention, that in his long and intense application to public duties he had impaired his health and greatly embarrassed his private affairs, but, but, he continued with emphasis . . . He never got any further. Senator Shafer, of Albany, who was unfriendly to the governor, jumped up and shouted: "Damn him, he has accepted!"

The convention, when finally brought to order, reaffirmed its complimentary nomination as a real one, with great enthusiasm and wild acclaim.

When the result was reported to Mr. Richmond at his office, I was told by one who was present that Richmond's picturesque vocabulary of indignation and denunciation was enriched to such a degree as to astonish and shock even the hardened Democrats who listened to the outburst.

A committee was appointed to wait on the governor and request him to appear before the convention. In a little while there stepped upon the platform the finest figure in the State or country. Horatio Seymour was not only a handsome man, with a highly intellectual and expressive face of mobile features, which added to the effect of his oratory, but he never appeared unless perfectly dressed and in the costume which was then universally regarded as the statesman's apparel. His patent-leather boots, his Prince Albert suit, his perfectly correct collar and tie were evidently new, and this was their first appearance. From head to foot he looked the aristocrat. In a few minutes he became the idol of that wild and overheated throng. His speech was a model of tact, diplomacy, and eloquence, with just that measure of restraint which increased the enthusiasm of the hearers. The convention, which had gathered for another purpose, another candidate, and a new policy, hailed with delight its old and splendid leader.

Commodore Vanderbilt had a great admiration for Dean Richmond. The commodore disliked boasters and braggarts intensely. Those who wished to gain his favor made the mistake, as a rule, of boasting about what they had done, and were generally met by the remark: "That amounts to nothing." Mr. Tillinghast, a western New York man and a friend of Richmond, was in the commodore's office one day, soon after Richmond died. Tillinghast was general superintendent of the New York Central and had been a sufferer from being stepped on by the commodore when he was lauding his own achievements and so took the opposite line of extreme moderation. The commodore asked Tillinghast, after praising Mr. Richmond very highly, "How much did he leave?" "Oh," said Tillinghast, "his estate is a great disappointment, and compared with what it was thought to be it is very little." "I am surprised," remarked the commodore, "but how much?" "Oh, between five or six millions," Tillinghast answered. For the first time in his life the commodore was thrown off his guard and said: "Tillinghast, if five or six millions of dollars is a disappointment, what do you expect in western New York?" At that time there were few men who were worth that amount of money.

Governor Seymour made a thorough canvass of the State, and I was appointed by our State committee to follow him. It was a singular experience to speak and reply to the candidate the day after his address. The local committee meets you with a very complete report of his speech. The trouble is that, except you are under great restraint, the urgency of the local committee and the inevitable temptations of the reply under such conditions, when your adversary is not present, will lead you to expressions and personalities which you deeply regret.

When the canvass was over and the governor was beaten, I feared that the pleasant relations which had existed between us were broken. But he was a thorough sportsman. He sent for and received me with the greatest cordiality, and invited me to spend a week-end with him at his home in Utica. There he was the most delightful of hosts and very interesting as a gentleman farmer. In the costume of a veteran agriculturist and in the farm wagon he drove me out mornings to his farm, which was so located that it could command a fine view of the Mohawk Valley. After the inspection of the stock, the crops, and buildings, the governor would spend the day discoursing eloquently and most optimistically upon the prosperity possible for the farmer. To his mind then the food of the future was to be cheese. There was more food value in cheese than in any known edible article, animal or vegetable. It could sustain life more agreeably and do more for longevity and health.

No one could have imagined, who did not know the governor and was privileged to listen to his seemingly most practical and highly imaginative discourse, that the speaker was one of the ablest party managers, shrewdest of politicians, and most eloquent advocates in the country, whose whole time and mind apparently were absorbed in the success of his party and the fruition of his own ambitions.

As we were returning home he said to me: "You have risen higher than any young man in the country of your age. You have a talent and taste for public life, but let me advise you to drop it and devote yourself to your profession. Public life is full of disappointments, has an unusual share of ingratitude, and its compensations are not equal to its failures. The country is full of men who have made brilliant careers in the public service and then been suddenly dropped and forgotten. The number of such men who have climbed the hill up State Street to the capitol in Albany, with the applause of admiring crowds whom none now can recall, would make a great army."

He continued by telling this story: "In the war of 1812 the governor and the legislature decided to bring from Canada to Albany the remains of a hero whose deeds had excited the admiration of the whole State. There was an imposing and continuous procession, with local celebrations all along the route, from the frontier to the capital. The ceremonies in Albany were attended by the governor, State officers, legislature, and judges, and the remains were buried in the capitol park. No monument was erected. The incident is entirely forgotten, no one remembers who the hero was, what were his deeds, nor the spot where he rests."

Years afterwards, when the State was building a new capitol and I was one of the commissioners, in excavating the grounds a skeleton was found. It was undoubtedly the forgotten hero of Governor Seymour's story.

When my term was about expiring with the year 1865 I decided to leave public life and resume the practice of my profession. I was at the crossroads of a political or a professional career. So, while there was a general assent to my renomination, I emphatically stated the conclusion at which I had arrived.

The Republican convention nominated for my successor as secretary of state General Francis C. Barlow, a very brilliant soldier in the Civil War. The Democratic convention adopted a patriotic platform of advanced and progressive views, and nominated at the head of their ticket for secretary of state General Henry W. Slocum. General Slocum had been a corps commander in General Sherman's army, and came out of the war among the first in reputation and achievement of the great commanders. It was a master stroke on the part

IN PUBLIC LIFE

of the Democratic leaders to place him at the head of their ticket. He was the greatest soldier of our State and very popular with the people. In addition to being a great commander, he had a charming personality, which fitted him for success in public life.

The Democrats also on the same ticket nominated for attorney-general John Van Buren. He was a son of President Van Buren and a man of genius. Although he was very erratic, his ability was so great that when serious he captured not only the attention but the judgment of people. He was an eloquent speaker and had a faculty of entrancing the crowd with his wit and of characterization of his opponent which was fatal. I have seen crowds, when he was elaborately explaining details necessary for the vindication of his position, or that of his party which did not interest them, to remain with close attention, hoping for what was certain to come, namely, one of those sallies of wit, which made a speech of Van Buren a memorable thing to have listened to.

Van Buren was noted for a reckless disregard of the confidences of private conversation. Once I was with him on the train for several hours, and in the intimacy which exists among political opponents who know and trust each other we exchanged views in regard to public measures and especially public men. I was very indiscreet in talking with him in my criticism of the leaders of my own party, and he equally frank and delightful in flaying alive the leaders of his party, especially Governor Seymour.

A few days afterwards he made a speech in which he detailed what I had said, causing me the greatest embarrassment and trouble. In retaliation I wrote a letter to the public, stating what he had said about Governor

Seymour. The Democratic ticket was beaten by fifteen thousand in a very heavy vote, and Van Buren always charged it to the resentment of Governor Seymour and his friends.

In our country public life is a most uncertain career for a young man. Its duties and activities remove him from his profession or business and impose habits of work and thought which unfit him for ordinary pursuits, especially if he remains long in public service. With a change of administration or of party popularity, he may be at any time dropped and left hopelessly stranded. On the other hand, if his party is in power he has in it a position of influence and popularity. He has a host of friends, with many people dependent upon him for their own places, and it is no easy thing for him to retire.

When I had decided not to remain any longer in public life and return home, the convention of my old district, which I had represented in the legislature, renominated me for the old position with such earnestness and affection that it was very difficult to refuse and to persuade them that it was absolutely necessary for me to resume actively my profession.

Our village of Peekskill, which has since grown into the largest village in the State, with many manufacturing and other interests, was then comparatively small. A large number of people gathered at the post-office every morning. On one occasion when I arrived I found them studying a large envelope addressed to me, which the postmaster had passed around. It was a letter from William H. Seward, secretary of state, announcing that the president had appointed me United States minister to Japan, and that the appointment had been sent to the Senate and confirmed by that body, and directing that I appear at the earliest possible moment at his office to receive instructions and go to my post. A few days afterwards I received a beautiful letter from Henry J. Raymond, then in Congress, urging my acceptance.

On arriving in Washington I went to see Mr. Seward, who said to me: "I have special reasons for securing your appointment from the president. He is rewarding friends of his by putting them in diplomatic positions for which they are wholly unfit. I regard the opening of Japan to commerce and our relations to that new and promising country so important, that I asked the privilege to select one whom I thought fitted for the position. Your youth, familiarity with public life, and ability seem to me ideal for this position, and I have no doubt you will accept."

I stated to him how necessary it was that after long neglect in public life of my private affairs I should return to my profession, if I was to make a career, but Mr. Seward brushed that aside by reciting his own success, notwithstanding his long service in our State and in Washington. "However," he continued, "I feared that this might be your attitude, so I have made an appointment for you to see Mr. Burlingame, who has been our minister to China, and is now here at the head of a mission from China to the different nations of the world."

Anson Burlingame's career had been most picturesque and had attracted the attention of not only the United States but of Europe. As a member of the House of Representatives he had accepted the challenge of a "fire-eater," who had sent it under the general view that no Northern man would fight. As minister to China he had so gained the confidence of the Chinese Government that he persuaded them to open diplomatic relations with the Western world, and at their request he had resigned his position from the United States and accepted the place of ambassador to the great powers, and was at the head of a large delegation, composed of the most important, influential, and representative mandarins of the old empire.

When I sent up my card to his room at the hotel his answer was: "Come up immediately." He was shaving and had on the minimum of clothes permissible to receive a visitor. He was expecting me and started in at once with an eloquent description of the attractions and importance of the mission to Japan. With the shaving brush in one hand and the razor in the other he delivered an oration. In order to emphasize it and have time to think and enforce a new idea, he would apply the brush and the razor vigorously, then pause and resume. I cannot remember his exact words, but have a keen recollection of the general trend of his argument.

He said: "I am surprised that a young man like you, unmarried and with no social obligations, should hesitate for a moment to accept this most important and attractive position. If you think these people are barbarians, I can assure you that they had a civilization and a highly developed literature when our forefathers were painted savages. The western nations of Europe, in order to secure advantages in this newly opened country for commerce, have sent their ablest representatives. You will meet there with the diplomats of all the great western nations, and your intimacy with them will be a university of the largest opportunity. You will come in contact with the best minds of Europe. You can make a great reputation in the keen rivalry of this situation by securing the best of the trade of Japan for your own country to its western coasts over the waters of the Pacific. You will be welcomed by the Japanese Government, and the minister of foreign affairs will assign you a palace to live in, with a garden attached so perfectly appointed and kept as to have been the envy of Shenstone. You will be attended by hundreds of beautiful and accomplished Japanese maidens."

When I repeated to a large body of waiting office-seekers who had assembled in my room what Mr. Burlingame had said, they all became applicants for the place.

There is no more striking evidence of the wonderful advance in every way of the Japanese Empire and its people than the conditions existing at that time and now. Then it took six months to reach Japan and a year for the round trip. Of course, there was no telegraphic or cable communication, and so it required a year for a message to be sent and answered. The Japanese army at that time was mostly clad in armor and its navy were junks.

In fifty years Japan has become one of the most advanced nations of the world. It has adopted and assimilated all that is best of Western civilization, and acquired in half a century what required Europe one thousand years to achieve. Its army is unexcelled in equipment and discipline, and its navy and mercantile marine are advancing rapidly to a foremost place. It demonstrated its prowess in the war with Russia, and its diplomacy and power in the recent war.

Japan has installed popular education, with common schools, academies, and universities, much on the American plan. It has adopted and installed every modern appliance developed by electricity—telegraph, cable, telephone, etc.

While I was greatly tempted to reverse my decision and go, my mother, who was in delicate health, felt that an absence so long and at such distance would be fatal, and so on her account I declined.

As I look back over the fifty years I can see plainly that four years, and probably eight, in that mission would have severed me entirely from all professional and business opportunities at home, and I might have of necessity become a place holder and a place seeker, with all its adventures and disappointments.

If I had seriously wanted an office and gone in pursuit of one, my pathway would have had the usual difficulties, but fickle fortune seemed determined to defeat my return to private life by tempting offers. The collectorship of the port of New York was vacant. It was a position of great political power because of its patronage. There being no civil service, the appointments were sufficiently numerous and important to largely control the party in the State of New York, and its political influence reached into other commonwealths. It was an office whose fees were enormous, and the emoluments far larger than those of any position in the country.

The party leaders had begun to doubt President Johnson, and they wanted in the collectorship a man in whom they had entire confidence, and so the governor and State officers, who were all Republicans, the Republican members of the legislature, the State committee, the two United States senators, and the Republican delegation of New York in the House of Representatives unanimously requested the president to appoint me.

President Johnson said to me: "No such recommendation and indorsement has ever been presented to me before." However, the breach between him and the party was widening, and he could not come to a decision.

One day he suddenly sent for Senator Morgan, Henry J. Raymond, Thurlow Weed, and the secretary of the treasury for a consultation. He said to them: "I have decided to appoint Mr. Depew." The appointment was made out by the secretary of the treasury, and the president instructed him to send it to the Senate the next morning. There was great rejoicing among the Republicans, as this seemed to indicate a favorable turn in the president's mind. Days and weeks passed, however, and when the veto of the Civil Rights Bill was overridden in the Senate and, with the help of the votes of the senators from New York, the breach between the president and his party became irreconcilable, the movement for his impeachment began, which ended in the most sensational and perilous trial in our political history.

On my way home to New York, after the vote of the New York senators had ended my hope for appointment, I had as a fellow traveller my friend, Professor Davies, from West Point. He was a brother of that eminent jurist, Henry E. Davies, a great lawyer and chief justice of our New York State Court of Appeals. Professor Davies said to me: "I think I must tell you why your nomination for collector was not sent to the Senate. I was in Washington to persuade the president, with whom I am quite intimate, to make another appointment. I was calling on Secretary Hugh McCulloch and his family in the evening of the day when the conference decided to appoint you. Secretary McCulloch said to me: 'The contest over the collectorship of the port of New York is settled, and Chauncey Depew's name will be sent to the Senate to-morrow morning.' I was at the White House," continued the professor, "the next morning before breakfast. The president received me at once because I said my mission was urgent and personal. I told him what the secretary of the treasury had told me and said: 'You are making a fatal mistake. You are going to break with your party and to have a party of your own. The collectorship of the port of New York is the key to your success. Depew is very capable and a partisan of his party. If you have any doubt, I beg of you to withhold the appointment until the question comes up in the Senate of sustaining or overriding of the veto of the Civil Rights Bill. The votes of the two New York senators will decide whether they are your friends or not.' The president thought that was reasonable, and you know the result."

There was at least one satisfaction in the professor's amazingly frank revelation: it removed all doubt why I had lost a great office and, for my age and circumstances, a large fortune.

President Andrew Johnson differed radically from any President of the United States whom it has been my good fortune to know. This refers to all from and including Mr. Lincoln to Mr. Harding. A great deal must be forgiven and a great deal taken by way of explanation when we consider his early environment and opportunities.

In the interviews I had with him he impressed me as a man of vigorous mentality, of obstinate wilfulness, and overwhelming confidence in his own judgment and the courage of his convictions. His weakness was alcoholism. He made a fearful exhibition of himself at the time of his inauguration and during the presidency, and especially during his famous trip "around the circle" he was in a bad way.

He was of humble origin and, in fact, very poor. It is said of him that he could neither read nor write until his wife taught him. He made a great career both as a member of the House of Representatives and a senator, and was of unquestionable influence in each branch. With reckless disregard for his life, he kept east Tennessee in the Union during the Civil War.

General Grant told me a story of his own experience with him. Johnson, he said, had always been treated with such contempt and ignored socially by the members of the old families and slave aristocracy of the South that his resentment against them was vindictive, and so after the surrender at Appomattox he was constantly proclaiming "Treason is odious and must be punished." He also wanted and, in fact, insisted upon ignoring Grant's parole to the Confederate officers, in order that they might be tried for treason. On this question of maintaining his parole and his military honor General Grant was inflexible, and said he would appeal not only to Congress but to the country.

One day a delegation, consisting of the most eminent, politically, socially, and in family descent, of the Southern leaders, went to the White House. They said: "Mr. President, we have never recognized you, as you belong to an entirely different class from ourselves, but it is the rule of all countries and in all ages that supreme power vested in the individual raises him, no matter what his origin, to supreme leadership. You are now President of the United States, and by virtue of your office our leader, and we recognize you as such." Then followed attention from these people whom he admired and envied, as well as hated, of hospitality and deference, of which they were past masters. It captivated him and changed his whole attitude towards them.

He sent for General Grant and said to him: "The war is over and there should be forgiveness and reconciliation. I propose to call upon all of the States recently in rebellion to send to Washington their United States senators and members of the House, the same as they did before the war. If the present Congress will not admit them, a Congress can be formed of these Southern senators and members of the House and of such Northern senators and representatives as will believe that I am right and acting under the Constitution. As President of the United States, I will recognize that Congress and communicate with them as such. As general of the army I want your support." General Grant replied: "That will create civil war, because the North will undoubtedly recognize the Congress as it now exists, and that Congress will assert itself in every way possible." "In that case," said the president, "I want the army to support the constitutional Congress which I am recognizing." General Grant said: "On the contrary, so far as my authority goes, the army will support the Congress as it is now and disperse the other." President Johnson then ordered General Grant to Mexico on a mission, and as he had no power to send a general of the army out of the United States, Grant refused to go.

Shortly afterwards Grant received a very confidential communication from General Sherman, stating that he had been ordered to Washington to take command of the army, and wanted to know what it meant. General Grant explained the situation, whereupon General Sherman announced to the president that he would take exactly the same position as General Grant had. The president then dropped the whole subject.

III

ABRAHAM LINCOLN

The secretaryship of the State of New York is a very delightful office. Its varied duties are agreeable, and the incumbent is brought in close contact with the State administration, the legislature, and the people.

We had in the secretary of state's office at the time I held the office, about fifty-eight years ago, very interesting archives. The office had been the repository of these documents since the organization of the government. Many years afterwards they were removed to the State Library. Among these documents were ten volumes of autograph letters from General Washington to Governor Clinton and others, covering the campaign on the Hudson in the effort by the enemy to capture West Point, the treason of Arnold, and nearly the whole of the Revolutionary War. In the course of years before these papers were removed to the State Library, a large part of them disappeared. It was not the fault of the administration succeeding me, but it was because the legislature, in its effort to economize, refused to make appropriation for the proper care of these invaluable historic papers. Most of Washington's letters were written entirely in his own hand, and one wonders at the phenomenal industry which enabled him to do so much writing while continuously and laboriously engaged in active campaigning.

In view of the approaching presidential election, the

legislature passed a law, which was signed by the governor, providing machinery for the soldiers' vote. New York had at that time between three and four hundred thousand soldiers in the field, who were scattered in companies, regiments, brigades, and divisions all over the South. This law made it the duty of the secretary of state to provide ballots, to see that they reached every unit of a company, to gather the votes and transmit them to the home of each soldier. The State government had no machinery by which this work could be done. I applied to the express companies, but all refused on the ground that they were not equipped. I then sent for old John Butterfield, who was the founder of the express business but had retired and was living on his farm near Utica. He was intensely patriotic and ashamed of the lack of enterprise shown by the express companies. He said to me: "If they cannot do this work they ought to retire." He at once organized what was practically an express company, taking in all those in existence and adding many new features for the sole purpose of distributing the ballots and gathering the soldiers' votes. It was a gigantic task and successfully executed by this patriotic old gentleman.

Of course, the first thing was to find out where the New York troops were, and for that purpose I went to Washington, remaining there for several months before the War Department would give me the information. The secretary of war was Edwin M. Stanton. It was perhaps fortunate that the secretary of war should not only possess extraordinary executive ability, but be also practically devoid of human weakness; that he should be a rigid disciplinarian and administer justice without mercy. It was thought at the time that these qualities were necessary to counteract, as far as possible, the tender-heartedness of President Lincoln. If the boy condemned to be shot, or his mother or father, could reach the president in time, he was never executed. The military authorities thought that this was a mistaken charity and weakened discipline. I was at a dinner after the war with a number of generals who had been in command of armies. The question was asked one of the most famous of these generals: "How did you carry out the sentences of your courts martial and escape Lincoln's pardons?" The grim old warrior answered: "I shot them first."

I took my weary way every day to the War Department, but could get no results. The interviews were brief and disagreeable and the secretary of war very brusque. The time was getting short. I said to the secretary: "If the ballots are to be distributed in time, I must have information at once." He very angrily refused and said: "New York troops are in every army, all over the enemy's territory. To state their location would be to give invaluable information to the enemy. How do I know if that information would be so safeguarded as not to get out?"

As I was walking down the long corridor, which was full of hurrying officers and soldiers returning from the field or departing for it, I met Elihu B. Washburne, who was a congressman from Illinois and an intimate friend of the president. He stopped me and said:

"Hello, Mr. Secretary, you seem very much troubled. Can I help you?" I told him my story.

"What are you going to do?" he asked. I answered: "To protect myself I must report to the people of New York that the provision for the soldiers' voting cannot be carried out because the administration refuses to give information where the New York soldiers are located."

"Why," said Mr. Washburne, "that would beat Mr. Lincoln. You don't know him. While he is a great statesman, he is also the keenest of politicians alive. If it could be done in no other way, the president would take a carpet-bag and go around and collect those votes himself. You remain here until you hear from me. I will go at once and see the president."

In about an hour a staff officer stepped up to me and asked: "Are you the secretary of state of New York?" I answered "Yes." "The secretary of war wishes to see you at once," he said. I found the secretary most cordial and charming.

"Mr. Secretary, what do you desire?" he asked. I stated the case as I had many times before, and he gave a peremptory order to one of his staff that I should receive the documents in time for me to leave Washington on the midnight train.

The magical transformation was the result of a personal visit of President Lincoln to the secretary of war. Mr. Lincoln carried the State of New York by a majority of only 6,749, and it was a soldiers' vote that gave him the Empire State.

The compensations of my long delay in Washington trying to move the War Department were the opportunity it gave me to see Mr. Lincoln, to meet the members of the Cabinet, to become intimate with the New York delegation in Congress, and to hear the wonderful adventures and stories so numerous in Washington.

The White House of that time had no executive offices as now, and the machinery for executive business was very primitive. The east half of the second story had one large reception-room, in which the president could always be found, and a few rooms adjoining for his secretaries and clerks. The president had very little protection or seclusion. In the reception-room, which was always crowded at certain hours, could be found members of Congress, office-seekers, and an anxious company of fathers and mothers seeking pardons for their sons condemned for military offenses, or asking permission to go to the front, where a soldier boy was wounded or sick. Every one wanted something and wanted it very bad. The patient president, wearied as he was with cares of state, with the situation on several hostile fronts, with the exigencies in Congress and jealousies in his Cabinet, patiently and sympathetically listened to these tales of want and woe. My position was unique. I was the only one in Washington who personally did not want anything, my mission being purely in the public interest.

I was a devoted follower of Mr. Seward, the secretary of state, and through the intimacies with officers in his department I learned from day to day the troubles in the Cabinet, so graphically described in the diary of the secretary of the navy Gideon Welles.

The antagonism between Mr. Seward and Mr. Chase, the secretary of the treasury, though rarely breaking out in the open, was nevertheless acute. Mr. Seward was devoted to the president and made every possible effort to secure his renomination and election. Mr. Chase was doing his best to prevent Mr. Lincoln's renomination and secure it for himself.

No president ever had a Cabinet of which the members were so independent, had so large individual followings, and were so inharmonious. The president's sole ambition was to secure the ablest men in the country for the departments which he assigned to them without regard to their loyalty to himself. One of Mr. Seward's secretaries would frequently report to me the acts of disloyalty or personal hostility on the part of Mr. Chase with the lament: "The old man—meaning Lincoln—knows all about it and will not do a thing."

I had a long and memorable interview with the president. As I stepped from the crowd in his reception-room, he said to me: "What do you want?" I answered: "Nothing, Mr. President, I only came to pay my respects and bid you good-by, as I am leaving Washington." "It is such a luxury," he then remarked, "to find a man who does not want anything. I wish you would wait until I get rid of this crowd."

When we were alone he threw himself wearily on a lounge and was evidently greatly exhausted. Then he indulged, rocking backward and forward, in a reminiscent review of different crises in his administration, and how he had met them. In nearly every instance he had carried his point, and either captured or beaten his adversaries by a story so apt, so on all fours, and such complete answers that the controversy was over. I remember eleven of these stories, each of which was a victory.

In regard to this story-telling, he said: "I am accused of telling a great many stories. They say that it lowers the dignity of the presidential office, but I have found that plain people (repeating with emphasis plain people), take them as you find them, are more easily influenced by a broad and humorous illustration than in any other way, and what the hypercritical few may think, I don't care."

In speaking Mr. Lincoln had a peculiar cadence in his

voice, caused by laying emphasis upon the key-word of the sentence. In answer to the question how he knew so many anecdotes, he answered: "I never invented a story, but I have a good memory and, I think, tell one tolerably well. My early life was passed among pioneers who had the courage and enterprise to break away from civilization and settle in the wilderness. The things which happened to these original people and among themselves in their primitive conditions were far more dramatic than anything invented by the professional story-tellers. For many years I travelled the circuit as a lawyer, and usually there was only one hotel in the county towns where court was held. The judge, the grand and petit juries, the lawyers, the clients, and witnesses would pass the night telling exciting or amusing occurrences, and these were of infinite variety and interest." He was always eager for a new story to add to his magazine of ammunition and weapons.

One night when there was a reception at the executive mansion Rufus C. Andrews, surveyor of the port of New York, and I went there together. Andrews was a good lawyer and had been a correspondent in New York of Mr. Lincoln, while he was active at the bar in Illinois. He was a confidential adviser of the president on New York matters and frequently at the executive mansion. As the procession moved past the president he stopped Andrews and, leaning over, spoke very confidentially to him. The conversation delayed the procession for some time. When Andrews and I returned to the hotel, our rooms were crowded with newspaper men and politicians wanting to know what the confidential conversation was about. Andrews made a great mystery of it and so did the press. He explained to me when we were alone that during his visit to the president the night before he told the president a new story. The president delayed him at the reception, saying: "Andrews, I forgot the point of that story you told me last night; repeat it now."

While Mr. Lincoln had the most logical of minds and his letters and speeches on political controversies were the most convincing of any statesman of his period, he rarely would enter into a long discussion in conversation; he either would end the argument by an apt story or illustration enforcing his ideas.

John Ganson, of Buffalo, was the leader of the bar in western New York. Though elected to the House of Representatives as a Democrat, he supported the war measures of the administration. He was a gentleman of the old school, of great dignity, and always immaculately dressed. He was totally bald and his face also devoid of hair. It was a gloomy period of the war and the reports from the front very discouraging. Congressman Ganson felt it his duty to see the president about the state of the country. He made a formal call and said to Mr. Lincoln: "Though I am a Democrat, I imperil my political future by supporting your war measures. I can understand that secrecy may be necessary in military operations, but I think I am entitled to know the exact conditions, good or bad, at the front."

Mr. Lincoln looked at him earnestly for a minute and then said: "Ganson, how clean you shave!" That ended the interview.

The first national convention I ever attended was held in Baltimore in 1864, when Mr. Lincoln was renominated. I have since been four times a delegate-at-large, representing the whole State, and many times a delegate representing a congressional district. Judge

W. H. Robertson, of Westchester County, and I went to the convention together. We thought we would go by sea, but our ship had a collision, and we were rescued by a pilot boat. Returning to New York, we decided to accept the security of the railroad. Judge Robertson was one of the shrewdest and ablest of the Republican politicians in the State of New York. He had been repeatedly elected county judge, State senator, and member of Congress, and always overcoming a hostile Democratic majority.

We went to Washington to see Mr. Seward first, had an interview with him at his office, and dined with him in the evening. To dine with Secretary Seward was an event which no one, and especially a young politician, ever forgot. He was the most charming of hosts and his conversation a liberal education.

There was no division as to the renomination of Mr. Lincoln, but it was generally conceded that the vice-president should be a war Democrat. The candidacy of Daniel S. Dickinson, of New York, had been so ably managed that he was far and away the favorite. He had been all his life, up to the breaking out of the Civil War, one of the most pronounced extreme and radical Democrats in the State of New York. Mr. Seward took Judge Robertson and me into his confidence. He was hostile to the nomination of Mr. Dickinson, and said that the situation demanded the nomination for vice-president of a representative from the border States, whose loyalty had been demonstrated during the war. He eulogized Andrew Johnson, of Tennessee, and gave a glowing description of the courage and patriotism with which Johnson, at the risk of his life, had advocated the cause of the Union and kept his State partially loyal.

He said to us: "You can quote me to the delegates, and they will believe I express the opinion of the president. While the president wishes to take no part in the nomination for vice-president, yet he favors Mr. Johnson."

When we arrived at the convention this interview with Mr. Seward made us a centre of absorbing interest and at once changed the current of opinion, which before that had been almost unanimously for Mr. Dickinson. It was finally left to the New York delegation.

The meeting of the delegates from New York was a stormy one and lasted until nearly morning. Mr. Dickinson had many warm friends, especially among those of previous democratic affiliation, and the State pride to have a vice-president was in his favor. Upon the final vote Andrew Johnson had one majority. The decision of New York was accepted by the convention and he was nominated for vice-president.

This is an instance of which I have met many in my life, where the course of history was changed on a very narrow margin. Political histories and the newspapers' discussions of the time assigned the success of Mr. Johnson to the efforts of several well-known delegates, but really it was largely if not wholly due to the message of Mr. Seward, which was carried by Judge Robertson and myself to the delegates.

The year of 1864 was full of changes of popular sentiment and surprises. The North had become very tired of the war. The people wanted peace, and peace at almost any price. Jacob Thompson and Clement C. Clay, ex-United States senators from the South, appeared at Niagara Falls, on the Canadian side, and either they or their friends gave out that they were there to treat for peace. In reference to them Mr. Lincoln said to me: "This effort was to inflame the peace sentiment of the North, to embarrass the administration, and to demoralize the army, and in a way it was successful. Mr. Greeley was hammering at me to take action for peace, and said that unless I met these men every drop of blood that was shed and every dollar that was spent I would be responsible for, that it would be a blot upon my conscience and soul. I wrote a letter to Mr. Greeley and said to him that those two ex-United States senators were Whigs and old friends of his, personally and politically, and that I desired him to go to Niagara Falls and find out confidentially what their credentials were and let me know."

The president stated that instead of Mr. Greeley doing it that way, he went there as an ambassador, and with an array of reporters established himself on the American side and opened negotiations with these two alleged envoys across the bridge. Continuing, Mr. Lincoln said: "I had reason to believe from confidential information which I had received from a man I trusted and who had interviewed Jefferson Davis, the president of the Confederacy, that these envoys were without authority, because President Davis had said to this friend of mine and of his that he would treat on no terms whatever but on absolute recognition of the independence of the Southern Confederacy. The attention of the whole country and of the army centred on these negotiations at Niagara Falls, and to stop the harm they were doing I recalled Mr. Greeley and issued my proclamation 'To Whom It May Concern,' in which I stated if there was anybody or any delegation at Niagara Falls, or anywhere else, authorized to represent the Southern Confederacy and to treat for peace, they had free conduct and safety to

Washington and return. Of course, they never came, because their mission was a subterfuge. But they made Greeley believe in them, and the result is that he is still attacking me for needlessly prolonging the war for purposes of my own."

At a Cabinet meeting one of the members said to Mr. Lincoln: "Mr. President, why don't you write a letter to the public stating these facts, and that will end Mr. Greeley's attacks?" The president answered: "Mr. Greeley owns a daily newspaper, a very widely circulated and influential one. I have no newspaper. The press of the country would print my letter, and so would the *New York Tribune.* In a little while the public would forget all about it, and then Mr. Greeley would begin to prove from my own letter that he was right, and I, of course, would be helpless to reply." He brought the Cabinet around to unanimous agreement with him by telling one of his characteristic stories.

This affair and the delays in the prosecution of the war had created a sentiment early in 1864 that the reelection of Mr. Lincoln was impossible. The leaders of both the conservative and the radical elements in the Republican party, Mr. Weed, on the one hand, and Mr. Greeley, on the other, frankly told the president that he could not be re-elected, and his intimate friend, Congressman Elihu B. Washburne, after a canvass of the country, gave him the same information.

Then came the spectacular victory of Farragut at Mobile and the triumphant march of Sherman through Georgia, and the sentiment of the country entirely changed. There was an active movement on foot in the interest of the secretary of the treasury, Chase, and fostered by him, to hold an independent convention before the regular Republican convention as a protest against the renomination of Mr. Lincoln. It was supported by some of the most eminent and powerful members of the party, who threw into the effort their means and influence. After these victories the effort was abandoned and Mr. Lincoln was nominated by acclamation. I recall as one of the excitements and pleasures of a lifetime the enthusiastic confidence of that convention when they acclaimed Lincoln their nominee.

Governor Seymour, who was the idol of his party, headed the New York delegation to the national Democratic convention to nominate the president, and his journey to that convention was a triumphal march. There is no doubt that at the time he had with him not only the enthusiastic support of his own party but the confidence of the advocates of peace. His own nomination and election seemed inevitable. However, in deference to the war sentiment, General McClellan was nominated instead, and here occurred one of those little things which so often in our country have turned the tide.

The platform committee, and the convention afterwards, permitted to go into the platform a phrase proposed by Clement C. Vallandigham, of Ohio, the phrase being, "The war is a failure." Soon after the adjournment of the convention, to the victories of Farragut and Sherman was added the spectacular campaign and victory of Sheridan in the Valley of Shenandoah. The campaign at once took on a new phase. It was the opportunity for the orator.

It is difficult now to recreate the scenes of that campaign. The people had been greatly disheartened. Every family was in bereavement, with a son lost and others still in the service. Taxes were onerous and economic and business conditions very bad. Then came this reaction, which seemed to promise an early victory for the Union. The orator naturally picked up the phrase, "The war is a failure"; then he pictured Farragut tied to the shrouds of his flag-ship; then he portrayed Grant's victories in the Mississippi campaign, Hooker's "battle above the clouds," the advance of the Army of Cumberland; then he enthusiastically described Sheridan leaving the War Department hearing of the battle in Shenandoah Valley, speeding on and rallying his defeated troops, reforming and leading them to victory, and finished with reciting some of the stirring war poems.

Mr. Lincoln's election under the conditions and circumstances was probably more due to that unfortunate phrase in the Democratic platform than to any other cause.

The tragedy of the assassination of Mr. Lincoln was followed by the most pathetic incident of American life —his funeral. After the ceremony at Washington the funeral train stopped at Philadelphia, New York, and Albany. In each of these cities was an opportunity for the people to view the remains.

I had charge in my official capacity as secretary of state of the train after it left Albany. It was late in the evening when we started, and the train was running all night through central and western New York. Its schedule was well known along the route. Wherever the highway crossed the railway track the whole population of the neighborhood was assembled on the highway and in the fields. Huge bonfires lighted up the scene. Pastors of the local churches of all denominations had united in leading their congregations for greeting and farewell for their beloved president. As we would reach a crossing there sometimes would be hundreds and at others thousands of men, women, and children on their knees, praying and singing hymns.

This continuous service of prayer and song and supplication lasted over the three hundred miles between Albany and Buffalo, from midnight until dawn.

IV

GENERAL GRANT

The fairies who distribute the prizes are practical jokers. I have known thousands who sought office, some for its distinction, some for its emoluments, and some for both; thousands who wanted promotion from places they held, and other thousands who wanted to regain positions they had lost, all of whom failed in their search.

I probably would have been in one of those classes if I had been seeking an office. I was determined, however, upon a career in railroad work until, if possible, I had reached its highest rewards. During that period I was offered about a dozen political appointments, most of them of great moment and very tempting, all of which I declined.

Near the close of President Grant's administration George Jones, at that time the proprietor and publisher of the *New York Times*, asked me to come and see him. Mr. Jones, in his association with the brilliant editor, Henry J. Raymond, had been a progressive and staying power of the financial side of this great journal. He was of Welsh descent, a very hardheaded, practical, and wise business man. He also had very definite views on politics and parties, and several times nearly wrecked his paper by obstinately pursuing a course which was temporarily unpopular with its readers and subscribers. I was on excellent terms with Mr. Jones and admired him. The *New York Times* became under his management one of the severest critics of General Grant's administration and of the president himself.

I went to his house and during the conversation Jones said to me: "I was very much surprised to receive a letter from the president asking me to come and see him at the White House. Of course I went, anticipating a disagreeable interview, but it turned out absolutely the reverse. The president was most cordial, and his frankness most attractive. After a long and full discussion, the president said the *Times* had been his most unsparing critic, but he was forced to agree with much the *Times* said; that he had sent for me to make a request; that he had come to the presidency without any preparation whatever for its duties or for civic responsibilities; that he was compelled to take the best advice he could find and surround himself with men, many of whom he had never met before, and they were his guides and teachers; that he, however, assumed the entire responsibility for everything he had done. He knew perfectly well, in the retrospect and with the larger experience he had gained, that he had made many mistakes. 'And now, Mr. Jones,' he continued, 'I have sent for you as the most powerful as well as, I think, the fairest of my critics, to ask that you will say in your final summing up of my eight years that, however many my errors or mistakes, they were faults of judgment, and that I acted conscientiously and in any way I thought was right and best.'

"I told the president I would be delighted to take that view in the *Times*. Then the president said that he would like to show his appreciation in some way which would be gratifying to me. I told him that I wanted nothing for myself, nor did any of my friends, in the line of patronage. Then he said he wanted my assistance because he was looking for the best man for United States district attorney for the district of New York. With my large acquaintance he thought that I should be able to tell him whom among the lawyers would be best to appoint. After a little consideration I recommended you.

"The president then said: 'Mr. Depew supported Greeley, and though he is back in the party and doing good service in the campaigns, I do not like those men. Nevertheless, you can tender him the office and ask for his immediate acceptance.'"

I told Mr. Jones what my determination was in regard to a career, and while appreciating most highly both his own friendship and the compliment from the president, I must decline.

General Grant's mistakes in his presidency arose from his possession of one of the greatest of virtues, and that is loyalty to one's friends. He had unlimited confidence in them and could not see, or be made to see, nor listen to any of their defects. He was himself of such transparent honesty and truthfulness that he gauged and judged others by his own standard. Scandals among a few of the officials of his administration were entirely due to this great quality.

His intimacy among his party advisers fell among the most extreme of organization men and political machinists. When, under the advice of Senator Conkling, he appointed Thomas Murphy collector of the port of New York, it was charged in the press that the collector removed employees at the rate of several hundred per day and filled their places with loyal supporters of the organization. This policy, which was a direct reversal of the ideas of civil-service reform which were then rapidly gaining strength, incurred the active hostility of civil-service reformers, of whom George William Curtis was the most conspicuous.

When General Grant came to reside in New York, after his tour around the world, he was overwhelmed with social attentions. I met him at dinners several times a week and was the victim of a characteristic coldness of manner which he had towards many people.

One St. Patrick's Day, while in Washington, I received an earnest telegraphic request from Judge John T. Brady and his brother-in-law, Judge Charles P. Daly, president of the Society of the Friendly Sons of St. Patrick, saying: "The Sons are to have their greatest celebration because they are to be honored by the presence of General Grant, who will also speak, and it is imperative that you come and help us welcome him."

I arrived at the dinner late and passed in front of the daïs to my seat at the other end, while General Grant was speaking. He was not easy on his feet at that time, though afterwards he became very felicitous in public speaking. He paused a moment until I was seated and then said: "If Chauncey Depew stood in my shoes, and I in his, I would be a much happier man."

I immediately threw away the speech I had prepared during the six hours' trip from Washington, and proceeded to make a speech on "Who can stand now or in the future in the shoes of General Grant?" I had plenty of time before my turn came to elaborate this idea, gradually eliminating contemporary celebrities until in the future the outstanding figure representing the period would be the hero of our Civil War and the restoration of the Union.

The enthusiasm of the audience, as the speech went on, surpassed anything I ever saw. They rushed over tables and tried to carry the general around the room. When the enthusiasm had subsided he came to me and with much feeling said: "Thank you for that speech; it is the greatest and most eloquent that I ever heard." He insisted upon my standing beside him when he received the families of the members, and took me home in his carriage.

From that time until his death he was most cordial, and at many dinners would insist upon my being assigned to a chair next to him.

Among strangers and in general conversation General Grant was the most reticent of men, but among those whom he knew a most entertaining conversationalist. He went over a wide field on such occasions and was interesting on all subjects, and especially instructive on military campaigns and commanders. He gave me as his judgment that among all the military geniuses of the world the greatest was General Philip Sheridan, and that Sheridan's grasp of a situation had no parallel in any great general of whom he knew.

I was with General Grant at his home the day before he went from New York to Mount McGregor, near Saratoga, where he died. I learned of the trip and went immediately to see him, and was met by his son, General Frederick D. Grant. I said to him: "I learn that your father is going to Mount McGregor to-morrow, and I have come to tender him a special train."

After all the necessary arrangements had been made he asked me to go in and see the general. Before doing this I asked: "How is he?" "Well," he answered, "he is dying, but it is of infinite relief to him to see people whom he knows and likes, and I know he wants to see you. Our effort is to keep his mind off from himself and interest him with anything which we think will be of relief to him, and if you have any new incidents do not fail to tell him."

When I entered the room the general was busy writing his "Memoirs." He greeted me very cordially, said he was glad to see me, and then remarked: "I see by the papers that you have been recently up at Hartford delivering a lecture. Tell me about it."

In reply I told him about a very interesting journey there; the lecture and supper afterwards, with Mark Twain as the presiding genius, concerning all of which he asked questions, wanting more particulars, and the whole story seemed to interest him. What seemed to specially please him was the incident when I arrived at the hotel, after the supper given me at the close of my lecture. It was about three o'clock in the morning, and I went immediately to bed, leaving a call for the early train to New York. At five o'clock there was violent rapping on the door and, upon opening it, an Irish waiter stood there with a tray on which were a bottle of champagne and a goblet of ice.

"You have made a mistake," I said to the waiter.

"No, sir," he answered, "I could not make a mistake about you."

"Who sent this?" I asked.

"The committee, sir, with positive instructions that you should have it at five o'clock in the morning," he answered.

"Well, my friend, I said, is it the habit of the good people of Hartford, when they have decided to go to New York on an early train to drink a bottle of champagne at five o'clock in the morning?"

He answered: "Most of them do, sir."

(Nobody at that time had dreamed of the Eighteenth Amendment and the Volstead law.)

With a smile General Grant then said: "Well, there are some places in Connecticut where that could not be done, as local option prevails and the towns have gone dry. For instance, my friend, Senator Nye, of Nevada, spoke through Connecticut in my interest in the last campaign. Nye was a free liver, though not a dissipated man, and, as you know, a very excellent speaker. He told me that when he arrived at one of the principal manufacturing towns he was entertained by the leading manufacturer at his big house and in magnificent style. The dinner was everything that could be desired, except that the only fluid was ice-water. After a long speech Nye, on returning to the house, had a reception, and the supper was still dry, except plenty of ice-water.

"Nye, completely exhausted, went to bed but could not sleep, nor could he find any stimulants. So, about six o'clock in the morning he dressed and wandered down to the dining-room. The head of the house came in and, seeing him, exclaimed: 'Why, senator, you are up early.' Nye replied: 'Yes, you know, out in Nevada we have a great deal of malaria, and I could not sleep.' 'Well,' said the host, 'this is a temperance town. We find it an excellent thing for the working people, and especially for the young men, but we have some malaria here, also, and for that I have a private remedy.' Whereupon he went to a closet and pulled out a bottle of brandy.

"After his host had left, Nye continued there in a refreshed and more enjoyable spirit. Soon his hostess came in and, much surprised, said: 'Why, senator, you are up early.' 'Yes,' he said, 'out in Nevada we have a great deal of malaria, and while I am on these speaking tours I have sharp attacks and cannot sleep. I had one last night.'

"'Well,' she remarked, 'this is a temperance town, and it is a good thing for the working people and the young men, but I have a touch of malaria now and then myself.' Then she went to the tea-caddy and pulled out a bottle of brandy. The senator by this time was in perfect harmony with himself and the whole world.

"When the boys came in (sons of the entertainer) they said: 'Senator, we hear that you are an expert on live stock, horses, cattle, etc. Won't you come out in the barn so we can show you some we regard as very fine specimens?' The boys took him out to the barn, shut the door, locked it, and whispered: 'Senator, we have no live stock, but we have a bottle here in the hay mow which we think will do you good.' And the senator wound up his narrative by saying: 'The wettest place that I know of is a dry town in Connecticut.'"

The next day General Grant went to Mount McGregor and, as we all know, a few days afterwards he lost his voice completely.

V

ROSCOE CONKLING

For a number of years, instead of taking my usual vacation in travel or at some resort, I spent a few weeks in the fall in the political canvass as a speaker. In the canvass of 1868 I was associated with Senator Roscoe Conkling, who desired an assistant, as the mass meetings usually wanted at least two and probably three hours of speaking, and he limited himself to an hour. General Grant was at the height of his popularity and the audiences were enormous. As we had to speak every day and sometimes several times a day, Mr. Conkling notified the committees that he would not speak out of doors, and that they must in all cases provide a hall.

When we arrived at Lockport, N. Y., the chairman of the committee, Burt Van Horn, who was the congressman from the district, told the senator that at least twenty thousand people from the town, and others coming from the country on excursion trains, had filled the Fair Grounds. Conkling became very angry and told the congressman that he knew perfectly well the conditions under which he came to Lockport, and that he would not speak at the Fair Grounds. A compromise was finally effected by which the senator was to appear upon the platform, the audience be informed that he would speak in the Opera House, and I was to be left to take care of the crowd. The departure of the senator from the grounds was very dramatic. He was enthusiastically applauded and a band preceded his carriage. For some reason I never had such a success as in addressing that audience. Commencing with a story which was new and effective, I continued for two hours without apparently losing an auditor.

Upon my return to the hotel I found the senator very indignant. He said that he had gone to the Opera House with the committee; that, of course, no meeting had been advertised there, but a band had been placed on the balcony to play, as if it were a dime museum attraction inside; that a few farmers' wives had straggled in to have an opportunity to partake from their baskets their luncheons, and that he had left the Opera House and returned to the hotel. The committee coming in and narrating what had occurred at the Fair Grounds, did not help his imperious temper. The committee begged for a large meeting, which was to be held in the evening, but Conkling refused and ordered me to do the same, and we left on the first train. The cordial relations which had existed up to that time were somehow severed and he became very hostile.

General Grant, as president, of course, never had had experience or opportunity to know anything of practical politics. It was said that prior to his election he had never voted but once, and that was before the war, when he voted the Democratic ticket for James Buchanan.

All the senators, representatives, and public men who began to press around him, seeking the appointment to office of their friends, were unknown to him personally. He decided rapidly whom among them he could trust, and once having arrived at that conclusion, his decision was irrevocable. He would stand by a friend, without regard to its effect upon himself, to the last ditch.

Of course, each of the two United States senators, Conkling and Fenton, wanted his exclusive favor. It is impossible to conceive of two men so totally different in every characteristic. Grant liked Conkling as much as he disliked Fenton. The result was that he transferred the federal patronage of the State to Senator Conkling.

Conkling was a born leader, very autocratic and dictatorial. He immediately began to remove Fenton officials and to replace them with members of his own organization. As there was no civil service at that time and public officers were necessarily active politicians, Senator Conkling in a few years destroyed the organization which Fenton had built up as governor, and became master of the Republican party in the State.

The test came at the State convention at Saratoga. Senator Conkling at that time had become hostile to me, why I do not know, nor could his friends, who were most of them mine also, find out. He directed that I must not be elected a delegate to the convention. The collector of the port of New York, in order to make that decree effective, filled my district in Westchester County with appointees from the Custom House.

Patronage, when its control is subject to a popular vote, is a boomerang. The appointment of a citizen in a town arouses the anger of many others who think they are more deserving. I appealed to the farmers with the simple question whether old Westchester should be controlled by federal authority in a purely State matter of their own. The result of the appeal was overwhelming, and when the district convention met, the Custom House did not have a single delegate.

The leader of the Custom House crowd came to me and said: "This is a matter of bread-and-butter and living with us. It is nothing to you. These delegates are against us and for you at the convention. Now, we have devised a plan to save our lives. It is that the three delegates elected shall all be friends of yours. You shall apparently be defeated. A resolution will be passed that if either delegate fails to attend or resigns, the other two may fill the vacancy. One of these will resign when the convention meets and you will be substituted in his place. In the meantime we will send out through the Associated Press that you have been defeated." I did not have the heart to see these poor fellows dismissed from their employment, and I assented to the proposition.

When we arrived at the convention Governor Cornell, then State chairman, called it to order. I arose to make a motion, when he announced: "You, sir, are not a member of this convention." My credentials, however, under the arrangement made in Westchester, convinced him that he was misinformed. The Conkling side selected for their chairman Andrew D. White, and the other side selected me. Upon careful canvass of the votes we had a clear majority.

There were several delegations which were controlled by federal office-holders. It is at this point that patronage becomes overwhelmingly effective. Several of those office-holders were shown telegrams from Washington, which meant their removal unless they did as directed by Senator Conkling. When the convention met the next day, the office-holders kept their heads on their shoulders, and my dear and valued old friend, Andrew D. White, was elected chairman of the convention.

I asked the leader of the federal crowd from Westchester how he explained my getting into the convention. "Oh," he said, "that was easy. Our people gained so many delegates by offers of patronage and threats of removal that when I told them you had bought my delegates away from me, they believed it without question, and we are all safe in our places in the Custom House." My success was entirely due to the farmers' indignation at federal dictation, and the campaign did not cost me a dollar.

Roscoe Conkling was created by nature for a great career. That he missed it was entirely his own fault. Physically he was the handsomest man of his time. His mental equipment nearly approached genius. He was industrious to a degree. His oratorical gifts were of the highest order, and he was a debater of rare power and resources. But his intolerable egotism deprived him of vision necessary for supreme leadership. With all his oratorical power and his talent in debate, he made little impression upon the country and none upon posterity. His position in the Senate was a masterful one, and on the platform most attractive, but none of his speeches appear in the schoolbooks or in the collections of great orations. The reason was that his wonderful gifts were wholly devoted to partisan discussions and local issues.

His friends regarded his philippic against George W. Curtis at the Republican State convention at Rochester as the high-water mark of his oratory. I sat in the seat next to Mr. Curtis when Conkling delivered his famous attack. His admirers thought this the best speech he ever made, and it certainly was a fine effort, emphasized by oratory of a high order, and it was received by them with the wildest enthusiasm and applause.

The assault upon Mr. Curtis was exceedingly bitter, the denunciation very severe, and every resource of sarcasm, of which Mr. Conkling was past master, was poured upon the victim. His bitterness was caused by Mr. Curtis's free criticism of him on various occasions. The speech lasted two hours, and it was curious to note its effect upon Mr. Curtis. Under the rules which the convention had adopted, he could not reply, so he had to sit and take it. The only feeling or evidence of being hurt by his punishment was in exclamations at different points made by his assailant. They were: "Remarkable!" "Extraordinary!" "What an exhibition!" "Bad temper!" "Very bad temper!"

In the long controversy between them Mr. Curtis had the advantages which the journalist always possesses. The orator has one opportunity on the platform and the publication the next day in the press. The editor—and Mr. Curtis was at that time editor of *Harper's Weekly*—can return every Saturday and have an exclusive hearing by an audience limited only by the circulation of his newspaper and the quotations from it by journalistic friends.

The speech illustrated Conkling's methods of preparation. I used to hear from the senator's friends very frequently that he had added another phrase to his characterization of Curtis. While he was a ready debater, yet for an effort of this kind he would sometimes devote a year to going frequently over the ground, and in each repetition produce new epigrams, quotable phrases, and characterizations.

There used to be an employee of the State committee named Lawrence. He was a man of a good deal of receptive intelligence and worshipped the senator. Mr.

Conkling discovered this quality and used Lawrence as a target or listening-post. I have often had Lawrence come to my office and say: "I had a great night. The senator talked to me or made speeches to me until nearly morning." He told me that he had heard every word of the Curtis philippic many times.

Lawrence told me of another instance of Conkling's preparation for a great effort. When he was preparing the speech, which was to bring his friends who had been disappointed at the convention to the support of General Garfield, he summoned Lawrence for clerical work at his home. Lawrence said that the senator would write or dictate, and then correct until he was satisfied with the effort, and that this took considerable time. When it was completed he would take long walks into the country, and in these walks recite the whole or part of his speech until he was perfect master of it.

This speech took four hours in delivery in New York, and he held the audience throughout this long period. John Reed, one of the editors of the *New York Times*, told me that he sat on the stage near Conkling and had in his hands the proofs which had been set up in advance and which filled ten columns of his paper. He said that the senator neither omitted nor interpolated a word from the beginning to the end. He would frequently refer apparently to notes on his cuffs, or little memoranda, not that he needed them, but it was the orator's always successful effort to create impression that his speech is extemporaneous, and the audience much prefer a speech which they think is such.

Senator Conkling held an important position in a critical period of our country's history. If his great powers had been devoted in the largest way to the national constructive problems of the time, he would have been the leader of the dominant party and president of the United States. Instead, he became the leader of a faction in his own State only, and by the merciless use of federal patronage absolutely controlled for twelve years the action of the State organization.

All the young men who appeared in the legislature or in county offices who displayed talent for leadership, independence, and ambition were set aside. The result was remarkable. While prior to his time there were many men in public life in the State with national reputation and influence, this process of elimination drove young men from politics into the professions or business, and at the close of Senator Conkling's career there was hardly an active member of the Republican party in New York of national reputation, unless he had secured it before Mr. Conkling became the autocrat of New York politics. The political machine in the Republican party in his Congressional district early in his career became jealous of his growing popularity and influence, both at home and in Congress. By machine methods they defeated him and thought they had retired him permanently from public life.

When I was elected secretary of state I received a note from Mr. Conkling, asking if I would meet him. I answered: "Yes, immediately, and at Albany." He came there with Ward Hunt, afterwards one of the associate justices of the Supreme Court of the United States. He delivered an intense attack upon machine methods and machine politics, and said they would end in the elimination of all independent thought, in the crushing of all ambition in promising young men, and ultimate infinite damage to the State and nation. "You," he said, "are a very young man for your present position, but you will soon be marked for destruction."

Then he stated what he wanted, saying: "I was defeated by the machine in the last election. They can defeat me now only by using one man of great talent and popularity in my district. I want you to make that man your deputy secretary of state. It is the best office in your gift, and he will be entirely satisfied."

I answered him: "I have already received from the chiefs of the State organization designations for every place in my office, and especially for that one, but the appointment is yours and you may announce it at once."

Mr. Conkling arose as if addressing an audience, and as he stood there in the little parlor of Congress Hall in Albany he was certainly a majestic figure. He said: "Sir, a thing that is quickly done is doubly done. Hereafter, as long as you and I both live, there never will be a deposit in any bank, personally, politically, or financially to my credit which will not be subject to your draft."

The gentleman whom he named became my deputy. His name was Erastus Clark. He was a man of ability and very broad culture, and was not only efficient in the performance of his duties, but one of the most delightful of companions. His health was bad, and his friends were always alarmed, and justifiably so, about him. Nevertheless, I met him years afterwards in Washington, when he was past eighty-four.

At Mr. Conkling's request Mr. Clark made an appointment for a mutual visit to Trenton Falls, a charming resort near Utica. We spent the week-end there, and I saw Mr. Conkling at his best. He was charming in reminiscence, in discussion, in his characterization of the leading actors upon the public stage, and in varying views of ambitions and careers.

When the patronage all fell into his hands after the election of General Grant, he pressed upon me the appointment of postmaster of the city of New York. It was difficult for him to understand that, while I enjoyed politics and took an active part in campaigns, I would not accept any office whatever. He then appointed one of the best of postmasters, who afterwards became postmaster-general, but who was also one of the most efficient of his lieutenants, General Thomas L. James.

When Mr. Conkling was a candidate for United States senator I was regarded as a confidential friend of Governor Fenton. The governor was one of the most secretive of men, and, therefore, I did not know his views as to the candidate, or whether he had preferences. I think he had no preferences but wished Conkling defeated, and at the same time did not want to take a position which would incur the enmity of him or his friends.

One night there was a great public demonstration, and, being called upon, I made a speech to the crowd, which included the legislature, to the effect that we had been voiceless in the United States Senate too long; that the greatest State in the Union should be represented by a man who had demonstrated his ability to all, and that man was Mr. Conkling. This created an impression that I was speaking for the governor as well as myself, and the effect upon the election was great. Mr. Conkling thought so, and that led to his pressing upon me official recognition.

How the breach came between us, why he became persistently hostile during the rest of his life, I never knew. President Arthur, Governor Cornell, and other of his intimate friends told me that they tried often to find out, but their efforts only irritated him and never received any response.

Senator Conkling's peculiar temperament was a source of great trouble to his lieutenants. They were all able and loyal, but he was intolerant of any exercise on their part of independent judgment. This led to the breaking off of all relations with the two most distinguished of them—President Arthur and Governor Cornell.

A breach once made could not be healed. A bitter controversy in debate with Mr. Blaine assumed a personal character. In the exchanges common in the heat of such debates Blaine ridiculed Conkling's manner and called him a turkey-cock. Mutual friends tried many times to bring them together. Blaine was always willing, but Conkling never.

Conkling had a controversy which was never healed with Senator Platt, who had served him long and faithfully and with great efficiency. During the twenty years in which Platt was leader, following Senator Conkling, he displayed the reverse qualities. He was always ready for consultation, he sought advice, and was tolerant of large liberty of individual judgment among his associates. He was always forgiving, and taking back into confidence those with whom he had quarrelled.

One summer I was taking for a vacation a trip to Europe and had to go aboard the steamer the night before, as she sailed very early in the morning. One of my staff appeared and informed me that a very serious attack upon the New York Central had been started in the courts and that the law department needed outside counsel and asked whom he should employ. I said: "Senator Conkling." With amazement he replied:

"Why, he has been bitterly denouncing you for months." "Yes, but that was politics," I said. "You know the most brilliant lawyer in the United States might come to New York, and unless he formed advantageous associations with some of the older firms he could get no practice. Now, this suit will be very conspicuous, and the fact that Senator Conkling is chief counsel for the Central will give him at once a standing and draw to him clients." His appearance in the case gave him immediate prominence and a large fee.

Senator Conkling's career at the bar was most successful, and there was universal sorrow when his life ended in the tragedy of the great blizzard.

VI

HORACE GREELEY

While secretary of state of New York, the decennial State census was taken, and the appointment of three thousand census takers involved as much pressure from congressmen, State senators, assemblymen, and local leaders as if the places had been very remunerative and permanent. I discovered what a power political patronage is in party organization, because it developed that the appointment of this large number of men, located in every town in the State, could easily have been utilized for the formation of a personal organization within the party.

I was exceedingly fond, as I am still and always have been, of political questions, issues affecting the general government, the State, or localities, party organizations, and political leaders. So, while devoted to my profession and its work and increasingly enjoying its labor and activities, politics became an interesting recreation. With no desire for and with a determination not to take any public office, to be called into party councils, to be at an occasional meeting of the State committee and a delegate to conventions were happy relief and excursions from the routine of professional work, as golf is to a tired business man or lawyer.

The nomination of General Grant for president by the Republicans and of Horatio Seymour by the Democrats had made New York the pivotal State in the national election. John T. Hoffman, the most popular among the younger Democrats, was their nominee for governor. The Republicans, with great unanimity, agreed upon John A. Griswold, a congressman from the Troy district. Griswold was the idol of his colleagues in the New York delegation in Congress, and his attractive personality and demonstrated business ability had made him a great favorite with politicians, business men, and labor. The canvass for his nomination had been conducted with great ardor by enthusiastic friends in all parts of the State, and the delegations were nearly all practically pledged to his nomination. No one dreamed that there would be an opposition candidate.

On the train to the convention John Russell Young, then managing editor of the *New York Tribune* under Mr. Greeley, came to me and said: "Mr. Greeley has decided to be a candidate at the convention for the nomination for governor. You are his friend, he lives in your assembly district in Westchester County, and wishes you to make the nomination speech."

I tried to argue the question with Young by portraying to him the situation and the utter hopelessness of any attempt to break the slate. He, however, insisted upon it, saying that all pledges and preferences would disappear because of Greeley's services to the party for so many years.

When we arrived at Syracuse and stated our determination to present Mr. Greeley's name, it was hilariously received as a joke. Efforts were made by friends of Mr. Greeley to persuade him not to undertake such an impossible task, but they could produce no effect.

Mr. Griswold was put in nomination by Mr. Demers, one of the most eloquent young men in the ministry of the State, and afterwards an editor of power, and his speech filled every requirement.

Then I presented Mr. Greeley. At first the audience was hostile, but as the recital of the great editor's achievements grew in intensity and heat, the convention began to applaud and then to cheer. A delegate hurled at me the question: "How about Greeley signing the bail of Jefferson Davis?" The sentiment seemed to change at once and cheers were followed by hisses. Then there was supreme silence, and I immediately shouted: "There are spots on the sun."

The effect was electrical. Delegates were on their feet, standing on chairs, the air was full of hats, and the cheers deafening for Greeley for some minutes. Mr. Demers, the preacher delegate, lost his equilibrium, rushed up to me, shaking his fist excitedly, and shouted: "Damn you! you have nominated him and beaten Griswold."

A recess was taken, and when the convention reconvened the ballot demonstrated that if the organization is given time it can always reform its shattered lines and show the efficiency of discipline.

When I met Mr. Greeley soon after, he said: "I cannot understand why I desired the nomination for governor, nor why anybody should want the office. There is nothing in it. No man now can name the ten last governors of the State of New York."

Having tried that proposition many times since on the average citizen, I have found that Mr. Greeley was absolutely right. Any one who does not think so can try to solve that problem himself.

The meeting of the Electoral College at the Capitol at Albany in 1864 was one of the most picturesque and interesting gatherings ever held in the State. People came from all parts of the country to witness the formality of the casting of the vote of New York for Abraham Lincoln. The members of the college were, most of them, men of great distinction in our public and civic life.

Horace Greeley was elected president of the college. The meeting was held in the Senate chamber. When Mr. Greeley took the chair, the desk in front of him made only his bust visible, and with his wonderfully intellectual face, his long gray hair brushed back, and his solemn and earnest expression, he was one of the most impressive figures I ever saw occupying the chair as a presiding officer.

One of the electors had failed to appear. Most of us knew that under pressure of great excitement he was unable to resist his convivial tendencies, but no one supposed that Mr. Greeley could by any possibility know of his weakness. After waiting some time one of the electors moved that the college take a recess for half a day. Mr. Greeley turned very pale and, before putting the question, made a little speech, something like this, in a voice full of emotion, I might almost say tears: "My brethren, we are met here upon the most solemn occasion of our lives in this crisis of the republic. Upon the regularity of what we do here this day may depend whether the republic lives or dies. I would, therefore, suggest that we sit here in silence until our absent brother, who is doubtless kept from us by some good reason, shall appear and take his seat."

The effect of this address upon the Electoral College and the surrounding audience was great. Many were in tears, and the women spectators, most of whom were in mourning for those lost during the war, were all crying.

As secretary of state it was my duty to have the papers all prepared for execution as soon as the college had voted, and to attach to them the great seal of the State, and then they were sent by special messenger to Washington to be delivered to the House of Representatives. Mr. Greeley, at the opening of the session, said to me: "Chauncey, as I am not very familiar with parliamentary law, I wish you would take a seat on the steps beside me here, so that I can consult you if necessary." After this effective and affecting speech he leaned down until he was close to my ear, and said: "Chauncey, how long do you think it will be before that d—— drunken fool will be able to return and take his seat?"

General Grant's administration soon aroused great opposition. Carl Schurz, Charles Francis Adams, and other leaders became very hostile to the administration and to a second term. The country was longing for peace. The "carpet-bag" governments of the South were full of corruption and incompetence and imposed upon the Southern States intolerable burdens of debt. The feeling was becoming general that there should be universal amnesty in order that the best and most capable people of the South could return to the management of their own affairs.

This led to the calling of a convention of the Republicans, which nominated Horace Greeley for president. I had no desire nor the slightest intention of being involved in this controversy, but was happily pursuing my profession, with increasing fondness for private life.

One day Commodore Vanderbilt, who had a strong

friendship for Mr. Greeley, but took no interest in politics, said to me: "Mr. Greeley has been to see me and is very anxious for you to assist him. If you can aid him in any way I wish you would."

Afterwards Mr. Greeley called at my house. "Chauncey," he said (he always called me Chauncey), "as you know, I have been nominated by the Liberal Republican convention for President of the United States. If I can get the indorsement of the Democratic party my election is assured. My Democratic friends tell me that in order to accomplish that I must demonstrate that I have a substantial Republican following. So we have called a meeting at Rochester, which is the capital of the strongest Republican counties of the State. It is necessary to have for the principal speaker some Republican of State and national reputation. I have selected you for that purpose."

To my protest that I did not wish to enter into the contest nor to take any part in active politics, he said very indignantly: "I have supported you in my paper and personally during the whole of your career. I thought that if anybody was capable of gratitude it is you, and I have had unfortunate experiences with many." I never was able to resist an appeal of this kind, so I said impulsively: "Mr. Greeley, I will go."

The meeting was a marvellous success for the purpose for which it was called. It was purely a Republican gathering. The crowd was several times larger than the hall could accommodate. Henry R. Selden, one of the judges of the Court of Appeals and one of the most eminent and respected Republicans of the State, presided. The two hundred vice-presidents and secretaries upon the platform I had known intimately for years as Republican leaders of their counties and districts. The demonstration so impressed the Democratic State leaders that at the national Democratic convention Mr. Greeley was indorsed.

There were two State conventions held simultaneously that year, one Democratic and one Liberal Republican. In the division of offices the Democratic party, being the larger, was given the governorship and the Liberal Republicans had the lieutenant-governorship. I was elected as the presiding officer of the Liberal Republican convention and also was made unanimously its nominee for lieutenant-governor. The Democratic convention nominated Francis Kernan, one of the most distinguished lawyers of the State, and afterwards United States senator.

If the election had been held early in the canvass there is little doubt but that Mr. Greeley would have carried the State by an overwhelming majority. His difficulty was that for a quarter of a century, as editor of the *New York Tribune*, he had been the most merciless, bitter, and formidable critic and opponent of the Democratic party. The deep-seated animosity against him was fully aroused as the campaign proceeded by a propaganda which placed in the hands of every Democrat these former slashing editorials of the *New York Tribune*. Their effect upon the Democratic voters was evident after a while, and when in the September election North Carolina went Republican, a great mass of Republicans, who had made up their minds to support Mr. Greeley, went back to their party, and he was overwhelmingly defeated.

In the early part of his canvass Mr. Greeley made a tour of the country. There have been many such travels by presidential candidates, but none like this. His march was a triumphal procession, and his audiences enormous and most enthusiastic. The whole country marvelled at his intellectual versatility. He spoke every day, and often several times a day, and each speech was absolutely new. There seemed to be no limit to his originality, his freshness, or the new angles from which to present the issues of the canvass. No candidate was ever so bitterly abused and so slandered.

A veteran speaker has in the course of his career original experiences. The cordiality and responsiveness of his audience is not always an index of their agreement with his argument. During the campaign Mr. Greeley came to me and said: "I have received encouraging accounts from the State of Maine. I have a letter from such a place"—naming it—"from the principal of the academy there. He writes me that the Congregational minister, who has the largest church in town, the bank president, the manufacturer, the principal lawyer, and himself are lifelong readers of the *Tribune*, and those steadfast Republicans intend to support me. He thinks if they can have a public meeting with a speaker of national reputation, the result might be an overturn in my favor in this community, which is almost unanimously Republican, that it may influence the whole State, and," continued Mr. Greeley, "he suggests you as the speaker, and I earnestly ask you to go."

When I arrived at the place I was entertained by the manufacturer. The audience crowded the largest hall in the town. The principal of the academy presided, the Congregational minister opened the exercises with a prayer, and I was introduced and received with great cordiality.

For such an audience my line of talk was praising General Grant as the greatest general of modern times, and how largely the preservation of the Union depended upon his military genius. Then to picture the tremendous responsibilities of the presidency and the impossibility of a man, however great as a soldier, with a lifetime of military education, environment, and experiences, succeeding in civil office, especially as great a one as the presidency of the United States. Then came, naturally, a eulogium of Horace Greeley, the maker of public opinion, the moulder of national policies, the most eloquent and resourceful leader of the Republican party since its formation. The audience cheered with great enthusiasm all these allusions to General Grant, and responded with equal fervor to my praise of Horace Greeley.

When I concluded they stood up and gave me cordial cheers, and the presiding officer came forward and said: "I now suggest that we close this meeting with three rousing cheers for Horace Greeley." The principal of the academy, the manufacturer, the minister, the lawyer, a very few of the audience, and several women responded. After this frost a farmer rose gradually, and as he began to let out link after link of his body, which seemed about seven feet tall, he reached his full height, and then in a voice which could be heard a mile shouted: "Three cheers for General Grant!" The response nearly took the roof off the house. I left the State the next morning and told Mr. Greeley that he could not carry Maine.

Among the amusing episodes of the campaign was one which occurred at an open-door mass meeting at Watertown, N. Y. John A. Dix had been nominated for governor on the Republican ticket, and I was speaking of him and his career. He had changed from one party to the other five or six times in the course of his long career, and each time received an office. There was great doubt as to his age, because in the American Encyclopædia the date of his birth was given as of a certain year, and in the French Encyclopædia, which published his biography when he was minister to France, a widely different date was given. In the full tide of partisan oratory I went over these changes of political activity, and how each one had been rewarded, also the doubt as to his age, and then I shouted: "I have discovered among the records of the Pilgrim Fathers that when they landed on Plymouth Rock they found John A. Dix standing on the rock and announcing that unless they made him justice of the peace he would join the Indians." An indignant farmer, who could not hold his wrath any longer, shouted: "That's a lie! The Pilgrims landed more than two hundred and fifty years ago." I saw that my interrupter had swallowed my bait, hook, and line, bob and sinker, pole and all, and shouted with great indignation: "Sir, I have narrated that historical incident throughout the State, from Montauk Point to Niagara Falls, and you are the first man who has had the audacity to question it."

Another farmer stepped up to the heckler and said: "Here is my hat, neighbor. You can keep it. I am going bareheaded for the rest of my life." In his uproarious laughter the crowd all joined. It was years before the questioning farmer could visit Watertown without encountering innumerable questions as to when the Pilgrims landed on Plymouth Rock.

The last meeting of the campaign was held at Mr. Greeley's home at Chappaqua in Westchester County.

We all knew that the contest was hopeless and defeat sure. I was one of the speakers, both as his neighbor and friend, and accompanied him to New York. A rough crowd on the train jeered him as we rode along. We went to his office, and there he spoke of the lies that had been told about him, and which had been believed by the public; of the cartoons which had misrepresented him, especially those of Tom Nast, and of which there were many lying about. Leaning upon his desk, a discouraged and hopeless man, he said: "I have given my life to the freeing of the slaves, and yet they have been made to believe that I was a slave driver. It has been made to appear, and people have been made to believe, that I was wrong or faithless, or on the other side of the reforms which I have advocated all my life. I will be beaten in the campaign and I am ruined for life." He was overcome with emotion, and it was the saddest interview I ever had with any one. It was really the breaking of a great heart. He died before the votes were counted.

There was instantly a tremendous revulsion of popular feeling in the country. He had lost his wife during the campaign, and the people woke up suddenly to the sorrows under which he had labored, to his genius as a journalist, to his activity as a reformer, and to a usefulness that had no parallel among his contemporaries. The president-elect, General Grant, and the vice-president-elect, Schuyler Colfax, attended the funeral, and without distinction of party his death was universally mourned.

After the election, in consultation on railroad affairs, Commodore Vanderbilt said to me, "I was very glad you were defeated," which was his way of saying that he did not want me either to leave the railroad or to have other duties which would impair my efficiency.

With the tragic death of Mr. Greeley the Liberal Republican movement ended. Most of us who had followed him resumed at once our Republican party relations and entered actively into its work in the next campaign. The revolt was forgiven, except in very few instances, and the Greeley men went back to their old positions in their various localities and became prominent in the official life of the State. I, as usual, in the fall took my vacation on the platform for the party.

VII

RUTHERFORD B. HAYES AND WILLIAM M. EVARTS

It is one of the tragedies of history that in the procession of events, the accumulation of incidents, year by year and generation by generation, famous men of any period so rapidly disappear.

At the close of the Civil War there were at least a score of generals in the North, and as many in the South, whose names were household words. About fifty-five years have passed since the war closed, and the average citizen knows only two of them—Grant and Lee.

One of the last acts of General Grant was to tender to Senator Conkling the position of chief justice of the Supreme Court of the United States. Conkling had gained from the senatorship and the leadership of his party a great reputation, to which subsequent service in the Senate could add little or nothing. He was in his early forties, in the prime of his powers, and he would have had before him, as chief justice of this great court, a long life of usefulness and distinction.

Conkling was essentially an advocate, and as an advocate not possessing the judicial temperament. While there was a great surprise that he declined this wonderful opportunity, we can see now that the environment and restrictions of the position would have made it impossible for this fiery and ambitious spirit. It was well known that General Grant, so far as he could influence the actions of the national Republican convention, was in favor of Senator Conkling as his successor. The senator's friends believed, and they made him believe, that the presidency was within his grasp.

When the national convention met it was discovered that the bitterness between the two leaders, Blaine and Conkling, made harmony impossible. The bitterness by that time was on Conkling's side against Blaine. With the latter's make-up, resentment could not last very long. It is an interesting speculation what might have happened if these two leaders had become friends. It is among the possibilities that both might have achieved the great object of their ambitions and been presidents of the United States.

The outstanding feature of that convention in the history of those interesting gatherings was the speech of Colonel Robert G. Ingersoll, nominating Mr. Blaine. In its effect upon the audience, in its reception by the country, and by itself as an effort of that kind, it stands unprecedented and unequalled.

As usual in popular conventions, where the antagonism of the leaders and the bitterness of their partisanship threatens the unity of the party, the result was the nomination of a "dark horse," and the convention closed its labors by presenting to the country General Rutherford B. Hayes.

President Hayes, although one of the most amiable, genial, and companionable of our presidents, with every quality to attach men to him and make warm friendships, was, nevertheless, one of the most isolated. He inherited all the business troubles, economic disorganization, and currency disturbances which grew out of the panic of 1873. He was met with more bankruptcy than had ever occurred in our business history.

With rare courage and the most perfect good nature, he installed essential reforms, which, in the then condition of party organization and public sentiment, practically offended everybody. He threw the extreme radicals of his party into a frenzy of rage by wiping out the "carpet-bag" governments and restoring self-government for the South. He inaugurated civil-service reform, but in doing so antagonized most of the senators and members of the House.

When he found that the collector of the port of New York, Chester A. Arthur, and the surveyor, Alonzo B. Cornell, were running their offices with their vast patronage on strictly machine lines, and that this had the general approval of party leaders, he removed them and appointed for their successors General Edwin A. Merritt and Silas W. Burt, with instructions to remove no one on account of politics, and to appoint no one except for demonstrated efficiency for the place. He pursued the same policy in the Internal Revenue and Post-Office Departments. This policy threatened the primacy of the Conkling machine.

President Hayes had a very strong Cabinet. The secretary of state, William M. Evarts, and the secretary of the treasury, John Sherman, were two of the ablest men in the country. Evarts was the leader of the national bar, and in crystallized mentality had no equal in the profession or outside of it. Sherman was the foremost and best-informed economist, and also a great statesman.

In close consultation with Sherman, Hayes brought about the resumption of specie payment. The "greenbackers," who were for unlimited paper, and the silver men, who were for unlimited coinage of silver, and who were very numerous, joined the insurgent brigade.

While Mr. Hayes retired from the presidency by what might be called unanimous consent, he had created conditions which made possible the success of his party in 1880.

It was a refreshing experience to meet the president during these troublous times. While everybody else was excited, he was perfectly calm. While most of the great men at the Capitol were raging, he, at the other end of the avenue, was placid and serene. He said once to me: "It is a novel experience when you do what you think right and best for the country to have it so generally criticised and disapproved. But the compensation is that you expect antagonism and disapproval and would think something was the matter with your decisions if you did not receive them."

The general abuse to which he was subjected from so many sources affected the public's view of him. After he had left the presidency he told me that he thought it was the duty of an ex-president to utilize the prestige which belonged to the office in the aid of education. "I have found," he said, "that it helps enormously in colleges and schools to have lectures, lessons, etc., in history and patriotism, and behind them the personality of an ex-president of the United States."

As an illustration of how distinguished men, when out of power, no longer interest our people, I remember I met Mr. Hayes one day in front of a fruit display of a well-known grocery establishment, and after cordial greeting said to the groceryman: "That is ex-President Hayes. Don't you want to meet him?" The groceryman replied: "I am not interested in him, but I have the finest collection of pears in the city and want to sell you some."

The Capitol was full of the rich and racy characterizations, epigrams, and sarcasms which Senator Conkling was daily pouring out upon President Hayes, and especially Secretary Evarts. By all the rules of senatorial courtesy in those machine days, a member of the Cabinet from New York should have been a friend of its United States senator. Mr. Evarts was too big a man to be counted in any other class or category except his own. Of course, all these criticisms were carried to both the president and the secretary of state. The president never mentioned them, and I never heard Evarts, though I met him frequently, make any reply but once.

Dining with Mr. Evarts, who entertained charmingly, a very distinguished English jurist among the guests, here on a special mission, said: "Mr. Secretary, I was at the Senate to-day and heard Senator Conkling speaking. His magnificent personal appearance, added to his fine oratory, must make him one of the most formidable advocates at your bar and in your courts." The English judge thought, of course, that Mr. Evarts, as the leader of the American Bar and always in the courts, would know every lawyer of distinction. Mr. Evarts dryly replied: "I never saw Mr. Conkling in court."

It is always dangerous to comment or narrate a racy story which involves the personal affliction of anybody. Dining with Mr. Evarts one night was also a very distinguished general of our Civil War, who had been an important figure in national politics. He was very curious to know about Mr. Tilden, and especially as to the truth of a report that Mr. Tilden had a stroke of paralysis, and appealed to me, as I was just from New York. I narrated a story which was current at the time that Mr. Tilden had denied the report by saying to a friend:

"They say I cannot lift my left hand to my head." He then put his right hand under the left elbow and shot the left one easily up to his face and said: "See there, my left has reached its goal."

I saw that Mr. Evarts was embarrassed at the anecdote and discovered afterwards that the distinguished guest had recently had a similar stroke on his left side and could propel his left arm and hand only with the assistance of his right.

My old bogie of being put into office arose again in the senatorial election of 1882. The legislature, for the first time in a generation, was entirely leaderless. The old organization had disappeared and a new one had not yet crystallized.

Mr. Evarts was anxious to be senator, and I pledged him my support. Evarts was totally devoid of the arts of popular appeal. He was the greatest of lawyers and the most delightful of men, but he could not canvass for votes. Besides, he was entirely independent in his ideas of any organization dictation or control, and resented both. He did not believe that a public man should go into public office under any obligations, and resented such suggestions.

A large body of representative men thought it would be a good thing for the country if New York could have this most accomplished, capable, and brilliant man in the United States Senate. They urged him strongly upon the legislature, none of whose members knew him personally, and Mr. Evarts would not go to Albany.

The members selected a committee to come down to New York and see Mr. Evarts. They went with the idea of ascertaining how far he would remember with gratitude those who elected him. Their visit was a miserable failure. They came in hot indignation to my office and said they did not propose to send such a cold and unsympathetic man as their representative to Washington and earnestly requested my consent to their nominating me at the caucus the next morning.

The committee telephoned to Albany and received the assent of every faction of their party to this proposition. Then they proposed that when the caucus met, Mr. Evarts, of course, should receive complimentary speeches from his friends. Meanwhile others would be nominated, and then a veteran member, whom they designated, should propose me in the interest of harmony and the union of the party, whereat the sponsors of the other candidate would withdraw their man, and I be nominated by acclamation. My answer was a most earnest appeal for Mr. Evarts. Then Mr. Evarts's friends rallied to his support and he was elected.

I place Mr. Evarts in the foremost rank as a lawyer, a wit, and a diplomat. He tried successfully the most famous cases of his time and repeatedly demonstrated his remarkable genius. As a general railway counsel and, therefore, as an administrator in the retaining of distinguished counsels, I met with many of the best men at the bar, but never any with such a complete and clarified intellect as William M. Evarts. The mysteries of the most complicated cases seemed simple, the legal difficulties plain, and the solution comprehensible to everybody under his analysis.

Mr. Evarts was the wittiest man I ever met. It is difficult to rehabilitate in the sayings of a wit the complete flavor of the utterance. It is easier with a man of humor. Evarts was very proud of his efforts as a farmer on his large estate in Vermont. Among his prizes was a drove of pigs. He sent to Chief Justice Morrison R. Waite a copy of his eulogy on Chief Justice Salmon P. Chase, Waite's predecessor, and at the same time a ham, saying in his letter: "My dear Chief Justice, I send you to-day one of my prize hams and also my eulogy on Chief Justice Chase, both the products of my pen."

The good things Mr. Evarts said would be talked of long after a dinner. I remember on one occasion his famous partner, Mr. Choate, who was a Harvard man, while Evarts was a graduate from Yale, introduced Mr. Evarts by saying that he was surprised that a Yale man, with all the prejudices of that institution against the superior advantages of Harvard, should have risked the coats of his stomach at a Harvard dinner. Mr. Evarts replied: "When I go to a Harvard dinner I always leave the coats of my stomach at home."

Mr. Evarts once told me when I was visiting him at his country place that an old man whom he pointed out, and who was sawing wood, was the most sensible philosopher in the neighborhood. Mr. Evarts said: "He is always talking to himself, and I asked him why." His answer was: "I always talk to myself in preference to talking to anybody else, because I like to talk to a sensible man and to hear a man of sense talk."

VIII

GENERAL GARFIELD

The triumph of the Democrats in Maine in the September election, 1880, had a most depressing effect upon the Republicans and an equally exhilarating one upon the Democrats. The paralyzing effect of the simple utterances in popular elections almost makes one think that every candidate should follow Matthew Quay's famous advice to his candidate for governor: "Beaver, keep your mouth shut."

In the campaign when General Winfield Scott ran for the presidency, he began an important communication by stating that he would answer as soon as he had taken a hasty plate of soup. That "hasty plate of soup" appeared in cartoons, was pictured on walls, etc., in every form of ridicule, and was one of the chief elements of his defeat.

When towards the close of the canvass Garfield had succeeded in making the tariff the leading issue, General Hancock was asked what were his views on the tariff. (You must remember that the general was a soldier and had never been in politics.) The general answered: "The tariff was a purely local issue in Pennsylvania." The whole country burst into a gale of laughter, and Hancock's campaign had a crack which was never mended.

There never were two more picturesque opponents than General Garfield and General Hancock. Hancock was the idol of the Army of the Potomac, and everybody remembered McClellan's despatch after one of the bloodiest battles of the Peninsula campaign: "Hancock was superb to-day." He was an exceedingly handsome man and one of the finest figures in uniform in the whole country.

General Garfield also presented a very fine appearance. He was a large man, well-proportioned, and with very engaging manners. He also had an unusual faculty for attractive public addresses, not only on politics, but many subjects, especially education and patriotism.

I never can forget when the news of Lincoln's assassination reached New York. The angry and dangerous crowd which surged up and down Broadway and through Wall Street threatened to wreck the banking and business houses which were supposed to be sympathetic with the Confederates.

Garfield suddenly appeared on the balcony of the Custom House in Wall Street and succeeded in stilling the crowd. With a voice that reached up to Trinity Church he urged calmness in thought and action, deprecated any violence, and then, in an impassioned appeal to hopefulness notwithstanding the tragedy, exclaimed impulsively: "God reigns and the Republic still lives."

I was requested by some friends to visit General Garfield and see how he felt on the political situation, which during the campaign of 1880 did not look hopeful. I took the next train, spent the day with him, and was back in New York the following day.

When I left the train at Cleveland in the morning the newsboys pushed at me a Cleveland Democratic daily, with a rooster's picture covering the whole front page, and the announcement that the Democrats had carried

Maine. The belief was universal then that "as Maine goes so goes the Union," and whichever party carried that State in the September election, the country would follow in the presidential contest in November.

I took the next train to Mentor, the residence of General Garfield. I found at the station a score or more of country wagons and carriages waiting for passengers. I said to the farmers: "Will any of you take me up to General Garfield's residence?" One of them answered: "We will all take you up this morning, but if you had come yesterday you would have had to wait your turn."

It was a startling instance of the variableness of public opinion. Delegations from everywhere, on their way to extend greetings to the candidate, had read the morning papers and turned back, deciding not to go.

I found Garfield struggling bravely to overcome the depression which he felt. He was in close touch with the situation everywhere, and discussed it with discrimination and hopefulness.

The most affecting incident occurred while I was talking with him. His mother passed through the room and, patting him on the back, said: "James, the neighbors think it is all right; they are raising a banner at the corner."

Two old soldier friends came in, and the noonday dinner was a rare intellectual feast. The general was a brilliant conversationalist. His mind turned first to the accidents of careers. He asked me if there was not a time in my early struggles when if Providence had offered a modest certainty I would not have exchanged the whole future for it, and then continued: "There was a period in my early struggles as a teacher when, if I had been offered the principalship of an endowed academy, with an adequate salary, with the condition that I must devote myself to its interests and abandon everything else, I am quite sure I would have accepted."

Of course, the hopeful application of this incident to the Maine defeat was that, no such offer having been made or accepted, he had made a glorious career in the army, rising to the head of the General Staff, and for twenty years had been the leading figure in the House of Representatives, and was now a recently elected United States senator and chosen candidate for president.

Then he turned to the instances where victory had been plucked from defeat in battles. After citing many instances he gave a word picture of the Battle of Chickamauga which was the finest thing of the kind I have ever heard or ever read.

After his two comrades left I told him of the interest which my friends were taking in his canvass, and that I would add their contribution to the campaign committee. The general instantly was exultant and jubilant. He fairly shouted: "Have I not proved to you all day that there is always a silver lining to the cloud, and that the darkest hour is just before dawn?"

It was one of the sources of General Garfield's success as an orator that he was very emotional and sentimental. He happily carried with him amid all struggles and disappointments, as well as successes in the making of a career, the buoyant, hopeful, companionable, and affectionate interests which characterize the ambitious senior who has just left college to take his plunge into the activities of life.

So far as our State was concerned, a great deal turned upon the attitude of Senator Conkling. His great and triumphant speech of four hours at the Academy of

Music in New York brought all his friends into line, but the greatest help which General Garfield received was from the generous, unselfish, and enthusiastic support of General Grant.

General Grant had been the leading candidate in the convention which finally nominated Garfield, but he voluntarily appeared upon the platform in several States and at Garfield's home. His brief but most effective speeches gathered around Garfield not only the whole of the old-soldier vote but those who had become disaffected or indifferent because of the result of the national Republican convention.

There probably was no canvass where the Republican orator ever had so many opportunities for the exercise of every faculty which he possessed. His candidate had made an excellent record as a soldier in the field and as a statesman in Congress, as an educator and a popular speaker on questions of vital interest, while the opposition presented abundant opportunities for attack.

After the presidential election came the meeting of the New York State legislature for the choosing of a United States senator. The legislature was overwhelmingly Republican, and the organization or machine Republicans were in a large majority. The assembly was organized and the appointment of committees used to make certain the election of an organization man.

A very unusual thing happened. The forces of the organization were divided between two candidates: Thomas C. Platt and Richard Crowley. Mr. Conkling had not declared his preference for either, as they were both devoted friends of his, though he had the power to have made a selection and have that selection accepted by the legislature. Vice-President-elect Chester A. Arthur appeared as manager for Mr. Crowley. Platt conducted his own canvass.

I was called to a meeting in New York, where Mr. Blaine, secretary of state, was present. Mr. Blaine said that administration managers had made a thorough canvass of the legislature and they had found that I was the only one who could control enough anti-organization votes to be elected, and, therefore, General Garfield and his friends had decided that I must enter the race. I did not want to do it, nor did I want the senatorship at that time. However, it seemed a plain duty.

A canvass showed that Mr. Platt, Mr. Crowley, and myself had about an equal number of votes. Of course, Mr. Blaine's object was, knowing that Senator Conkling would be hostile to the administration, to prevent his having a colleague who would join with him, and thus place the State of New York against the policies of the incoming president.

After the canvass had been going on for some time, Mr. Platt came to me and asked why I was in it. I told him frankly that I was in it to see, if possible, that the senator-elect should support the administration. He said: "Very well, I will do that."

I immediately called together my supporters. Mr. Platt appeared before them and stated that if elected he would support the president and his administration in every respect. He was asked if he would vote for the confirmation of appointees whom the president might select who were specially in disfavor with Senator Conkling, conspicuously Senator William H. Robertson. Mr. Platt said, "Yes, I will." My friends all went over to him and he was elected.

General Garfield was inaugurated in March, 1881, and

his difficulties began with his Cabinet. Senator Conkling, who saw clearly that with Blaine in the Cabinet his organization was in danger in New York, did not want any of his friends to accept a Cabinet position. The navy was offered to Levi P. Morton, but at the request of Senator Conkling he declined.

When the time came for appointments in the Custom House of New York, General Garfield sent in the name of William H. Robertson, who was the leader of the anti-machine forces in the State. Mr. Conkling at once demanded that Mr. Platt should join with him in inducing the Senate to reject the nomination. Under the rule of senatorial courtesy the Senate would undoubtedly have done this if the two New York senators had acted together. Mr. Platt told Mr. Conkling of his pledge to the members of the legislature, and that he must abide by it, and, as he told me, suggested to Mr. Conkling that, as he always had been his friend and did not want any breach with him, the only thing to be done, consistent with honor, was for both of them to resign and go back to the legislature for re-election, with a mandate which should enable them to reject the appointment of Judge Robertson and all similar appointments.

As the legislature was overwhelmingly Republican, and the organization had a large majority, it seemed to both senators that they would be returned immediately. But it is singular how intense partisanship will blind the ablest and shrewdest politicians. Senators Conkling and Platt were among the ablest and most capable political managers of their time. What they did not reckon with was that the people of the State of New York, or, rather, the Republicans of the State, having just elected a president, would not view favorably the legislature of the

State sending two senators to embarrass their own administration. There was hardly a newspaper in the State or in the country that did not take a hostile attitude.

Mr. Blaine again came to New York and insisted upon my entering the canvass, and that I was the only one who could get the whole of the anti-organization vote.

With the Democrats voting for their own candidate, and the anti-organization men voting for me, it was impossible for any one to have a majority. The fight was most bitter. The ineffectual ballotting went on every day for months. Then Garfield was assassinated. The leader of the Conkling forces came to me and said: "You have a majority of the Republican members now voting for you. Of course, the antagonism has become so great on your candidacy that we cannot vote for you, but if you will withdraw, we will go into caucus."

I instantly accepted the proposition, saw my own people, and we selected Warner Miller to represent the administration, and Congressman Lapham, a very able and capable lieutenant of Mr. Conkling, to represent the organization. The caucus unanimously nominated them and they were elected. Senator Conkling immediately settled in New York to practise law and retired from political activities.

It is the irony of fate that General Garfield, who did more than any other statesman to bring the public from its frenzy after the murder of Lincoln back to a calm and judicious consideration of national conditions, should himself be the victim, so soon after his inauguration, of an assassin.

Lincoln was assassinated in April, after his second inauguration in March, while Garfield was shot in the railway station at Washington July 2, following his inauguration. The president was removed to a cottage at Long Branch, N. J., and lingered there with great suffering for over two months.

I was living at Long Branch that summer and going up and down every day to my office in New York. The whole country was in alternate emotions of hope and despair as the daily bulletins announced the varying phases of the illustrious patient's condition. The people also were greatly impressed at his wonderful self-control, heroic patience, endurance, and amiability.

It was the experience of a lifetime in the psychology of human nature to meet, night after night, the people who gathered at the hotel at Long Branch. Most of them were office-seekers. There were those who had great anticipations of Garfield's recovery, and others, hidebound machinists and organization men, who thought if Garfield died and Vice-President Arthur became president, he would bring in the old order as it existed while he was one of its chief administrators.

There were present very able and experienced newspaper men, representing every great journal in the country. The evening sessions of these veteran observers of public men were most interesting. Their critical analysis of the history and motives of the arriving visitors would have been, if published, the most valuable volume of "Who's Who" ever published. When President Garfield died the whole country mourned.

IX

CHESTER A. ARTHUR

Chester A. Arthur immediately succeeded to the presidency. It had been my good fortune to know so well all the presidents, commencing with Mr. Lincoln, and now the occupant of the White House was a lifelong friend.

President Arthur was a very handsome man, in the prime of life, of superior character and intelligence, and with the perfect manners and courtesies of a trained man of the world. A veteran statesman who had known most of our presidents intimately and been in Congress under many of them said, in reviewing the list with me at the recent convention at Chicago: "Arthur was the only gentleman I ever saw in the White House."

Of course, he did not mean exactly that. He meant that Arthur was the only one of our presidents who came from the refined social circles of the metropolis or from other capitals, and was past master in all the arts and conventionalities of what is known as "best society." He could have taken equal rank in that respect with the Prince of Wales, who afterwards became King Edward VII.

The "hail-fellow-well-met" who had been on familiar terms with him while he was the party leader in New York City, found when they attempted the old familiarities that, while their leader was still their friend, he was President of the United States.

CHESTER A. ARTHUR

Arthur, although one of the most rigid of organization and machine men in his days of local leadership, elevated the party standards by the men whom he drew around himself. He invited into party service and personal intimacy a remarkable body of young, exceedingly able and ambitious men. Many of those became distinguished afterwards in public and professional life. The ablest of them all was a gentleman who, I think, is now universally recognized both at home and abroad as the most efficient and accomplished American diplomat and lawyer—Elihu Root.

There is no career so full of dramatic surprises as the political. President Hayes put civil-service reform upon its feet, and without the assistance of necessary laws vigorously enforced its principles. Among the victims of his enforcement was General Arthur, whom he relieved as collector of the port of New York. To the surprise of every one and the amazement of his old friends, one of the first acts of President Arthur was to demand the enactment of a civil-service law, which had originated with the Civil Service Association, and whose most prominent members were George William Curtis and Carl Schurz.

The president's urgency secured the passage of the measure. He then appointed a thoroughgoing Civil Service Commission, and during his term lived up to every requirement of the system. In doing this he alienated all his old friends, and among them General Grant, ex-Senator Conkling, Thomas C. Platt, and also Mr. Blaine, whom he had asked to remain in the Cabinet as secretary of state. Among them was also John Sherman, whom he had equally wished to retain as secretary of the treasury.

Arthur's administration, both in domestic affairs and in its foreign policies, meets the approval of history and the impartial judgment of posterity. But he was not big enough, nor strong enough, to contend with the powerful men who were antagonized, especially by his civil-service-reform tendencies. When the Republican convention met in 1884 and nominated a new ticket, it was universally recognized by everybody, including the president, that his political career had closed.

President Arthur was one of the most delightful of hosts, and he made the White House the centre of refined hospitality and social charm. He was a shrewd analyst of human nature and told stories full of humor and dramatic effect of some of his contemporaries.

General Arthur, while Republican party leader in New York, invited me to a dinner given him by a friend who had just returned from a hunting trip with a large collection of fine game. With the exception of myself, all the guests were active leaders in the State machine.

During the dinner the general said to me: "While we draft you every fall to help in our canvass, after we have nominated our ticket we miss you in our councils, and we need you."

"Well," I replied, "I do not know what the matter is, nor why Senator Conkling should have a continuing hostility, which I only feel when the time comes around to elect delegates to the State convention."

The general continued: "We are unable to find out either. However, it is absurd, and we are going to see that you are a delegate to the national convention, and we want you to be at the State convention at Utica."

I went to Albany, knowing that there would be a conference at the Executive Mansion, with General Arthur,

Governor Cornell, and Senator Conkling, to lay out a programme for the convention. I met the then secretary of the State committee, Mr. Johnson, and told him about my conversation with General Arthur. He said he was going to attend the conference and would report to me.

When Mr. Johnson returned he told me that General Arthur, Governor Cornell, and others had strongly urged my being a delegate, and that Senator Conkling became very indignant and said that he did not want me back in the organization, and that it was a matter of indifference on what side I was. It is needless to say that I did not attend the convention at Utica.

Mr. Johnson also told me that among other things decided upon was that if General Grant should be nominated for a third term, the old machine under Senator Conkling would be made stronger than ever; that the men who had come to the front during President Hayes's administration as members of the State Senate and assembly and of Congress would be retired, and that another State paper would be established which would wipe out the *Albany Evening Journal*, because it had sustained President Hayes and his policies.

While the convention was in session at Utica I had an interview with Mr. George Dawson, who was editor of the *Albany Evening Journal*, and he became convinced that he had nothing to lose by entering at once into an open antagonism, if there was any way by which it could be made effective.

I said to Mr. Dawson: "The only salvation for those who have been benefited during the era of liberty occasioned by President Hayes's civil-service policies is to prevent the national convention adopting the unit rule."

The unit rule is that if the majority of the delegates from any State make a decision, the chairman of the delegation shall cast the entire vote of the delegation from the State for the result arrived at by the majority, whether it be a candidate or a policy. Under the unit rule I have seen a bare majority of one vote for a candidate, and then the chairman of the delegation cast the entire vote for the candidate, though the minority were very hostile to him.

The delegates of the State convention at Utica returned to Albany that night. Many of them were State senators whose decapitation was assured if the old machine supported by federal patronage was revived. State Senator Webster Wagner was one of them. He and I chartered a train and invited the whole State delegation to go with us to Chicago. In the preliminary discussions, before the national convention met, twenty-six out of seventy-eight delegates decided to act independently.

Wayne MacVeagh, a lifelong friend of mine, had a strong following in the Pennsylvania delegation, and after he learned our position brought over also his people. Emory Storrs, who led the Illinois delegation, came to me and said that if we would not boom Elihu B. Washburne, who was a candidate for the nomination, we would have the Illinois vote. The result of the canvass was that the convention decided against the unit rule. This released so many individual delegates to independent action that the field was cleared and nobody had a majority. The leading candidates were General Grant, James G. Blaine, and John Sherman.

In the history of convention oratory the nominating speeches of Senator Conkling for General Grant, and

James A. Garfield for John Sherman take the highest rank. Conkling took a lofty position on the platform. His speech was perfectly prepared, delivered with great dramatic effect, and received universal applause on the floor and in the gallery.

General Garfield, on the other hand, also a fine-looking man and a practised orator, avoided the dramatic element, in which he could not compete with Conkling, but delivered a speech along the line of the average thought and general comprehension of his audience that made a great impression. It was a common remark: "He has nominated himself."

There were among the audience thousands of Blaine enthusiasts. No public man since Lincoln ever had such enthusiastic, devoted, and almost crazy followers as Mr. Blaine. These enthusiasts were waiting to raise the roof and secure the nomination of their candidate when the chosen orator should present their favorite.

The gentleman selected to present Mr. Blaine was eminent in business and great enterprises, but I doubt if he had ever spoken before except to a board of directors. Of course, in that vast hall such a man was fearfully handicapped and could not be very well heard. He closed by naming his candidate somewhat like this: "I now have the pleasure and honor of proposing as the candidate of this convention that eminent statesman, James S. Blaine." Nearly every one in the convention knew that Mr. Blaine's middle name was Gillespie.

The Blaine followers, whose indignation had been growing throughout the speech, because they expected the very highest type of oratory for their favorite, shouted in chorus, "G., you fool, G.!"

When General Garfield was voted for, he indignantly

repudiated the votes as an imputation upon his honor, as he was there to nominate his friend, John Sherman. Senator George F. Hoar, of Massachusetts, presided at the convention. He interrupted Garfield by calling him to order, as it was not in order to interrupt the calling of the roll, and he did so for fear that Garfield would go so far as to say he would not accept the nomination if it were made. On the last ballot State after State, each striving to get ahead of the other, changed its vote from Sherman or Blaine to Garfield, and he was nominated.

I sat close to him as a visitor to the Ohio delegation. It was a curious exhibit of the ambition of a lifetime suddenly and unexpectedly realized by a highly sensitive and highly wrought-up man. He was so overcome that he practically had to be carried out of the convention by his friends.

Senator Conkling was very indignant at the result and expressed his anger with his usual emphasis and picturesqueness. The Ohio leaders were then anxious to placate New York, but Conkling would have nothing to do with them. They then came to us, who had been opposed to the unit rule, and wanted suggestions as to which New Yorker they should select for vice-president. Levi P. Morton was suggested. Mr. Morton said he would accept if Senator Conkling was willing to agree to it, and that he would not act without the senator's acquiescence, as he was an organization man. The senator refused his consent, and told Mr. Morton that no friend of his would go on the ticket.

It was then suggested that they try General Arthur, who was Conkling's first lieutenant and chairman of the Republican State Committee of New York. Senator Conkling made the same answer to General Arthur, but he frankly said to Conkling: "Such an honor and opportunity comes to very few of the millions of Americans, and to that man but once. No man can refuse it, and I will not." And so General Arthur was nominated for vice-president.

X

GROVER CLEVELAND

Grover Cleveland was a remarkable man. He had more political courage of the General Jackson type than almost any man who ever held great responsible positions. He defied Tammany Hall while governor of the State, and repeatedly challenged the strongest elements of his party while president. Threats of defeat or retaliation never moved him. If he had once made up his mind and believed he was right, no suggestions of expediency or of popularity had any influence on him.

In personal intercourse he made friends and had great charm. The campaign against him when he ran for governor of New York was ruthlessly conducted. I considered the actions of his enemies as unfair and that they would react in the canvass. I studiously discredited all in my speeches, and begged our people not to feature them.

I knew Mr. Cleveland, and as an evidence of my appreciation of his character and ability, when the office of general counsel of the New York Central Railroad at Buffalo became vacant, I offered it to him, saying: "I am exceedingly anxious that you should accept this place. I think, by an adjustment of the administration of your office, you can retain your private practice, and this will add about fifteen thousand dollars a year to your income."

Mr. Cleveland replied: "I have a very definite plan of life and have decided how much work I can do without impairing my health, and how much of additional responsibility I can assume. I have accumulated about seventy-five thousand dollars and my practice yields me an income which is sufficient for my wants and a prudent addition for my old age to my capital. No amount of money whatever would tempt me to add to or increase my present work."

I doubt if there were many lawyers in the United States who had that philosophy or control of their ambitions. His annual income from his profession was considerably less than the compensation offered by the general counselship of the New York Central.

Cleveland was most satisfactory as president in his quick and decisive judgment upon matters presented to him. There were no delays, no revisions; in fact, no diplomatic methods of avoiding a disagreeable decision. He told you in the briefest time and in the clearest way what he would do.

A great social leader and arbiter in social affairs in New York was very desirous that the president should reverse his judgment in regard to an appointment affecting a member of his family. I gave him a letter which procured him a personal and confidential interview. When he came back to me he said: "That is the most extraordinary man I ever saw. After he had heard me through, he said he understood the matter thoroughly and would not change his opinion or action. He has no social position and never had. I tried to present its attractions and my ability to help him in that regard, but he only laughed; yes, he positively laughed."

While President Hayes had difficulty with civil-service reform and incurred the hostility of the Republican organization and machine men, the situation with him was far less difficult than it was with Cleveland, who was a sincere civil-service reformer, and also an earnest Democrat. While a Democratic senator from Ohio, Mr. Pendleton, had passed a bill during the Hayes administration for reform in the civil service, the great majority of the Democratic party believed in Secretary Marcy's declaration that "to the victors belong the spoils."

There was an aggravation, also, growing out of the fact that the Democrats had been out of office for twenty-four years. We can hardly visualize or conceive now of their hunger for office. The rule for rescuing people dying of starvation is to feed them in very small quantities, and frequently. By trying this, the president became one of the most unpopular of men who had ever held office; in fact, so unpopular among the Democratic senators and members of the House that a story which Zebulon Vance, of North Carolina, told went all over the country and still survives. Vance, who had a large proportion of the citizens of North Carolina on his waiting list, and could get none of them appointed, said that the situation, which ought to be one of rejoicing at the election of a president by his own party, was like that of a client of his who had inherited a farm from his father. There were so many difficulties about the title and getting possession of it and delay, that the son said: "I almost wished father had not died."

However, Mr. Cleveland, in his deliberate way did accomplish the impossible. He largely regained favor with his party by satisfying their demands, and at the same time so enlarged the scope of civil-service requirements as to receive the commendation of the two great leaders of the civil-service movement—George William Curtis and Carl Schurz.

President Cleveland entered upon his second term with greater popularity in the country than most of his predecessors. When he retired from office, it was practically by unanimous consent. It is among the tragedies of public life that he lost entirely the confidence of his party and, in a measure, of the whole people by rendering to his country the greatest public service.

A strike of the men on the railroads tied up transportation. Railroads are the arteries of travel, commerce, and trade. To stop them is to prevent the transportation of provisions or of coal, to starve and freeze cities and communities. Cleveland used the whole power of the federal government to keep free the transportation on the railways and to punish as the enemies of the whole people those who were trying to stop them. It was a lesson which has been of incalculable value ever since in keeping open these great highways.

He forced through the repeal of the silver purchasing law by every source and pressure and the unlimited use of patronage. His party were almost unanimous for the silver standard and resented this repeal as a crime, but it saved the country from general bankruptcy. Except in the use of patronage to help his silver legislation, he offended his party by improving the civil service and retaining Theodore Roosevelt as head of the Civil Service Commission. These crises required from the president an extraordinary degree of courage and steadfastness.

While Mr. Cleveland was in such unprecedented popular disfavor when he retired to private life, his fame as president increases through the years, and he is rapidly assuming foremost position in the estimation of the people.

Mr. Cleveland had a peculiar style in his speeches and public documents. It was criticised as labored and that of an essayist. I asked him, after he had retired to private life, how he had acquired it. He said his father was a clergyman and he had been educated by him largely at home. His father was very particular about his compositions and his English, so that he acquired a ministerial style. The result of this was that whenever any of the members of the local bar died, he was called upon to write the obituary resolutions.

To take a leap over intervening years: After Mr. Cleveland retired from his second term I used to meet him very frequently on social occasions and formal celebrations. He soon left the practice of law and settled in Princeton, where he did great and useful service, until he died, as trustee of the university and a lecturer before the students.

Riding in the same carriage with him in the great procession at the funeral of General Sherman, he reminisced most interestingly in regard to his experiences while president. Every little while there would break out a cheer and then a shout in the crowd of one of the old campaign cries: "Grover, Grover, four years more." Mr. Cleveland remarked: "I noticed while president a certain regularity and recrudescence of popular applause, and it was the same in every place I visited." That cry, "Grover, Grover, four years more!" would occur every third block, and during our long ride the mathematical tradition was preserved.

XI

BENJAMIN HARRISON

The year 1888 was one of singular experience for me. I was working very hard in my professional duties and paying no attention to public affairs.

The district conventions to send delegates to the national convention at Chicago began electing their delegates and alternates, and passing resolutions instructing them to vote for me as their candidate for president.

After several districts had thus acted I was asked to meet in Whitelaw Reid's office in the Tribune Building Thomas C. Platt, our State leader, and United States Senator Frank Hiscock. Platt demanded to know why I was making this canvass without consulting the organization or informing them. I told him I was doing nothing whatever by letter, telegram, or interview; that I had seen no one, and no one had been to see me.

Mr. Platt, who had been all his life accomplishing things through the organization, was no believer in spontaneous uprisings, and asked me frankly: "Are you a candidate?" I told him I was not, because I did not believe I could be nominated with the present condition of the public mind in regard to railways, and I was president of one of the largest systems.

Then it was suggested that I permit the *Tribune*, which was the party organ, to state that I was not a candidate and did not want to be. The next morning the *Tribune* had that fully explained. The conventions kept on convening and instructing their delegates the same way.

Another conference was called, and then I was asked to make the statement that if nominated I would not accept, and if elected I would decline. I said to my conferees: "Gentlemen, there is no American living big enough to say that. In the first place, it is gross egotism to think such a thing might happen." The result was that the organization accepted the situation.

The only way that I can account for this unanimous action of the party in its conventions in the congressional districts of the State is the accumulative result of appreciation of unselfish work for the party. Every fall, for a quarter of a century, I had been on the platform in every part of the State, and according to my means was a contributor to the State and local canvass. During this period I had asked nothing and would accept nothing. If I may apply so large a phrase to a matter so comparatively unimportant, I would deny the often quoted maxim that "republics are ungrateful."

When the convention met there was an overwhelming sentiment for Mr. Blaine, but his refusal was positive and absolute. I had always been a warm supporter and friend of Mr. Blaine, and his followers were very friendly to me.

What were called "the Granger States," and especially Iowa, had become very hostile to railway management and railway men. They were passing laws which were practically confiscatory of railway securities. The committees from those States visited all other State delegations and spoke in bitter terms of my candidacy. The strength of my candidacy was that New York was unanimously for me, except for one vote from New York

City, and no nominee could hope to be elected unless he could carry New York.

After receiving ninety-nine votes, I found that on the next ballot my vote would be very largely increased, and decided to retire. I called together the New York delegation and stated my position, and the reason for it. A considerable debate took place. The motion was made and unanimously carried that the four delegates at large should meet and see if they could agree upon a candidate who would command the support of the entire delegation of the State. The object was, of course, to make the State, with its larger number of delegates than any other commonwealth, a deciding factor in the selection.

The delegates at large were: Thomas C. Platt, Senator Frank Hiscock, Warner Miller, and myself. When we met, Platt and Hiscock declared for Senator Allison of Iowa. Warner Miller with equal warmth announced that he was for John Sherman.

A heated controversy arose between Mr. Platt and Mr. Miller, during which Mr. Platt said that neither he nor any of his friends would vote for Sherman if he was nominated. Senator Hiscock, who was always a pacifier, interrupted them, saying: "Mr. Depew has said nothing as yet. I suggest that we hear his views."

Mr. Platt and Mr. Miller responded to this suggestion and I replied: "Gentlemen, New York has given to me its cordial and practically unanimous support, and I have felt under the circumstances that I should follow and not lead. The situation which has grown out of this discussion here eliminates two candidates. Without the aid of Senator Platt and his friends, Mr. Sherman could not carry New York. Iowa has gone to the extreme of radical legislation which threatens the investment in securities of her railroads, and New York is such a capitalistic State that no man identified with that legislation could carry a majority of the vote of its people, and that makes Allison impossible. There is one candidate here who at present apparently has no chance, but who, nevertheless, seems to me to possess more popular qualifications than any other, and that is General Benjamin Harrison, of Indiana. I do not know him, never met him, but he rose from the humblest beginnings until he became the leader of the bar of his State. He enlisted in the Civil War as a second lieutenant, and by conspicuous bravery and skill upon the battle-field came out as brigadier-general. As United States senator he became informed about federal affairs. His grandfather, President William H. Harrison, had one of the most picturesque campaigns in our history. There are enough survivors of that 'hard cider and log cabin' canvass to make an attractive contribution on the platform at every meeting, and thus add a certain historic flavor to General Harrison's candidacy."

After some discussion the other three agreed. We reported our conclusion to the delegation, which by an overwhelming majority assented to the conclusions of the four delegates at large. This decision settled the question in the convention, and after a few ballots General Harrison was nominated. New York was awarded the vice-presidency and selected Levi P. Morton.

During Harrison's administration I was absorbed in my duties as president of the New York Central Railroad, and was seldom in Washington. But soon after his inauguration he sent to me a member of Congress from Indiana with a special message. This congressman said: "I come from President Harrison, and he has instructed me to offer you a place in his Cabinet. He is anxious to have you in his official family."

I told him that I was not prepared to enter public life, and while I was exceedingly gratified by the offer, it was impossible for me to accept.

The congressman said: "I am a poor man, but cannot understand how anybody can refuse to be member of the Cabinet of the President of the United States. If such an offer was made to me, and the conditions of our overruling Providence were that I and my family should live in want and poverty for the rest of our lives, I would accept without hesitation."

I had met Benjamin Harrison as we passed through Indianapolis on business during the canvass, for the first time. I was much impressed with him, but his austerity appeared to those who called upon him while present upon official business. I found him one of the most genial and agreeable of men, and this impression was intensified when I met him at the White House. At his own table and family dinners he was one of the most charming of hosts. He had, unfortunately, a repellent manner and a harsh voice. In meeting those who came to him for official favors this made him one of the most unpopular presidents with senators and members of the House of Representatives.

On the platform as a public speaker he had few equals. He was most lucid and convincing, and had what few orators possess, which was of special use to him in campaigning and touring the country as president, the ability to make a fresh speech every day and each a good one. It was a talent of presenting questions from many angles, each of which illuminated his subject and captivated his audience. It was said of him by a senator who was his friend, and the remark is quoted by Senator Hoar, that if he spoke to an audience of ten thousand people, he would make every one of them his friend, but if he were introduced to each of them afterwards, each would depart his enemy. I think that his manner, which was so unfortunate, came from the fact that his career had been one of battle, from his early struggles to his triumphant success.

A short time before the national convention met in 1892 Senator Frank Hiscock came to me and said that President Harrison had requested him to ask me to lead his forces on the floor in the convention. I said to him that I was a loyal organization man and did not want to quarrel with our leader, Senator Platt. Then he told me that he had seen Platt, who remarked that no one could help Harrison, and that I would conduct the campaign in better spirit than any one, and so he had no objection to my accepting the position. There was one obstacle which I wished removed. I was devoted to Mr. Blaine and not only was one of his political supporters but very fond of him personally. Mr. Blaine happened to be in the city, and I immediately called upon him. His health was then very bad.

"Mr. Blaine," I said to him, "if you are a candidate, you know I will support you with the greatest of pleasure, but if not, then I will accept the invitation of the president."

Mr. Blaine was most cordial. He said that he had no objections whatever to my taking the commission, but he doubted if the president could be renominated, and that he could not be re-elected if nominated. Harrison had made an excellent president, but his manner of treating people who came to him had filled the country with bitter and powerful enemies, while his friends were very few. Then he mentioned several other possible candidates, but evidently doubted the success of the Republican party in the election. In regard to himself he said: "If I should accept the nomination I could not endure the labors of the canvass and its excitements. It would kill me." That diagnosis of his condition was correct and was demonstrated by the fact that he died soon after the election, but long before he could be inaugurated if elected.

All organization leaders of the party were united against the nomination of President Harrison. The leaders were Platt, Quay, and Clarkson, who was also chairman of the national committee. They were the greatest masters of organization and of its management we ever had in politics, especially Platt and Quay. Their methods were always secret, so I decided that the only hope of success for President Harrison was in the greatest publicity.

The position I had accepted soon became known, and I began to give the fullest interviews, each one an argument for the renomination of the president. I went to Chicago a few days in advance of the convention, was met there by correspondents of the press, some fifty of them, and gave them a talk in a body, which made a broadside in the morning papers, each correspondent treating it in his own way, as his own individual interview.

This statement or, rather, argument, was intended to be read and succeeded in being so by the delegates from everywhere who were on their way to the convention and had to pass through Chicago. The convention was held in Minneapolis. I received from that city an invitation to address a gathering of New Yorkers who had settled in the West to speak before two patriotic audiences, and to make the address at the dedication of the great hall where the convention was to meet.

It was evident that before these engagements had been concluded, every delegate would have attended some of these meetings, and, therefore, with the relationship between a speaker and his audience, I would be practically the only man in the convention who was personally known to every member. This relationship was an enormous benefit in conducting the canvass.

The great organization leaders were difficult of access and carried on their campaign through trusted members of each State delegation. My rooms were wide open for everybody. On account of the conflicting statements made by members of the State delegations, it was very difficult to make an accurate and detailed list of those who were for the president, and those who were for Mr. Blaine. It occurred to me that it would help to call a meeting of the Harrison delegates. Many thought it was hazardous, as it might develop a majority the other way.

The meeting was attended, however, by every delegate, those opposed coming out of curiosity. Taking the chair, I asked some member of each delegation to arise and state how many votes he believed could be relied upon from his State. Of course the statement of each delegate was often loudly challenged by others from his State who were present. When the result was announced it showed a majority of three for General Harrison. A veteran campaigner begged me to announce it as fifty, but I refused. "No," I said, "the closeness of the vote when there is every opportunity for manipulation would carry conviction."

An old gentleman who stood beside me had a gold-headed ebony cane. I seized it and rapped it on the table with such force that it broke in two and announced that the figures showed absolute certainty of President Harrison's renomination. I doubt if there was a reliable majority, but the announcement of this result brought enough of those always anxious to get on the band-wagon to make it certain.

Soon after arriving home I received a letter from the owner of the cane. He wrote: "I was very angry when you broke my cane. It was a valued birthday present from my children. It is now in a glass case in my library, and on the case is this label: 'This cane nominated a president of the United States.'"

Mr. McKinley, then Governor of Ohio, presided at the convention. I stood close beside him when I made my speech for Harrison's renomination. While thoroughly prepared, the speech was in a way extemporaneous to meet calls or objections. In the midst of a sentence McKinley said to me in a loud voice: "You are making a remarkably fine speech." The remark threw me off my balance as an opposition would never have done. I lost the continuity and came near breaking down, but happily the applause gave me time to get again upon the track.

Among my colleagues in the New York delegation was James W. Husted. General Husted was very ill and unable to leave his room during the convention. He sent for me one morning and said: "I have just had a call from Governor McKinley. He says that you have the power to nominate him, and that Harrison cannot be nominated. If you will direct the Harrison forces for him, he will be the next president."

I told Husted I was enlisted for the war and, while having a great admiration for McKinley, it was impossible.

Soon after arriving home I received an invitation from the president to visit him at Washington. I took the night train, arriving there in the morning. My appointment was to lunch with him.

During the morning Stephen B. Elkins, then secretary of war, called and asked me to take a walk. While we were walking he told me that the president was going to offer me the secretaryship of state, in succession to Mr. Blaine, and that I ought to accept. He then led me to the State Department and pointed to the portraits on the walls of the different secretaries, commencing with Thomas Jefferson. Elkins said that to be in that list was a greater distinction than to be on the walls of the White House, because these men are of far greater eminence.

After luncheon the president invited me into the Blue Room, and with a great deal of emotion said: "You are the only man who has ever unselfishly befriended me. It was largely through your efforts that I became president, and I am greatly indebted to you for my renomination. I have tried my best to show my appreciation by asking you into my Cabinet and otherwise, but you have refused everything I have heretofore offered. I now want to give you the best I have, which is secretary of state. It is broken bread, because if I am not re-elected it will be only till the 4th of March, but if I am re-elected it will be for four years more. I personally want you in my Cabinet."

I told the president it was impossible for me to accept; that even if I resigned my presidency of the railroad, coming directly from that position would bring the railroad question, which was very acute, into the canvass. He said he did not think there was anything in that, but I realized that if he was defeated his defeat would be charged to having made that mistake.

He then said: "Well, how about it if I am re-elected?" I told him that I would regard the appointment the greatest of honors, and the associations the most pleasurable of a lifetime.

"Very well," he said; "I will appoint Mr. John W. Foster, who has been doing excellent service for the State Department, until next 4th of March, and you can prepare to come here upon that date."

The most painful thing that was connected with the canvass at Minneapolis before the convention was the appearance of Mr. Blaine as a candidate. He had resigned from the Cabinet and yielded to the pressure of his friends to become a candidate.

Notwithstanding my interview and what he had said, he sent no word whatever to me, and personally I had no information and no notification that his candidacy was authorized by himself. What gave, however, much authority to the statement that he would accept the nomination was the appearance of his son, Emmons, among those who were endeavoring to bring it about.

There has never been a statesman in our public life, except Henry Clay, who had such devoted friends as Mr. Blaine. While Henry Clay never reached the presidency and was fairly defeated in his attempt, there is no doubt that Mr. Blaine was elected in 1884, and that notwithstanding the Burchard misfortune, he would still have been a victor except for transparent frauds in New York.

General Harrison was by far the ablest and profoundest lawyer among our presidents. None of them equalled him as an orator. His State papers were of a very high order. When history sums up the men who have held the great place of president of the United States, General Harrison will be among the foremost.

He retired from office, like many of our presidents, a comparatively poor man. After retirement he entered at once upon the practice of his profession of the law and almost immediately became recognized as one of the leaders of the American bar.

XII

JAMES G. BLAINE

I have spoken in every national canvass, beginning with 1856. It has been an interesting experience to be on the same platform as an associate speaker with nearly every man in the country who had a national reputation. Most of them had but one speech, which was very long, elaborately prepared, and so divided into sections, each complete in itself, that the orator was equipped for an address of any length, from fifteen minutes to four hours, by selection or consolidation of these sections. Few of them would trust themselves to extemporaneous speaking. The most versatile and capable of those who could was James G. Blaine. He was always ready, courted interruptions, and was brilliantly effective. In a few sentences he had captured his audience and held them enthralled. No public man in our country, except, perhaps, Henry Clay, had such devoted following.

Mr. Blaine had another extraordinary gift, which is said to belong only to kings; he never forgot any one. Years after an introduction he would recall where he had first met the stranger and remember his name. This compliment made that man Blaine's devoted friend for life.

I had an interesting experience of his readiness and versatility when he ran for president in 1884. He asked me to introduce him at the different stations, where he was to deliver long or short addresses. After several of these occasions, he asked: "What's the next station,

Chauncey?" I answered: "Peekskill." "Well," he said, "what is there about Peekskill?" "I was born there," I answered. "Well," he said, rising, "I always thought that you were born at Poughkeepsie." "No, Peekskill." Just then we were running into the station, and, as the train stopped, I stepped forward to introduce him to the great crowd which had gathered there from a radius of fifty miles. He pushed me back in a very dramatic way, and shouted: "Fellow citizens, allow me to make the introduction here. As I have many times in the last quarter of a century travelled up and down your beautiful Hudson River, with its majestic scenery made famous by the genius of Washington Irving, and upon the floating palaces not equalled anywhere else in the world, or when the steamer has passed through this picturesque bay and opposite your village, I have had emotions of tenderness and loving memories, greater than those impressed by any other town, because I have said to myself: 'There is the birthplace of one of my best friends, Chauncey Depew.'"

Local committees who desire to use the candidate to help the party in their neighborhood and also their county tickets are invariably most unreasonable and merciless in their demands upon the time of the candidate. They know perfectly well that he has to speak many times a day; that there is a limit to his strength and to his vocal cords, and yet they will exact from him an effort which would prevent his filling other engagements, if they possibly can. This was notoriously the case during Mr. Blaine's trip through the State of New York and afterwards through the country. The strain upon him was unprecedented, and, very naturally, he at times showed his irritation and some temper.

The local committees would do their best with the railroad company and with Blaine's managers in New York to prolong his stay and speech at each station. He would be scheduled according to the importance of the place for five, ten, fifteen, twenty, or thirty minutes.

Before we reached Albany he asked me to accompany him to the end of our line at Buffalo, and make the introduction as usual at the stations. The committee would sometimes succeed in changing the programme and make the stays longer at their several places. Mr. Blaine's arrangement with me was that after he had decided how long he would speak, I should fill up the time, whether it was longer or shorter. That would often enlarge my speech, but I was young and vigorous and had no responsibilities.

I remember one committee, where the train was scheduled for ten minutes, succeed in having it delayed an hour, and instead of a brief address from the platform of the car, carried the presidential party to a stand in the central square where many thousands had gathered. In the first place, this city was not on Mr. Blaine's schedule, and as it was late in the afternoon, after a fatiguing day, he therefore told the committee peremptorily that ten minutes was his limit. Then he said to me: "Chauncey, you will have to fill out the hour."

Mr. Blaine's wonderful magnetism, the impression he made upon every one, and his tactful flattery of local pride, did a great deal to remove the prejudices against him, which were being fomented by a propaganda of a "mugwump" committee in New York. This propaganda, as is usually the case, assailed his personal integrity.

Notwithstanding the predictions made at the time, he

was nominated, and it was subsequently repeated that he would not carry New York. From my own experience of many years with the people of the State and from the platform view-point, I felt confident that he would have a majority in the election.

It was a few days before the close of the canvass, when I was in the western part of the State, I received an urgent telegram from Mr. Blaine to join him on the train, which was to leave the Grand Central Station in New York early next morning for his tour of New England. Upon arrival I was met by a messenger, who took me at once to Mr. Blaine's car, which started a few minutes afterwards.

There was an unusual excitement in the crowd, which was speedily explained. The best account Mr. Blaine gave me himself in saying: "I felt decidedly that everything was well in New York. It was against my judgment to return here. Our national committee, however, found that a large body of Protestant clergymen wanted to meet me and extend their support. They thought this would offset the charges made by the 'mugwump' committee. I did not believe that any such recognition was necessary. However, their demands for my return and to meet this body became so importunate that I yielded my own judgment.

"I was engaged in my room with the committee and other visitors when I was summoned to the lobby of the hotel to meet the clergymen. I had prepared no speech; in fact, had not thought up a reply. When their spokesman, Reverend Doctor Burchard, began to address me, my only hope was that he would continue long enough for me to prepare an appropriate response. I had a very definite idea of what he would say and so paid little attention to his speech. In the evening the reporters began rushing in and wanted my opinion of Doctor Burchard's statement that the main issue of the campaign was 'Rum, Romanism, and Rebellion.' If I had heard him utter these words, I would have answered at once, and that would have been effective, but I am still in doubt as to what to say about it now. The situation is very difficult, and almost anything I say is likely to bitterly offend one side or the other. Now I want you to do all the introductions and be beside me to-day as far as possible. I have become doubtful about everybody and you are always sure-footed." I have treasured that compliment ever since.

As we rode through the streets of New Haven the Democrats had placed men upon the tops of the houses on either side, and they threw out in the air thousands of leaflets, charging Blaine with having assented to the issue which Doctor Burchard had put out—"Rum, Romanism, and Rebellion." They so filled the air that it seemed a shower, and littered the streets.

A distinguished Catholic prelate said to me: "We had to resent an insult like that, and I estimate that the remark has changed fifty thousand votes." I know personally of about five thousand which were changed in our State, but still Blaine lost New York and the presidency by a majority against him of only one thousand one hundred and forty-nine votes.

Whenever I visited Washington I always called upon Mr. Blaine. The fascination of the statesman and his wonderful conversational power made every visit an event to be remembered. On one occasion he said to me: "Chauncey, I am in very low spirits to-day. I have read over the first volume of my 'Twenty Years in

Congress,' which is just going to the printer, and destroyed it. I dictated the whole of it, but I find that accuracy and elegance can only be had at the end of a pen. I shall rewrite the memoirs in ink. In these days composition by the typewriter or through the stenographer is so common." There will be many who differ with Mr. Blaine.

XIII

WILLIAM McKINLEY

In the canvass of 1896 the Republican organization of the State of New York decided, if possible, to have the national convention nominate Levi P. Morton for president. Mr. Morton won popular favor as vice-president, and the canvass for him looked hopeful. But a new man of extraordinary force and ability came into this campaign, and that man was Mark Hanna, of Ohio. Mr. Hanna was one of the most successful of our business men. He had a rare genius for organization, and possessed resourcefulness, courage, and audacity. He was most practical and at the same time had imagination and vision. While he had taken very little part in public affairs, he had rather suddenly determined to make his devoted friend, William McKinley, president of the United States.

In a little while every State in tne Union felt the force of Mr. Hanna's efforts. He applied to politics the methods by which he had so successfully advanced his large manufacturing interests. McKinley clubs and McKinley local organizations sprang up everywhere under the magic of Hanna's management. When the convention met it was plain that McKinley's nomination was assured.

The New York delegation, however, decided to present Morton's name and submit his candidacy to a vote. I was selected to make a nominating speech. If there is any hope, an orator on such an occasion has inspiration.

But if he knows he is beaten he cannot put into his effort the fire necessary to impress an audience. It is not possible to speak with force and effect unless you have faith in your cause.

After Mr. McKinley was nominated I moved that the nomination be made unanimous. The convention called for speech and platform so insistently that their call had to be obeyed. The following is an account from a newspaper of that date of my impromptu speech. The story which is mentioned in the speech was told to me as I was ascending the platform by Senator Proctor of Vermont.

"I am in the happy position now of making a speech for the man who is going to be elected. (Laughter and applause.) It is a great thing for an amateur, when his first nomination has failed, to come in and second the man who has succeeded. New York is here with no bitter feeling and with no disappointment. We recognize that the waves have submerged us, but we have bobbed up serenely. (Loud laughter.) It was a cannon from New York that sounded first the news of McKinley's nomination. They said of Governor Morton's father that he was a New England clergyman, who brought up a family of ten children on three hundred dollars a year, and was, notwithstanding, gifted in prayer. (Laughter.) It does not make any difference how poor he may be, how out of work, how ragged, how next door to a tramp anybody may be in the United States to-night, he will be 'gifted in prayer' at the result of this convention. (Cheers and laughter.)

"There is a principle dear to the American heart. It is the principle which moves American spindles, starts the industries, and makes the wage-earners sought for, instead of seeking employment. That principle is embodied in McKinley. His personality explains the nomination to-day. And his personality will carry into the presidential chair the aspirations of the voters of America, of the families of America, of the homes of America, protection to American industry and America for Americans." (Cheers.)

As every national convention, like every individual, has its characteristics, the peculiar distinction of the Republican convention of 1896 was its adoption of the gold standard of value. An amazing and illuminating part of our political literature of that time is the claim which various statesmen and publicists make to the authorship of the gold plank in the platform.

Senator Foraker, who was chairman of the committee on resolutions, devotes a considerable part of his interesting autobiography to the discussion of this question. He is very severe upon all those who claim to have originated the idea. I have been asked by several statesmen to enforce their claims to its authorship.

The silver craze had not yet subsided. Bimetallism had strong advocates and believers in our convention. I think even our candidate was not fully convinced at that time of the wisdom of the declaration. It went into the platform rather as a venture than an article of faith, but to the surprise of both the journalists and campaign orators, it turned out that the people had become converted to the gold standard, and it proved to be the strongest and most popular declaration of the convention.

When the campaign opened the genius of Mark Hanna soon became evident. He organized a campaign of education such as had never been dreamed of, much less attempted. Travelling publicity agents, with wagonloads of pamphlets, filled the highways and the byways, and no home was so isolated that it did not receive its share. Columns in the newspapers, especially the country papers, were filled with articles written by experts, and the platform was never so rich with public speakers.

Such a campaign is irresistible. Its influence is felt by everybody; its arguments become automatically and almost insensibly the common language of the people. But the expense is so terrific that it will never again be attempted. There was no corruption or purchase of votes in Mr. Hanna's management. It was publicity and again publicity, but it cost nearly five millions of dollars. To reach the one hundred and ten million of people in the United States in such a way would involve a sum so vast that public opinion would never permit any approach to it.

Mr. McKinley's front-porch campaign was a picturesque and captivating feature. The candidate was a handsome man and an eloquent speaker, with a cordial and sympathetic manner which won everybody. Delegations from all parts of the country and representing every phase of American life appeared at Mr. McKinley's residence. His address to them was always appropriate and his reception made the visitors his fast friends.

I received a personal request to visit him, and on the occasion he said to me: "In certain large agricultural sections there is a very dangerous revolt in our party, owing to the bad conditions among the farmers. Wheat and corn are selling below the cost of production. I wish you would go down among them and make speeches explaining the economic conditions which have produced this result, and how we propose to and will remedy it."

"Mr. McKinley," I said, "my position as a railroad president, I am afraid, would antagonize them."

"On the contrary, your very position will draw the largest audiences and receive the greater attention."

The result proved that he was correct.

I recall one meeting in particular. There were thousands present, all farmers. In the midst of my speech one man arose and said: "Chauncey Depew, we appreciate your coming here, and we are very anxious to hear you. Your speech is very charming and interesting, but I want to put this to you personally. We here are suffering from market conditions for the products of our farms. The prices are so low that we have difficulty in meeting the interest on our mortgages and paying our taxes, no matter how seriously we economize. Now you are the president of one of the greatest railroads in the country. It is reported that you are receiving a salary of fifty thousand dollars a year. You are here in a private car. Don't you think that the contrast between you and us makes it difficult for us poor farmers to give you the welcome which we would like?"

I saw at once I had lost my audience. I then ventured upon a statement of conditions which I have often tried and always successfully. I said: "My friend, what you say about me is true. Now, as to my career, I was born and brought up in a village similar to the one which is near you here. My father gave me my education and nothing else with which to begin life. As a young lawyer I was looking for clients and not for office. I made up my mind that there were no opportunities offered in the village, but that the chances of success were in the service of corporations. The result is that I have accomplished what you have described. Now, my friend, I believe that you have a promising boy. I also believe that to your pride and satisfaction he is going through the neighboring college here, and that you intend on account of his brightness and ability to make him a lawyer. When he is admitted to the bar, do you expect him to try to do what I have accomplished and make an independent position in life, or fail?"

The farmer shouted: "Chauncey, you are all right. Go ahead and keep it up."

My arguments and presentation were no better than many another speaker's, but, as Mr. McKinley predicted, they received an attention and aroused a discussion, because of what the old farmer had said, that no other campaigner could command.

Mr. McKinley sent for me again and said: "Sentiment is a wonderful force in politics. Mr. Bryan, my opponent, has made a remarkable speaking tour through our State. He started in the early morning from Cleveland with a speech. His train made many stops on the way to Cincinnati, where he arrived in the evening, and at each place he addressed large audiences, traversing the State from one side to the other. His endurance and versatility have made a great impression upon our people. To meet and overcome that impression, I have asked you to come here and repeat Bryan's effort. You are so much older than he is—I think we may claim nearly twice his age—that if you can do it, and I hope you can, that sentiment will be dissipated."

I traversed Mr. Bryan's route, stopped at the same stations and delivered speeches to similar audiences of about the same length. On arriving in Cincinnati in the evening I was met by a committee, the chairman of which said: "We have followed you all along from Cleveland, where you started at seven o'clock this morning, and it is fine. Now Mr. Bryan, when he arrived here, had no meeting. We have seven thousand people in the Music Hall, and if you will go there and speak five minutes it will make your trip a phenomenal success."

I went to the Music Hall, of course had a wonderful time and wild ovation, and spoke for an hour. The next day I was none the worse for this twelve hours' experience.

President McKinley had spent most of his life in the House of Representatives. He loved the associations and life of Congress. The most erratic and uncertain of bodies is Congress to an executive who does not understand its temper and characteristics. McKinley was past master of this. Almost every president has been greatly relieved when Congress adjourned, but Mr. McKinley often expressed to me his wish that Congress would always be in session, as he never was so happy as when he could be in daily contact with it. His door was open at all times to a senator or a member of the House of Representatives. If either failed to see him at least once a week, the absentee usually received a message stating that the president desired him to call. He was very keen in discovering any irritation on the part of any senator or member about any disappointment or fancied slight, and always most tactfully managed to straighten the matter out. He was quite as attentive and as particular with the opposition as with members of his own party.

President McKinley had a wonderful way of dealing with office-seekers and with their friends and supporters. A phrase of his became part of the common language of the capital. It was: "My dear fellow, I am most anxious to oblige you, but I am so situated that I cannot give you what you want. I will, however, try to find you something equally as good." The anxious caller for favors, if he or his congressman failed to get the office desired, always carried away a flower or a bouquet given by the president, with a complimentary remark to be remembered. It soon came to be understood among applicants for office that a desired consulship in England could not be granted, but one of equal rank in South Africa was possible.

There were many good stories in the Senate of his tact in dealing with the opposition. A Southern senator, who as a general had made a distinguished record in the Civil War on the Confederate side, was very resentful and would frequently remark to his friends "that our president unfortunately is not a gentleman, and in his ancestry is some very common blood."

Mr. McKinley persuaded some of the senator's Southern colleagues to bring him to the White House. He expressed his regret to the senator that he should have offended him in any way and asked what he had done. The senator replied: "You have appointed for the town where my sister lives a nigger, and a bad nigger at that, for postmaster, and my sister has to go to him for her letters and stamps." The president arranged for the transfer of this postmaster and the appointment of a man recommended by the senator. The senator then went to his friends and said: "Have I remarked to you at any time that our president was not a gentleman and had somewhere in his ancestry very common blood? If I did I recall the statement and apologize. Mr. McKinley is a perfect gentleman."

All the measures which the president wished passed,

unless they were absolutely partisan, always received afterwards the support of the Southern senator.

I was in the Senate during a part of his term and nearly every day at the White House, where his reception was so cordial and his treatment of the matter presented so sympathetic that it was a delight to go there, instead of being, as usual, one of the most disagreeable tasks imposed upon a senator.

He had a way of inviting one to a private conference and with impressing you with its confidential character and the trust he reposed in your advice and judgment which was most flattering.

Entertainments at the White House were frequent, and he managed to make each dinner an event to be most pleasantly remembered. I think, while he was very courteous to everybody, he was more than usually so to me because of an incident prior to his inauguration.

A well-known journalist came to my office one day and said: "I am just from Canton, where I have been several days with the president. I discussed with him federal appointments—among others, the mission to England, in which I am interested because my father is an Englishman, and both my father and I are exceedingly anxious to have you take the post, and Mr. McKinley authorized me to ask you if you would accept the mission."

The embassy to England presented peculiar attraction to me, because I knew personally the Prince of Wales and most of the leading English statesmen and public men. The journalist said that if I accepted he would sound the press. This he did, and the response was most flattering from journals of all political views.

About the time of the inauguration Vice-President

Hobart, who was a cordial friend of mine, said to me: "There is something wrong about you with the president. It is very serious, and you can expect no recognition from the administration." I was wholly at a loss to account for the matter and would not investigate any further. Not long afterwards the vice-president came to me and said: "I have found out the truth of that matter of yours and have explained it satisfactorily to the president, who deeply regrets that he was misled by a false report from a friend in whom he had confidence." Soon after the president made me the offer of the mission to Germany. I did not understand the language and felt that I could be of little service there, and so declined.

When President McKinley was lying seriously wounded at Buffalo from the shot of the anarchist Czolgosz, I went there to see if anything could be done for his comfort. For some time there was hope he would recover, and that it would be better for him to go to Washington. I made every arrangement to take him to the capital if the doctors decided it could be done. But suddenly, as is always the case with wounds of that kind, a crisis arrived in which he died.

Vice-President Roosevelt was camping in the Adirondacks. A message reached him, and the next morning he arrived in Buffalo. The Cabinet of Mr. McKinley decided that the vice-president should be at once inaugurated as president. Colonel Roosevelt was a guest at the house of Mr. Ainsley Wilcox. He invited me to witness his inauguration, which occurred the same evening. It was a small company gathered in the parlor of Mr. Wilcox's house. Elihu Root, secretary of state, choking with emotion and in a voice full of tears, made a speech which was a beautiful tribute to the dead president and a clear statement of the necessity of immediate action to avoid an interregnum in the government. John Raymond Hazel, United States district judge, administered the oath, and the new president delivered a brief and affecting answer to Mr. Root's address.

This inauguration was in pathetic and simple contrast to that which had preceded at the Capitol at Washington. Among the few present was Senator Mark Hanna. He had been more instrumental than any one in the United States in the selection of Mr. McKinley for president and his triumphant election. Mr. McKinley put absolute trust in Hanna, and Hanna was the most powerful personality in the country. No two men in public life were ever so admirably fitted for each other as President McKinley and Senator Hanna. The day before the death of the president Hanna could look forward to four years of increasing power and usefulness with the president who had just been re-elected. But as he walked with me from Mr. Wilcox's house that night, he felt keenly that he never could have any such relation with Colonel Roosevelt. He was personally exceedingly fond of Mr. McKinley, and to his grief at the death of his friend was added a full apprehension of his changed position in American public life.

XIV

THEODORE ROOSEVELT

The bullet of the assassin had ended fatally, and McKinley was no more. Theodore Roosevelt, vice-president, became president. Few recognized at the time there had come into the presidency of the United States one of the most remarkable, capable, and original men who ever occupied the White House.

During the following seven years President Roosevelt not only occupied but filled the stage of public affairs in the United States. Even now, two years or more after his death, with the exception of President Wilson, Roosevelt is the best known American in the world. It is difficult to predict the future because of the idealization which sometimes though rarely occurs in regard to public men, but Colonel Roosevelt is rapidly taking a position as third, with Washington and Lincoln as the other two.

My relations with Colonel Roosevelt were always most interesting. His father, who was a cordial friend of mine, was one of the foremost citizens of New York. In all civic duties and many philanthropies he occupied a first place. The public activities of the father had great influence in forming the character and directing the ambitions of his son.

Mr. Roosevelt entered public life very early and, as with everything with him, always in a dramatic way. One of the interesting characters of New York City was Frederick Gibbs, who was an active politician and a district leader. Gibbs afterwards became the national committeeman from New York on the Republican national committee. When he died he left a collection of pictures which, to the astonishment of everybody, showed that he was a liberal and discriminating patron of art.

Gibbs had a district difficult to manage, because, commencing in the slums it ran up to Fifth Avenue. It was normally Democratic, but he managed to keep his party alive and often to win, and so gained the reputation that he was in league with Tammany. He came to me one day and said: "Our organization has lost the confidence of the 'highbrows.' They have not a great many votes, but their names carry weight and their contributions are invaluable in campaigns. To regain their confidence we are thinking of nominating for member of the legislature young Theodore Roosevelt, who has just returned from Harvard. What do you think of it?"

Of course, I advocated it very warmly. "Well," he said, "we will have a dinner at Delmonico's. It will be composed entirely of 'highbrows.' We wish you to make the principal speech, introducing young Roosevelt, who, of course, will respond. I will not be at the dinner, but I will be in the pantry."

The dinner was a phenomenal success. About three hundred in dress suits, white vests, and white neckties were discussing the situation, saying: "Where did these stories and slanders originate in regard to our district, about its being an annex of Tammany and with Tammany affiliations? We are the district, and we all know each other."

Young Roosevelt, when he rose to speak, looked about eighteen years old, though he was twenty-three. His speech was carefully prepared, and he read it from a manuscript. It was remarkable in the emphatic way in which he first stated the evils in the city, State, and national governments, and how he would correct them if he ever had the opportunity. It is a curious realization of youthful aspirations that every one of those opportunities came to him, and in each of them he made history and permanent fame.

The term of office of Frank Black, Governor of the State of New York, was about expiring. Black was a man of great ability and courage. The people had voted nine millions of dollars to improve the Erie Canal. There were persistent rumors of fraud in the work. Governor Black ordered an investigation through an able committee which he appointed. The committee discovered that about a million dollars had been wasted or stolen. Black at once took measures to recover the money if possible and to prosecute the guilty. The opposition took advantage of this to create the impression in the public mind of the corruption of the Republican administration. The acute question was: "Should Governor Black be renominated?"

Colonel Roosevelt had just returned from Cuba, where he had won great reputation in command of the Rough Riders, and he and his command were in camp on Long Island.

Senator Platt, the State leader, was accustomed to consult me, and his confidence in my judgment was the greater from the fact that he knew that I wanted nothing, while most of the people who surrounded the leader were recipients of his favor, and either the holders of offices or expecting some consideration. He asked me to come and see him at Manhattan Beach. As usual, he entered at once upon the question in hand by saying:

"I am very much troubled about the governorship. Frank Black has made an excellent governor and did the right thing in ordering an investigation of the Canal frauds, but the result of the investigation has been that in discovering frauds the Democrats have been able to create a popular impression that the whole State administration is guilty. The political situation is very critical in any way. Benjamin Odell, the chairman of our State committee, urges the nomination of Colonel Roosevelt. As you know, Roosevelt is no friend of mine, and I don't think very well of the suggestion. Now, what do you think?"

I instantly replied: "Mr. Platt, I always look at a public question from the view of the platform. I have been addressing audiences ever since I became a voter, and my judgment of public opinion and the views of the people are governed by how they take or will take and act upon the questions presented. Now, if you nominate Governor Black and I am addressing a large audience—and I certainly will—the heckler in the audience will arise and interrupt me, saying: 'Chauncey, we agree with what you say about the Grand Old Party and all that, but how about the Canal steal?' I have to explain that the amount stolen was only a million, and that would be fatal. If Colonel Roosevelt is nominated, I can say to the heckler with indignation and enthusiasm: 'I am mighty glad you asked that question. We have nominated for governor a man who has demonstrated in public office and on the battlefield that he is a fighter for the right, and always victorious. If he is selected, you know and we all know from his demonstrated characteristics, courage and ability, that every thief will be caught and punished, and every dollar that can be found restored to the public treasury.' Then I will follow the colonel leading his Rough Riders up San Juan Hill and ask the band to play the 'Star-Spangled Banner.'"

Platt said very impulsively: "Roosevelt will be nominated."

When the State convention met to nominate a State ticket, I was selected to present the name of Colonel Roosevelt as a candidate for governor. I have done that a great many times in conventions, but have never had such a response. As I went on reciting the achievements of Roosevelt, his career, his accomplishments, and his great promise, the convention went wild with enthusiasm. It was plain that no mistake had been made in selecting him as the candidate.

During the campaign he made one of the most picturesque canvasses the State has ever experienced. He was accompanied in his travels by a large staff of orators, but easily dominated the situation and carried the audience with him. He was greatly amused at a meeting where one of his Rough Riders, who was in the company, insisted upon making a speech. The Rough Rider said: "My friends and fellow citizens, my colonel was a great soldier. He will make a great governor. He always put us boys in battle where we would be killed if there was a chance, and that is what he will do with you."

Roosevelt as governor was, as always, most original. New York was an organization State, with Mr. Platt as leader, and with county leaders of unusual ability and strength. Governors had been accustomed to rely upon the organization both for advice and support. Roosevelt could not bear any kind of control. He sought advice in every direction and then made up his mind.

This brought him often in conflict with local leaders and sometimes with the general organization.

On one occasion the State chairman, who was always accustomed to be in Albany during the closing day of the legislature, to prevent in the haste and confusion, characteristic of legislation at this time, the passage of bad or unpopular measures, bade the governor good-by at midnight, as the legislature was to adjourn the following day with the understanding that lawmaking was practically over.

A large real-estate delegation arrived the next morning, with the usual desire to relieve real-estate from taxation by putting it somewhere else. They came with a proposition to place new burdens upon public utilities. It was too late to formulate and introduce a measure on a question so important, but there was a bill which had been in the legislature most of the session and never received serious consideration. The governor sent an emergency message to the legislature, which had remaining only one hour of life to pass that bill.

Next day the tremendous interest in public utilities was panic-stricken because the bill was so crude that it amounted to confiscation. The governor, when applied to, said: "Yes, I know that the bill is very crude and unfit to become a law, but legislation on this subject is absolutely necessary. I will do this: I have thirty days before I must make up my mind to sign the bill, or let it become a law without my signature. Within that thirty days I will call the legislature together again. Then you can prepare and submit to me a proper bill, and if we can agree upon it, I will present it to the legislature. If the legislature passes that measure I will sign it, but if it does not, I will let the present measure, bad as it is, become a law."

The result of the threat was that a very good and timely act was presented in regard to the taxation of public utilities, a measure which largely increased municipal and State revenues. I know of no governor in my time who would have had the originality and the audacity to accomplish what he desired by such drastic operation.

Roosevelt's administration was high-minded and patriotic. But by his exercise of independent judgment and frequently by doing things without consulting the leaders, State or local, he became exceedingly unpopular with the organization. It was evident that it would be very difficult to renominate him. It was also evident that on account of his popularity with the people, if he failed in the renomination, the party would be beaten. So it was unanimously decided to put him on the national ticket as vice-president.

The governor resisted this with all his passionate energy. He liked the governorship. He thought there were many things which he could do in another term, and he believed and so stated that the vice-presidency was a tomb. He thought that nobody could be resurrected when once buried in that sarcophagus.

The national Republican convention of 1904 was a ratification meeting. President McKinley's administration had been exceedingly popular. The convention met practically to indorse McKinley's public acts and renominate him for another term. The only doubtful question was the vice-presidency. There was a general accord of sentiment in favor of Governor Roosevelt, which was only blocked by his persistent refusal.

Roosevelt and I were both delegates at large, and that position gave him greater opportunity to emphasize his disinclination. A very intimate friend of his called upon me and begged that I would use all my influence to prevent the colonel's nomination. This friend said to me: "The governor's situation, officially and personally, makes it impossible for him to go to Washington. On the official side are his unfinished legislation and the new legislation greatly needed by the State, which will add enormously to his reputation and pave the way for his future. He has very little means. As governor his salary is ample. The Executive Mansion is free, with many contributory advantages, and the schools of Albany admirable for the education of his six children. While in Washington the salary of vice-president is wholly inadequate to support the dignity of the position, and it is the end of a young man of a most promising career."

I knew what the friend did not know, and it was that Mr. Roosevelt could not be governor again. I was so warmly attached to him and so anxious for his future that I felt it was my duty to force his nomination if possible.

Governor Odell was chairman of the delegation for all convention purposes, but in the distribution of honors I was made the presiding officer at its meetings. The delegation met to consider the vice-presidency. Several very eloquent speeches were made in favor of Mr. Roosevelt, but in an emphatic address he declined the nomination. He then received a unanimous vote, but again declined. A delegate then arose and suggested that he reconsider his determination, and several others joined most earnestly in this request. Roosevelt was deeply affected, but, nevertheless, firmly declined.

I knew there was a member of the delegation who had

canvassed it to secure the honor in case Roosevelt became impossible, and that the next motion would be the nomination of this aspirant. So I abruptly declared the meeting adjourned. I did this in the hope that during the night, with the pressure brought to bear upon him, the colonel would change his mind. In the morning Mr. Roosevelt surrendered his convictions and agreed to accept the nomination.

In every convention there is a large number of men prominent in their several delegations who wish to secure general attention and publicity. As there were no disputes as to either candidate or platform, these gentlemen all became anxious to make speeches favoring the candidates, McKinley and Roosevelt. There were so many of these speeches which, of course, were largely repetitions, that the convention became wearied and impatient. The last few were not heard at all on account of the confusion and impatience of the delegates. While one orator was droning away, a delegation from a Western State came over to me and said: "We in the extreme West have never heard you speak, and won't you oblige us by taking the platform?"

I answered: "The audience will not stand another address." Roosevelt, who sat right in front of me, then remarked: "Yes, they will from you. These speeches have pretty nearly killed the ticket, and if it keeps up the election is over, and McKinley and I are dead." He then seized me and almost threw me on the platform.

The novelty of the situation, which was suddenly grasped by the delegates, commanded attention. I recalled what Mr. Lincoln had once said to me, defending his frequent use of anecdotes, and this is what he said: "Plain people, take them as you find them, are more easily influenced through the medium of a broad and humorous illustration than in any other way."

I had heard a new story, a rare thing, and began with the narration of it. Alongside the chairman sat Senator Thurston. He was a fine speaker, very ornate and highly rhetorical. He never indulged in humor or unbent his dignity and formality. I heard him say in a sepulchral voice to the chairman: "Great God, sir, the dignity and solemnity of this most important and historical occasion is to be ruined by a story." Happily the story was a success and gave the wearied audience two opportunities to hear my speech. Their laughter was internal relief, and it was giving the external relief of changing their positions for new and more restful ones.

My friend, John M. Thurston, came to Philadelphia with a most elaborate and excellent oration. Sitting in the audience on three different occasions, I heard it with as much pleasure the last time as I had the first.

When Mr. Roosevelt as vice-president came to preside over the Senate, it was soon evident that he would not be a success. His talents were executive and administrative. The position of the presiding officer of the United States Senate is at once easy and difficult. The Senate desires impartiality, equable temper, and knowledge of parliamentary law from its presiding officer. But it will not submit to any attempt on the part of the presiding officer to direct or advise it, and will instantly resent any arbitrary ruling. Of course, Mr. Roosevelt presided only at a few meetings before the final adjournment. When Congress met again he was President of the United States.

Senators and members soon found that there was a change at the White House. No two men were ever so radically different in every respect as McKinley and Roosevelt. Roosevelt loved to see the people in a mass and rarely cared for private or confidential interviews. He was most hospitable and constantly bringing visitors to luncheon when the morning meetings in the executive offices had closed, and he had not had a full opportunity to hear or see them.

Senator Hanna was accustomed to have a few of his colleagues of the Senate dine with him frequently, in order to consult on more effective action upon pending measures. President Roosevelt, who knew everything that was going on, often burst into Hanna's house after dinner and with the utmost frankness submitted the problems which had arisen at the White House, and upon which he wished advice or, if not advice, support—more frequently support.

Any one who attended the morning conferences, where he saw senators and members of the House, and the public, was quite sure to be entertained. I remember on one occasion I had been requested by several friends of his, men of influence and prominence in New York, to ask for the appointment of minister to a foreign government for a journalist of some eminence. When I entered the Cabinet room it was crowded, and the president knew that I was far from well, so he at once called my name, asked how I was and what I wanted. I told him that I had to leave Washington that day on the advice of my doctor for a rest, and what I wanted was to present the name of a gentleman for appointment as a minister, if I could see him for five minutes.

The president exclaimed: "We have no secrets here. Tell it right out." I then stated the case. He asked who was behind the applicant. I told him. Then he said, "Yes, that's all right," to each one until I mentioned also the staff of the gentleman's newspaper, which was one of the most prominent and powerful in the country but a merciless critic of the president. He shouted at once: "That settles it. Nothing which that paper wishes will receive any consideration from me." Singularly enough, the paper subsequently became one of his ardent advocates and supporters.

On another occasion I was entering his private office as another senator was coming out of the Cabinet room, which was filled. He called out: "Senator Depew, do you know that man going out?" I answered: "Yes, he is a colleague of mine in the Senate." "Well," he shouted, "he is a crook." His judgment subsequently proved correct.

Mr. Roosevelt and his wife were all their lives in the social life of the old families of New York who were admitted leaders. They carried to the White House the culture and conventions of what is called the best society of the great capitals of the world. This experience and education came to a couple who were most democratic in their views. They loved to see people and met and entertained every one with delightful hospitality.

Roosevelt was a marvel of many-sidedness. Besides being an executive as governor of a great State and administrator as civil-service commissioner and police commissioner of New York, he was an author of popular books and a field naturalist of rare acquirements. He was also a wonderful athlete. I often had occasion to see him upon urgent matters, and was summoned to his gymnasium, where he was having a boxing match with a well-known pugilist, and getting the better of his antagonist, or else launching at his fencing master. The athletics would cease, to be resumed as soon as he had in his quick and direct way disposed of what I presented.

Horseback riding was a favorite exercise with him, and his experience on his Western ranch and in the army had made him one of the best riders in the world. The foreign diplomats in Washington, with their education that their first duty was to be in close touch with the chief magistrate, whether czar, queen, king, or president, found their training unequal to keeping close to President Roosevelt, except one, and he told me with great pleasure that though a poor rider he joined the president in his horseback morning excursions. Sometimes, he said, when they came to a very steep, high, and rough hill the president would shout, "Let us climb to the top," and the diplomat would struggle over the stones, the underbrush, and gullies, and return to his horse with torn garments after sliding down the hill. At another time, when on the banks of the Potomac, where the waters were raging rapids, the president said, "We will go to that island in the middle of the river," and immediately plunge in. The diplomat followed and reached the island after wading and swimming, and with great difficulty returned with sufficient strength to reach home. He had an attack of pneumonia from this unusual exposure, but thereafter was the envy and admiration of his colleagues and increased the confidence of his own government by this intimacy with the president.

The president's dinners and luncheons were unique because of his universal acquaintance with literary and scientific people. There were generally some of them present. His infectious enthusiasm and hearty cordiality drew out the best points of each guest. I was present at a large dinner one evening when an instance occurred which greatly amused him. There were some forty guests. When they were seated, the president noticed four vacant chairs. He sent one of his aides to ascertain the trouble. The aide discovered an elderly senator standing with his wife, and another senator and a lady looking very disconsolate. The aged senator refused to take out a lady as his card directed or leave his wife to a colleague. He said to the president's aide, who told him that dinner was waiting and what he had to do: "When I eat I eat with my wife, or I don't eat at all." The old gentleman had his way.

The president had one story which he told often and with much glee. While he was on the ranch the neighbors had caught a horse thief and hung him. They soon discovered that they had made a mistake and hung the wrong man. The most diplomatic among the ranchers was selected to take the body home and break the news gently to his wife. The cowboy ambassador asked the wife: "Are you the wife of ——?" She answered "Yes." "Well," said the ambassador, "you are mistaken. You are his widow. I have his body in the wagon. You need not feel bad about it, because we hung him thinking he was the horse thief. We soon after found that he was innocent. The joke is on us."

Mr. Roosevelt was intensely human and rarely tried to conceal his feelings. He was to address the New York State Fair at Syracuse. The management invited me as a United States Senator from New York to be present. There were at least twenty thousand on the fair ground, and Mr. Roosevelt read his speech, which he had elaborately prepared, detailing his scheme for harmonizing the relations between labor and capital. The speech was long and very able and intended for publication all over the country. But his audience, who were farmers, were not much interested in the subject. Besides, they had been wearied wandering around the grounds and doing the exhibits, waiting for the meeting to begin. I know of nothing so wearisome to mind and body as to spend hours going through the exhibits of a great fair. When the president finished, the audience began calling for me. I was known practically to every one of them from my long career on the platform.

Knowing Roosevelt as I did, I was determined not to speak, but the fair management and the audience would not be denied. I paid the proper compliments to the president, and then, knowing that humor was the only possible thing with such a tired crowd, I had a rollicking good time with them. They entered into the spirit of the fun and responded in a most uproarious way. I heard Roosevelt turn to the president of the fair and say very angrily: "You promised me, sir, that there would be no other speaker."

When I met the president that evening at a large dinner given by Senator Frank Hiscock, he greeted me with the utmost cordiality. He was in fine form, and early in the dinner took entire charge of the discussion. For three hours he talked most interestingly, and no one else contributed a word. Nevertheless, we all enjoyed the evening, and not the least the president himself.

I used to wonder how he found time, with his great activities and engagements, to read so much. Publishers frequently send me new books. If I thought they would interest him I mentioned the work to him, but invariably he had already read it.

When my first term as senator expired and the question of my re-election was before the legislature, President Roosevelt gave me his most cordial and hearty support.

Events to his credit as president, which will be monuments in history, are extraordinary in number and importance. To mention only a few: He placed the Monroe Doctrine before European governments upon an impregnable basis by his defiance to the German Kaiser, when he refused to accept arbitration and was determined to make war on Venezuela. The president cabled: "Admiral Dewey with the Atlantic Fleet sails to-morrow." And the Kaiser accepted arbitration. Raissuli, the Moroccan bandit, who had seized and held for ransom an American citizen named Perdicaris, gave up his captive on receipt of this cable: "Perdicaris alive or Raissuli dead." He settled the war between Russia and Japan and won the Nobel prize for peace.

Roosevelt built the Panama Canal when other efforts had failed for five hundred years. As senator from his own State, I was in constant consultation with him while he was urging legislation necessary to secure the concession for the construction of the canal. The difficulties to be overcome in both Houses seemed insurmountable, and would have been so except for the marvellous resourcefulness and power of the president.

When the Republican convention met in 1908, I was again delegate at large. It was a Roosevelt convention and crazy to have him renominated. It believed that he could overcome the popular feeling against a third term. Roosevelt did not think so. He believed that in order to make a third term palatable there must be an interval of another and different administration. When the convention found that his decision was unalterably not to accept the nomination himself, it was prepared to accept any one he might advise. He selected his secretary of war and most intimate friend, William Howard Taft. Taft had a delightful personality, and won distinction upon the bench, and had proved an admirable administrator as governor of the Philippine Islands. After Mr. Taft's election the president, in order that the new president and his administration might not be embarrassed by his presence and prestige, went on a two years' trip abroad.

During that trip he was more in the popular mind at home and abroad than almost any one in the world. If he reviewed the German army with the Kaiser, the press was full of the common characteristics and differences between the two men and of the unprecedented event of the guest giving advice to the Kaiser.

When he visited England he told in a public speech of his experience in Egypt, and recommended to the English Government that, if they expected to continue to govern Egypt, to begin to govern it.

All France was aghast and then hilarious when, in an address before the faculties of Sorbonne, he struck at once at the weak point of the future and power of France, and that was race suicide.

XV

UNITED STATES SENATE

My twelve years in the Senate were among the happiest of my life. The Senate has long enjoyed the reputation of being the best club in the world, but it is more than that. My old friend, Senator Bacon, of Georgia, often said that he preferred the position of senator to that of either President or Chief Justice of the United States. There is independence in a term of six years which is of enormous value to the legislative work of the senator. The member of the House, who is compelled to go before his district every two years, must spend most of his time looking after his re-election. Then the Senate, being a smaller body, the associations are very close and intimate. I do not intend to go into discussion of the measures which occupied the attention of the Senate during my time. They are a part of the history of the world. The value of a work of this kind, if it has any value, is in personal incidents.

One of the most delightful associations of a lifetime, personally and politically, was that with Vice-President James S. Sherman. During the twenty-two years he was in the House of Representatives he rarely was in the City of New York without coming to see me. He became the best parliamentarian in Congress, and was generally called to the chair when the House met in committee of the whole. He was intimately familiar with every political movement in Washington, and he had a rare talent for discriminatory description, both of events and analysis of the leading characters in the Washington drama. He was one of the wisest of the advisers of the organization of his party, both national and State.

When President Roosevelt had selected Mr. Taft as his successor he made no indication as to the vice-presidency. Of course, the nomination of Mr. Taft under such conditions was a foregone conclusion, and when the convention met it was practically unanimous for Roosevelt's choice. Who was the best man to nominate for vice-president in order to strengthen the ticket embarrassed the managers of the Taft campaign. The Republican congressmen who were at the convention were practically unanimous for Sherman, and their leader was Uncle Joe Cannon. We from New York found the Taft managers discussing candidates from every doubtful State. We finally convinced them that New York was the most important, but they had gone so far with State candidates that it became a serious question how to get rid of them without offending their States.

The method adopted by one of the leading managers was both adroit and hazardous. He would call up a candidate on the telephone and say to him: "The friends of Mr. Taft are very favorable to you for vice-president. Will you accept the nomination?" The candidate would hesitate and begin to explain his ambitions, his career and its possibilities, and the matter which he would have to consider. Before the prospective candidate had finished, the manager would say, "Very sorry, deeply regret," and put up the telephone.

When the nomination was made these gentlemen who might have succeeded would come around to the manager and say impatiently and indignantly: "I was all right. Why did you cut me off?" However, those gentlemen have had their compensation. Whenever you meet one of them he will say to you: "I was offered the vice-presidency with Taft but was so situated that I could not accept."

One evening during the convention a wind and rain storm drove everybody indoors. The great lobby of Congress Hall was crowded, and most of them were delegates. Suddenly there was a loud call for a speech, and some husky and athletic citizen seized and lifted me on to a chair. After a story and a joke, which put the crowd into a receptive mood, I made what was practically a nominating speech for Sherman. The response was intense and unanimous. When I came down from a high flight as to the ability and popularity to the human qualities of "Sunny Jim," I found "Sunny Jim" such a taking characterization, and it was echoed and re-echoed. I do not claim that speech nominated Sherman, only that nearly everybody who was present became a most vociferous advocate for Sherman for vice-president.

The position of vice-president is one of the most difficult in our government. Unless the president requests his advice or assistance, he has no public function except presiding over the Senate. No president ever called the vice-president into his councils. McKinley came nearest to it during his administration, with Hobart, but did not keep it up.

President Harding has made a precedent for the future by inviting Vice-President Coolidge to attend all Cabinet meetings. The vice-president has accepted and meets regularly with the Cabinet.

Sherman had one advantage over other vice-presidents in having been for nearly a quarter of a century a leader in Congress. Few, if any, who ever held that office have been so popular with the Senate and so tactful and influential when they undertook the very difficult task of influencing the action of a Senate, very jealous of its prerogatives and easily made resentful and hostile.

Among my colleagues in the Senate were several remarkable men. They had great ability, extraordinary capacity for legislation, and, though not great orators, possessed the rare faculty of pressing their points home in short and effective speeches. Among them was Senator Frye, of Maine. He was for many years chairman of the great committee on commerce. Whatever we had of a merchant marine was largely due to his persistent efforts. He saved the government scores of millions in that most difficult task of pruning the River and Harbor Bill. He possessed the absolute confidence of both parties, and was the only senator who could generally carry the Senate with him for or against a measure. While wise and the possessor of the largest measure of common sense, yet he was one of the most simple-minded of men. I mean by this that he had no guile and suspected none in others. Whatever was uppermost in his mind came out. These characteristics made him one of the most delightful of companions and one of the most harmonious men to work with on a committee.

Clement A. Griscom, the most prominent American ship owner and director, was very fond of Senator Frye. Griscom entertained delightfully at his country home near Philadelphia. He told me that at one time Senator Frye was his guest over a week-end. To meet the senator at dinner on Saturday evening, he had invited great bankers, lawyers, and captains of industry of Philadelphia. Their conversation ran from enterprises and combinations involving successful industries and exploitations to individual fortunes and how they were accumulated. The atmosphere was heavy with millions and billions. Suddenly Griscom turned to Senator Frye and said: "I know that our successful friends here would not only be glad to hear but would learn much if you would tell us of your career." "It is not much to tell," said Senator Frye, "especially after these stories which are like chapters from the 'Arabian Nights.' I was very successful as a young lawyer and rising to a leading practice and head of the bar of my State when I was offered an election to the House of Representatives. I felt that it would be a permanent career and that there was no money in it. I consulted my wife and told her that it meant giving up all prospects of accumulating a fortune or independence even, but it was my ambition, and I believed I could perform valuable service to the public, and that as a career its general usefulness would far surpass any success at the bar. My wife agreed with me cordially and said that she would economize on her part to any extent required.

"So," the senator continued, "I have been nearly thirty years in Congress, part of this time in the House and the rest in the Senate. I have been able on my salary to meet our modest requirements and educate our children. I have never been in debt but once. Of course, we had to calculate closely and set aside sufficient to meet our extra expenses in Washington and our ordinary one at home. We came out a little ahead every year but one. That year the president very unexpectedly called an extra session, and for the first time in twenty years I was in debt to our landlord in Washington."

Griscom told me that this simple narrative of a statesman of national reputation seemed to make the monumental achievements of his millionaire guests of little account.

Senator Frye's genial personality and vivid conversation made him a welcome guest at all entertainments in Washington. There was a lady at the capital at that time who entertained a great deal and was very popular on her own account, but she always began the conversation with the gentleman who took her out by narrating how she won her husband. I said one day to Senator Frye: "There will be a notable gathering at So-and-So's dinner to-night. Are you going?" He answered: "Yes, I will be there; but it has been my lot to escort to dinner this lady"—naming her—"thirteen times this winter. She has told me thirteen times the story of her courtship. If it is my luck to be assigned to her to-night, and she starts that story, I shall leave the table and the house and go home."

Senator Aldrich, of Rhode Island, was once called by Senator Quay the schoolmaster of the Senate. As the head of the finance committee he had commanding influence, and with his skill in legislation and intimate knowledge of the rules he was the leader whenever he chose to lead. This he always did when the policy he desired or the measure he was promoting had a majority, and the opposition resorted to obstructive tactics. As there is no restriction on debate in the Senate, or was none at my time, the only way the minority could defeat the majority was by talking the bill to death. I never knew this method to be used successfully but once, because in the trial of endurance the greater number wins. The only successful talk against time was by Senator Carter, of Montana. Carter was a capital debater. He was invaluable at periods when the discussion had become very bitter and personal. Then in his most suave way he would soothe the angry elements and bring the Senate back to a calm consideration of the question. When he arose on such occasions, the usual remark among those who still kept their heads was: "Carter will now bring out his oil can and pour oil upon the troubled waters"— and it usually proved effective.

Senator George F. Hoar, of Massachusetts, seemed to be a revival of what we pictured in imagination as the statesmen who framed the Constitution of the United States, or the senators who sat with Webster, Clay, and Calhoun. He was a man of lofty ideals and devotion to public service. He gave to each subject on which he spoke an elevation and dignity that lifted it out of ordinary senatorial discussions. He had met and knew intimately most of the historical characters in our public life for fifty years, and was one of the most entertaining and instructive conversationalists whom I ever met.

On the other hand, Senator Benjamin Tillman, of South Carolina, who was an ardent admirer of Senator Hoar, was his opposite in every way. Tillman and I became very good friends, though at first he was exceedingly hostile. He hated everything which I represented. With all his roughness, and at the beginning his brutality, he had a singular streak of sentiment.

I addressed the first dinner of the Gridiron Club at its organization and have been their guest many times since. The Gridiron Club is an association of the newspaper correspondents at Washington, and their dinners several times a year are looked forward to with the utmost interest and enjoyed by everybody privileged to attend.

The Gridiron Club planned an excursion to Charleston, S. C., that city having extended to them an invitation. They invited me to go with them and also Senator Tillman. Tillman refused to be introduced to me because I was chairman of the board of directors of the New York Central Railroad, and he hated my associations and associates. We had a wonderful welcome from the most hospitable of cities, the most beautifully located City of Charleston. On the many excursions, luncheons, and gatherings, I was put forward to do the speaking, which amounted to several efforts a day during our three days' visit. The Gridiron stunt for Charleston was very audacious. There were many speakers, of course, including Senator Tillman, who hated Charleston and the Charlestonians, because he regarded them as aristocrats and told them so. There were many invited to speak who left their dinners untasted while they devoted themselves to looking over their manuscripts, and whose names were read in the list at the end of the dinner, but their speeches were never called for.

On our way home we stopped for luncheon at a place outside of Charleston. During the luncheon an earthquake shook the table and rattled the plates. I was called upon to make the farewell address for the Gridiron Club to the State of South Carolina. Of course the earthquake and its possibilities gave an opportunity for pathos as well as humor, and Tillman was deeply affected. When we were on the train he came to me and with great emotion grasped my hand and said: "Chauncey Depew, I was mistaken about you. You are a damn good fellow." And we were good friends until he died.

I asked Tillman to what he owed his phenomenal rise

and strength in the conservative State of South Carolina. He answered: "We in our State were governed by a class during the colonial period and afterwards until the end of the Civil War. They owned large plantations, hundreds of thousands of negroes, were educated for public life, represented our State admirably, and did great service to the country. They were aristocrats and paid little attention to us poor farmers, who constituted the majority of the people. The only difference between us was that they had been colonels or generals in the Revolutionary War, or delegates to the Continental Congress or the Constitutional Convention, while we had been privates, corporals, or sergeants. They generally owned a thousand slaves, and we had from ten to thirty. I made up my mind that we should have a share of the honors, and they laughed at me. I organized the majority and put the old families out of business, and we became and are the rulers of the State."

Among the most brilliant debaters of any legislative body were Senators Joseph W. Bailey, of Texas, and John C. Spooner, of Wisconsin. They would have adorned and given distinction to any legislative body in the world. Senator Albert J. Beveridge, of Indiana, and Senator Joseph B. Foraker, of Ohio, were speakers of a very high type. The Senate still has the statesmanship, eloquence, scholarship, vision, and culture of Senator Lodge, of Massachusetts.

One of the wonders of the Senate was Senator W. M. Crane, of Massachusetts. He never made a speech. I do not remember that he ever made a motion. Yet he was the most influential member of that body. His wisdom, tact, sound judgment, encyclopædic knowledge of public affairs and of public men made him an authority.

Senator Hanna, who was a business man pure and simple, and wholly unfamiliar with legislative ways, developed into a speaker of remarkable force and influence. At the same time, on the social side, with his frequent entertainments, he did more for the measures in which he was interested. They were mainly, of course, of a financial and economic character.

One of the characters of the Senate, and one of the upheavals of the Populist movement was Senator Jeff. Davis, of Arkansas. Davis was loudly, vociferously, and clamorously a friend of the people. Precisely what he did to benefit the people was never very clear, but if we must take his word for it, he was the only friend the people had. Among his efforts to help the people was to denounce big business of all kinds and anything which gave large employment or had great capital. I think that in his own mind the ideal state would have been made of small landowners and an occasional lawyer. He himself was a lawyer.

One day he attacked me, as I was sitting there listening to him, in a most vicious way, as the representative of big corporations, especially railroads, and one of the leading men in the worst city in the world, New York, and as the associate of bankers and capitalists. When he finished Senator Crane went over to his seat and told him that he had made a great mistake, warned him that he had gone so far that I might be dangerous to him personally, but in addition to that, with my ridicule and humor, I would make him the laughing-stock of the Senate and of the country. Jeff, greatly alarmed, waddled over to my seat and said: "Senator Depew, I hope you did not take seriously what I said. I did not mean anything against you. I won't do it again, but I thought that you would not care, because it won't hurt you, and it does help me out in Arkansas." I replied: "Jeff, old man, if it helps you, do it as often as you like." Needless to say, he did not repeat.

I have always been deeply interested in the preservation of the forests and a warm advocate of forest preservers. I made a study of the situation of the Appalachian Mountains, where the lumberman was doing his worst, and millions of acres of fertile soil from the denuded hills were being swept by the floods into the ocean every year. I made a report from my committee for the purchase of this preserve, affecting, as it did, eight States, and supported it in a speech. Senator Eugene Hale, a Senate leader of controlling influence, had been generally opposed to this legislation. He became interested, and, when I had finished my speech, came over to me and said: "I never gave much attention to this subject. You have convinced me and this bill should be passed at once, and I will make the motion." Several senators from the States affected asked for delay in order that they might deliver speeches for local consumption. The psychological moment passed and that legislation could not be revived until ten years afterwards, and then in a seriously modified form.

I worked very hard for the American mercantile marine. A subsidy of four million dollars a year in mail contracts would have been sufficient, in addition to the earnings of the ships, to have given us lines to South and Central America, Australia, and Asia.

Shakespeare's famous statement that a rose by any other name would smell as sweet has exceptions. In the psychology of the American mind the word subsidy is fatal to any measure. After the most careful investigation, while I was in the Senate, I verified this statement, that a mail subsidy of four millions a year would give to the United States a mercantile marine which would open new trade routes for our commerce. This contribution would enable the ship-owners to meet the losses which made it impossible for them to compete with the ships of other countries, some having subsidies and all under cheaper expenses of operation. It would not all be a contribution because part of it was a legitimate charge for carrying the mails. The word subsidy, however, could be relied upon to start a flood of fiery oratory, charging that the people of the United States were to be taxed to pour money into the pockets of speculators in New York and financial crooks in Wall Street.

We have now created a mercantile marine through the Shipping Board which is the wonder and amazement of the world. It has cost about five hundred millions. Part of it is junk already, and a part available is run at immense loss, owing to discriminatory laws. Recently a bill was presented to Congress for something like sixty millions of dollars to make up the losses in the operations of our mercantile marine for the year. While a subsidy of four millions under private management would have been a success but was vetoed as a crime, the sixty millions are hailed as a patriotic contribution to public necessity.

A river and harbor bill of from thirty to fifty millions of dollars was eagerly anticipated and enthusiastically supported. It was known to be a give and take, a swap and exchange, where a few indispensable improvements had to carry a large number of dredgings of streams, creeks, and bayous, which never could be made navigable. Many millions a year were thrown away in these

UNITED STATES SENATE

river and harbor bills, but four millions a year to restore the American mercantile marine aroused a flood of indignant eloquence, fierce protest, and wild denunciation of capitalists, who would build and own ships, and it was always fatal to the mercantile marine.

Happily the war has, among its benefits, demonstrated to the interior and mountain States that a merchant marine is as necessary to the United States as its navy, and that we cannot hope to expand and retain our trade unless we have the ships.

I remember one year when the river and harbor bill came up for passage on the day before final adjournment. The hour had been fixed by both Houses, and, therefore, could not be extended by one House. The administration was afraid of the bill because of the many indefensible extravagances there were in it. At the same time, it had so many political possibilities that the president was afraid to veto it. Senator Carter was always a loyal administration man, and so he was put forward to talk the bill to death. He kept it up without yielding the floor for thirteen hours, and until the hour of adjournment made action upon the measure impossible.

I sat there all night long, watching this remarkable effort. The usual obstructor soon uses up all his own material and then sends pages of irrelevant matter to the desk for the clerk to read, or he reads himself from the pages of the *Record*, or from books, but Carter stuck to his text. He was a man of wit and humor. Many items in the river and harbor bill furnished him with an opportunity of showing how creeks and trout streams were to be turned by the magic of the money of the Treasury into navigable rivers, and inaccessible ponds were to be dredged into harbors to float the navies of the world.

The speech was very rich in anecdotes and delightful in its success by an adroit attack of tempting a supporter of the measure into aiding the filibuster by indignantly denying the charge which Carter had made against him. By this method Carter would get a rest by the folly of his opponent. The Senate was full and the galleries were crowded during the whole night, and when the gavel of the vice-president announced that no further debate was admissible and the time for adjournment had arrived, and began to make his farewell speech, Carter took his seat amidst the wreck of millions and the hopes of the exploiters, and the Treasury of the United States had been saved by an unexpected champion.

The country does not appreciate the tremendous power of the committees, as legislative business constantly increases with almost geometrical progression. The legislation of the country is handled almost entirely in committees. It requires a possible revolution to overcome the hostility of a committee, even if the House and the country are otherwise minded. Some men whose names do not appear at all in the *Congressional Record*, and seldom in the newspapers, have a certain talent for drudgery and detail which is very rare, and when added to shrewdness and knowledge of human nature makes such a senator or representative a force to be reckoned with on committees. Such a man is able to hold up almost anything.

I found during my Washington life the enormous importance of its social side. Here are several hundred men in the two Houses of Congress, far above the average in intelligence, force of character, and ability to accomplish things. Otherwise they would not have been elected. They are very isolated and enjoy far beyond those who have the opportunity of club life, social attentions. At dinner the real character of the guest comes out, and he is most responsive to these attentions. Mrs. Depew and I gave a great many dinners, to our intense enjoyment and, I might say, education. By this method I learned to know in a way more intimate than otherwise would have been possible many of the most interesting characters I have ever met.

Something must be done, and that speedily, to bridge the widening chasm between the Executive and the Congress. Our experience with President Wilson has demonstrated this. As a self-centred autocrat, confident of himself and suspicious of others, hostile to advice or discussion, he became the absolute master of the Congress while his party was in the majority.

The Congress, instead of being a co-ordinate branch, was really in session only to accept, adopt, and put into laws the imperious will of the president. When, however, the majority changed, there being no confidence between the executive and the legislative branch of the government, the necessary procedure was almost paralyzed. The president was unyielding and the Congress insisted upon the recognition of its constitutional rights. Even if the president is, as McKinley was, in close and frequent touch with the Senate and the House of Representatives, the relation is temporary and unequal, and not what it ought to be, automatic.

Happily we have started a budget system; but the Cabinet should have seats on the floor of the Houses, and authority to answer questions and participate in debates. Unless our system was radically changed, we could not adopt the English plan of selecting the members of the Cabinet entirely from the Senate and the House. But we could have an administration always in close touch with the Congress if the Cabinet members were in attendance when matters affecting their several departments were under discussion and action.

I heard Senator Nelson W. Aldrich, who was one of the shrewdest and ablest legislators of our generation, say that if business methods were applied to the business of the government in a way in which he could do it, there would be a saving of three hundred millions of dollars a year. We are, since the Great War, facing appropriations of five or six billions of dollars a year. I think the saving of three hundred millions suggested by Senator Aldrich could be increased in proportion to the vast increase in appropriations.

There has been much discussion about restricting unlimited debates in the Senate and adopting a rigid closure rule. My own recollection is that during my twelve years unlimited discussion defeated no good measure, but talked many bad ones to death. There is a curious feature in legislative discussion, and that is the way in which senators who have accustomed themselves to speak every day on each question apparently increase their vocabulary as their ideas evaporate. Two senators in my time, who could be relied upon to talk smoothly as the placid waters of a running brook for an hour or more every day, had the singular faculty of apparently saying much of importance while really developing no ideas. In order to understand them, while the Senate would become empty by its members going to their committee rooms, I would be a patient listener. I finally gave that up because, though endowed with reasonable intelligence and an intense desire for knowledge, I never could grasp what they were driving at.

XVI

AMBASSADORS AND MINISTERS

The United States has always been admirably represented at the Court of St. James. I consider it as a rare privilege and a delightful memory that I have known well these distinguished ambassadors and ministers who served during my time. I was not in England while Charles Francis Adams was a minister, but his work during the Civil War created intense interest in America. It is admitted that he prevented Great Britain from taking such action as would have prolonged the war and endangered the purpose which Mr. Lincoln was trying to accomplish, namely, the preservation of the Union. His curt answer to Lord John Russell, "This means war," changed the policy of the British Government.

James Russell Lowell met every requirement of the position, but, more than that, his works had been read and admired in England before his appointment. Literary England welcomed him with open arms, and official England soon became impressed with his diplomatic ability. He was one of the finest after-dinner speakers, and that brought him in contact with the best of English public life. He told me an amusing instance. As soon as he was appointed, everybody who expected to meet him sent to the book stores and purchased his works. Among them, of course, was the "Biglow Papers." One lady asked him if he had brought Mrs. Biglow with him.

The secretary of the embassy, William J. Hoppin, was a very accomplished gentleman. He had been president of the Union League Club, and I knew him very well. I called one day at the embassy with an American living in Europe to ask for a favor for this fellow countryman. The embassy was overwhelmed with Americans asking favors, so Hoppin, without looking at me or waiting for the request, at once brought out his formula for sliding his visitors on an inclined plane into the street. He said: "Every American—and there are thousands of them—who comes to London visits the embassy. They all want to be invited to Buckingham Palace or to have cards to the House of Lords or the House of Commons. Our privileges in that respect are very few, so few that we can satisfy hardly anybody. Why Americans, when there is so much to see in this old country from which our ancestry came, and with whose literature we are so familiar, should want to try to get into Buckingham Palace or the Houses of Parliament is incomprehensible. There is a very admirable cattle show at Reading. I have a few tickets and will give them to you, gentlemen, gladly. You will find the show exceedingly interesting."

I took the tickets, but if there is anything of which I am not a qualified judge, it is prize cattle. That night, at a large dinner given by a well-known English host, my friend Hoppin was present, and at once greeted me with warm cordiality. Of course, he had no recollections of the morning meeting. Our host, as usual when a new American is present, wanted to know if I had any fresh American stories, and I told with some exaggeration and embroidery the story of the Reading cattle show. Dear old Hoppin was considerably embarrassed at the chafing he received, but took it in good part, and thereafter the embassy was entirely at my service.

Mr. Edward J. Phelps was an extraordinary success.

He was a great lawyer, and the Chief Justice of the Supreme Court of the United States told me that there was no one who appeared before that Court whose arguments were more satisfactory and convincing than those of Mr. Phelps. He had the rare distinction of being a frequent guest at the Benchers' dinners in London. One of the English judges told me that at a Benchers' dinner the judges were discussing a novel point which had arisen in one of the cases recently before them. He said that in the discussion in which Mr. Phelps was asked to participate, the view which the United States minister presented was so forcible that the decision, which had been practically agreed upon, was changed to meet Mr. Phelps's view. I was at several of Mr. Phelps's dinners. They were remarkable gatherings of the best in almost every department of English life.

At one of his dinners I had a delightful talk with Browning, the poet. Browning told me that as a young man he was several times a guest at the famous breakfasts of the poet and banker, Samuel Rogers. Rogers, he said, was most arbitrary at these breakfasts with his guests, and rebuked him severely for venturing beyond the limits within which he thought a young poet should be confined.

Mr. Browning said that nothing gratified him so much as the popularity of his works in the United States. He was especially pleased and also embarrassed by our Browning societies, of which there seemed to be a great many over here. They sent him papers which were read by members of the societies, interpreting his poems. These American friends discovered meanings which had never occurred to him, and were to him an entirely novel view of his own productions. He also mentioned that every one sent him presents and souvenirs, all of them as appreciations and some as suggestions and help. Among these were several cases of American wine. He appreciated the purpose of the gifts, but the fluid did not appeal to him.

He told me he was a guest at one time at the dinners given to the Shah of Persia. This monarch was a barbarian, but the British Foreign Office had asked and extended to him every possible courtesy, because of the struggle then going on as to whether Great Britain or France or Russia should have the better part of Persia. France and Russia had entertained him with lavish military displays and other governmental functions, which a democratic country like Great Britain could not duplicate. So the Foreign Office asked all who had great houses in London or in the country, and were lavish entertainers, to do everything they could for the Shah.

Browning was present at a great dinner given for the Shah at Stafford House, the home of the Duke of Sutherland, and the finest palace in London. Every guest was asked, in order to impress the Shah, to come in all the decorations to which they were entitled. The result was that the peers came in their robes, which they otherwise would not have thought of wearing on such an occasion, and all others in the costumes of honor significant of their rank. Browning said he had received a degree at Oxford and that entitled him to a scarlet cloak. He was so outranked, because the guests were placed according to rank, that he sat at the foot of the table. The Shah said to his host: "Who is that distinguished gentleman in the scarlet cloak at the other end of the table?" The host answered: "That is one of our greatest poets." "That is no place for a poet," remarked the Shah; "bring him up here and let him sit next to me." So at the royal command the poet took the seat of honor. The Shah said to Browning: "I am mighty glad to have you near me, for I am a poet myself."

It was at this dinner that Browning heard the Shah say to the Prince of Wales, who sat at the right of the Shah: "This is a wonderful palace. Is it royal?" The Prince answered: "No, it belongs to one of our great noblemen, the Duke of Sutherland." "Well," said the Shah, "let me give you a point. When one of my noblemen or subjects gets rich enough to own a palace like this, I cut off his head and take his fortune."

A very beautiful English lady told me that she was at Ferdinand Rothschild's, where the Shah was being entertained. In order to minimize his acquisitive talents, the wonderful treasures of Mr. Rothschild's house had been hidden. The Shah asked for an introduction to this lady and said to her: "You are the most beautiful woman I have seen since I have been in England. I must take you home with me." "But," she said, "Your Majesty, I am married." "Well," he replied, "bring your husband along. When we get to Teheran, my capital, I will take care of him."

Mr. Phelps's talent as a speaker was quite unknown to his countrymen before he went abroad. While he was a minister he made several notable addresses, which aroused a great deal of interest and admiration in Great Britain. He was equally happy in formal orations and in the field of after-dinner speeches. Mrs. Phelps had such a phenomenal success socially that, when her husband was recalled and they left England, the ladies of both the great parties united, and through Lady Rosebery, the leader of the Liberal, and Lady Salisbury, of the Conservative, women, paid her a very unusual and complimentary tribute.

During John Hay's term as United States minister to Great Britain my visits to England were very delightful. Hay was one of the most charming men in public life of his period. He had won great success in journalism, as an author, and in public service. At his house in London one would meet almost everybody worth while in English literary, public, and social life.

In the hours of conversation with him, when I was posting him on the latest developments in America, his comment upon the leading characters of the time were most racy and witty. Many of them would have embalmed a statesman, if the epigram had been preserved, like a fly in amber. He had officially a very difficult task during the Spanish War. The sympathies of all European governments were with Spain. This was especially true of the Kaiser and the German Government. It was Mr. Hay's task to keep Great Britain neutral and prevent her joining the general alliance to help Spain, which some of the continental governments were fomenting.

Happily, Mr. Balfour, the British foreign minister, was cordially and openly our friend. He prevented this combination against the United States.

During part of my term as a senator John Hay was secretary of state. To visit his office and have a discussion on current affairs was an event to be remembered. He made a prediction, which was the result of his own difficulties with the Senate, that on account of the two-thirds majority necessary for the ratification of a treaty, no important treaty sent to the Senate by the president would ever again be ratified. Happily this gloomy view has not turned out to be entirely correct.

Mr. Hay saved China, in the settlement of the indemnities arising out of the Boxer trouble, from the greed of the great powers of Europe. One of his greatest achievements was in proclaiming the open door for China and securing the acquiescence of the great powers. It was a bluff on his part, because he never could have had the active support of the United States, but he made his proposition with a confidence which carried the belief that he had no doubt on that subject. He was fortunately dealing with governments who did not understand the United States and do not now. With them, when a foreign minister makes a serious statement of policy, it is understood that he has behind him the whole military, naval, and financial support of his government. But with us it is a long road and a very rocky one, before action so serious, with consequences so great, can receive the approval of the war-making power in Congress.

I called on Hay one morning just as Cassini, the Russian ambassador, was leaving. Cassini was one of the shrewdest and ablest of diplomats in the Russian service. It was said that for twelve years he had got the better of all the delegations at Pekin and controlled that extraordinary ruler of China, the dowager queen. Cassini told me that from his intimate associations with her he had formed the opinion that she was quite equal to Catherine of Russia, whom he regarded as the greatest woman sovereign who ever lived.

Hay said to me: "I have just had a very long and very remarkable discussion with Cassini. He is a revelation in the way of secret diplomacy. He brought to me the voluminous instructions to him of his government on our open-door policy. After we had gone over them carefully, he closed his portfolio and, pushing it aside, said: 'Now, Mr. Secretary, listen to Cassini.' He immediately presented an exactly opposite policy from the one in the instructions, and a policy entirely favorable to us, and said: 'That is what my government will do.'" It was a great loss to Russian diplomacy when he died so early.

As senator I did all in my power to bring about the appointment of Whitelaw Reid as ambassador to Great Britain. He and I had been friends ever since his beginning in journalism in New York many years before. Reid was then the owner and editor of the *New York Tribune*, and one of the most brilliant journalists in the country. He was also an excellent public speaker. His long and intimate contact with public affairs and intimacy with public men ideally fitted him for the appointment. He had already served with great credit as ambassador to France.

The compensation of our representatives abroad always has been and still is entirely inadequate to enable them to maintain, in comparison with the representatives of other governments, the dignity of their own country. All the other great powers at the principal capitals maintain fine residences for their ambassadors, which also is the embassy. Our Congress, except within the last few years, has always refused to make this provision. The salary which we pay is scarcely ever more than one-third the amount paid by European governments in similar service.

I worked hard while in the Senate to improve this situation because of my intimate knowledge of the question. When I first began the effort I found there was a very strong belief that the whole foreign service was an unnecessary expense. When Mr. Roosevelt first became president, and I had to see him frequently about diplomatic appointments, I learned that this was his view. He said to me: "This foreign business of the government, now that the cable is perfected, can be carried on between our State Department and the chancellery of any government in the world. Nevertheless, I am in favor of keeping up the diplomatic service. All the old nations have various methods of rewarding distinguished public servants. The only one we have is the diplomatic service. So when I appoint a man ambassador or minister, I believe that I am giving him a decoration, and the reason I change ambassadors and ministers is that I want as many as possible to possess it."

The longer Mr. Roosevelt remained president, and the closer he came to our foreign relations, the more he appreciated the value of the personal contact and intimate knowledge on the spot of an American ambassador or minister.

Mr. Reid entertained more lavishly and hospitably than any ambassador in England ever had, both at his London house and at his estate in the country. He appreciated the growing necessity to the peace of the world and the progress of civilization of closer union of English-speaking peoples. At his beautiful and delightful entertainments Americans came in contact with Englishmen under conditions most favorable for the appreciation by each of the other. The charm of Mr. and Mrs. Whitelaw Reid's hospitality was so genuine, so cordial, and so universal, that to be their guest was an event for Americans visiting England. There is no capital in the world where hospitality counts for so much as in London, and no country where the house-party brings people together under such favorable conditions. Both the city and the country homes of Mr. and Mrs. Reid were universities of international good-feeling. Mr. Reid, on the official side, admirably represented his country and had the most intimate relations with the governing powers of Great Britain.

I recall with the keenest pleasure how much my old friend, Joseph H. Choate, did to make each one of my visits to London during his term full of the most charming and valuable recollections. His dinners felt the magnetism of his presence, and he showed especial skill in having, to meet his American guests, just the famous men in London life whom the American desired to know.

Choate was a fine conversationalist, a wit and a humorist of a high order. His audacity won great triumphs, but if exercised by a man less endowed would have brought him continuously into trouble. He had the faculty, the art, of so directing conversation that at his entertainments everybody had a good time, and an invitation always was highly prized. He was appreciated most highly by the English bench and bar. They recognized him as the leader of his profession in the United States. They elected him a Bencher of the Middle Temple, the first American to receive that honor after an interval of one hundred and fifty years. Choate's witticisms and repartees became the social currency of dinner-tables in London and week-end parties in the country.

Choate paid little attention to conventionalities, which count for so much and are so rigidly enforced, especially in royal circles. I had frequently been at receptions, garden-parties, and other entertainments at Buckingham Palace in the time of Queen Victoria and also of King

Edward. At an evening reception the diplomats representing all the countries in the world stand in a solemn row, according to rank and length of service. They are covered with decorations and gold lace. The weight of the gold lace on some of the uniforms of the minor powers is as great as if it were a coat of armor. Mr. Choate, under regulations of our diplomatic service, could only appear in an ordinary dress suit.

While the diplomats stand in solemn array, the king and queen go along the line and greet each one with appropriate remarks. Nobody but an ambassador and minister gets into that brilliant circle. On one occasion Mr. Choate saw me standing with the other guests outside the charmed circle and immediately left the diplomats, came to me, and said: "I am sure you would like to have a talk with the queen." He went up to Her Majesty, stated the case and who I was, and the proposition was most graciously received. I think the royalties were pleased to have a break in the formal etiquette. Mr. Choate treated the occasion, so far as I was concerned, as if it had been a reception in New York or Salem, and a distinguished guest wanted to meet the hosts. The gold-laced and bejewelled and highly decorated diplomatic circle was paralyzed.

Mr. Choate's delightful personality and original conversational powers made him a favorite guest everywhere, but he also carried to the platform the distinction which had won for him the reputation of being one of the finest orators in the United States.

Choate asked at one time when I was almost nightly making speeches at some entertainment: "How do you do it?" I told him I was risking whatever reputation I had on account of very limited preparation, that I did not let these speeches interfere at all with my business, but that they were all prepared after I had arrived home from my office late in the afternoon. Sometimes they came easy, and I reached the dinner in time; at other times they were more difficult, and I did not arrive till the speaking had begun. Then he said: "I enjoy making these after-dinner addresses more than any other work. It is a perfect delight for me to speak to such an audience, but I have not the gift of quick and easy preparation. I accept comparatively few of the constant invitations I receive, because when I have to make such a speech I take a corner in the car in the morning going to my office, exclude all the intruding public with a newspaper and think all the way down. I continue the same process on my way home in the evening, and it takes about three days of this absorption and exclusiveness, with some time in the evenings, to get an address with which I am satisfied."

The delicious humor of these efforts of Mr. Choate and the wonderful way in which he could expose a current delusion, or what he thought was one, and produce an impression not only on his audience but on the whole community, when his speech was printed in the newspapers, was a kind of effort which necessarily required preparation. In all the many times I heard him, both at home and abroad, he never had a failure and sometimes made a sensation.

Among the many interesting characters whom I met on shipboard was Emory Storrs, a famous Chicago lawyer. Storrs was a genius of rare talent as an advocator. He also on occasions would make a most successful speech, but his efforts were unequal. At one session of the National Bar Association he carried off all the honors at their banquet. Of course, they wanted him the next year, but then he failed entirely to meet their expectations. Storrs was one of the most successful advocates at the criminal bar, especially in murder cases. He rarely failed to get an acquittal for his client. He told me many interesting stories of his experiences. He had a wide circuit, owing to his reputation, and tried cases far distant from home.

I remember one of his experiences in an out-of-the-way county of Arkansas. The hotel where they all stopped was very primitive, and he had the same table with the judge. The most attractive offer for breakfast by the landlady was buckwheat-cakes. She appeared with a jug of molasses and said to the judge: "Will you have a trickle or a dab?" The judge answered: "A dab." She then ran her fingers around the jug and slapped a huge amount of molasses on the judge's cakes. Storrs said: "I think I prefer a trickle." Whereupon she dipped her fingers again in the jug and let the drops fall from them on Storrs's cakes. The landlady was disappointed because her cakes were unpopular with such distinguished gentlemen.

Once Storrs was going abroad on the same ship with me on a sort of semi-diplomatic mission. He was deeply read in English literature and, as far as a stranger could be, familiar with the places made famous in English and foreign classics.

He was one of the factors, as chairman of the Illinois delegation, of the conditions which made possible the nomination of Garfield and Arthur. In the following presidential campaign he took an active and very useful part. Then he brought all the influences that he could use, and they were many, to bear upon President Arthur to make him attorney-general. Arthur was a strict formalist and could not tolerate the thought of having such an eccentric genius in his Cabinet. Storrs was not only disappointed but hurt that Arthur declined to appoint him.

To make him happy his rich clients—and he had many of them—raised a handsome purse and urged him to make a European trip. Then the president added to the pleasure of his journey by giving him an appointment as a sort of roving diplomat, with special duties relating to the acute trouble then existing in regard to the admission of American cattle into Great Britain. They were barred because of a supposed infectious disease.

Storrs's weakness was neckties. He told me that he had three hundred and sixty-five, a new one for every day. He would come on deck every morning, display his fresh necktie, and receive a compliment upon its color and appropriateness, and then take from his pocket a huge water-proof envelope. From this he would unroll his parchment appointment as a diplomat, and the letters he had to almost every one of distinction in Europe. On the last day, going through the same ceremony, he said to me: "I am not showing you these things out of vanity, but to impress upon you the one thing I most want to accomplish in London. I desire to compel James Russell Lowell, our minister, to give me a dinner."

Probably no man in the world could be selected so antipathetic to Lowell as Emory Storrs. Mr. Lowell told me that he was annoyed that the president should have sent an interloper to meddle with negotiations which he had in successful progress to a satisfactory conclusion. So he invited Storrs to dinner, and then Storrs took no further interest in his diplomatic mission.

Mr. Lowell told me that he asked Storrs to name whoever he wanted to invite. He supposed from his general analysis of the man that Storrs would want the entire royal family. He was delighted to find that the selection was confined entirely to authors, artists, and scientists.

On my return trip Mr. Storrs was again a fellow passenger. He was very enthusiastic over the places of historic interest he had visited, and eloquent and graphic in descriptions of them and of his own intense feelings when he came in contact with things he had dreamed of most of his life.

"But," he said, "I will tell you of my greatest adventure. I was in the picture-gallery at Dresden, and in that small room where hangs Raphael's 'Madonna.' I was standing before this wonderful masterpiece of divine inspiration when I felt the room crowded. I discovered that the visitors were all Americans and all looking at me. I said to them: 'Ladies and gentlemen, you are here in the presence of the most wonderful picture ever painted. If you study it, you can see that there is little doubt but with all his genius Raphael in this work had inspiration from above, and yet you, as Americans, instead of availing yourselves of the rarest of opportunities, have your eyes bent on me. I am only a Chicago lawyer wearing a Chicago-made suit of clothes.'

"A gentleman stepped forward and said: 'Mr. Storrs, on behalf of your countrymen and countrywomen present, I wish to say that you are of more interest to us than all the works of Raphael put together, because we understand that James Russell Lowell, United States Minister to Great Britain, gave you a dinner.'"

One other incident in my acquaintance with Mr. Storrs was original. I heard the story of it both from him and Lord Coleridge, and they did not differ materially. Lord Coleridge, Chief Justice of England, was a most welcome visitor when he came to the United States. He received invitations from the State Bar Associations everywhere to accept their hospitality. I conducted him on part of his trip and found him one of the most able and delightful of men. He was a very fine speaker, more in our way than the English, and made a first-class impression upon all the audiences he addressed.

At Chicago Lord Coleridge was entertained by the Bar Association of the State of Illinois. Storrs, who was an eminent member of the bar of that State, came to him and said: "Now, Lord Coleridge, you have been entertained by the Bar Association. I want you to know the real men of the West, the captains of industry who have created this city, built our railroads, and made the Great West what it is." Coleridge replied that he did not want to go outside bar associations, and he could not think of making another speech in Chicago. Storrs assured him it would be purely a private affair and no speeches permitted.

The dinner was very late, but when they sat down Lord Coleridge noticed a distinguished-looking gentleman, instead of eating his dinner, correcting a manuscript. He said: "Mr. Storrs, I understood there was to be no speaking." "Well," said Storrs, "you can't get Americans together unless some one takes the floor. That man with the manuscript is General and Senator John A. Logan, one of our most distinguished citizens." Just then a reporter came up to Storrs and said: "Mr. Storrs, we have the slips of your speech in our office, and it is now set up with the laughter and applause in their proper places. The editor sent me up to see if you wanted to add anything." Of course Lord Coleridge was in for it and had to make another speech.

The cause of the lateness of the dinner is the most original incident that I know of in historic banquets. Storrs received great fees and had a large income, but was very careless about his business matters. One of his creditors obtained a judgment against him. The lawyer for this creditor was a guest at this dinner and asked the landlord of the hotel if the dinner had been paid for in advance. The landlord answered in the affirmative, and so the lawyer telephoned to the sheriff, and had the dinner levied upon. The sheriff refused to allow it to be served until the judgment was satisfied. There were at least a hundred millions of dollars represented among the guests, packers, elevator men, real-estate operators, and grain operators, but millionaires and multimillionaires in dress suits at a banquet never have any money on their persons. So it was an hour or more before the sheriff was satisfied. Lord Coleridge was intensely amused and related the adventure with great glee.

Several years afterwards Lord Coleridge had some difficulty in his family which came into the courts of England. I do not remember just what it was all about, but Storrs, in reading the gossip which came across the cable, decided against the chief justice. Lord Coleridge told me he received from Storrs a cable reading something like this: "I have seen in our papers about your attitude in the suit now pending. I therefore inform you that as far as possible I withdraw the courtesies which I extended to you in Chicago." In this unique way Storrs cancelled the dinner which was given and seized by the sheriff years ago.

I met Storrs many times, and he was always not only charming but fascinating. He was very witty, full of anecdotes, and told a story with dramatic effect. Except for his eccentricities he might have taken the highest place in his profession. As it was, he acquired such fame that an admirer has written a very good biography of him.

XVII

GOVERNORS OF NEW YORK STATE

There is nothing more interesting than to see the beginning of a controversy which makes history. It is my good fortune to have been either a spectator or a participant on several occasions.

William M. Tweed was at the height of his power. He was the master of New York City, and controlled the legislature of the State. The rapid growth and expansion of New York City had necessitated a new charter, or very radical improvements in the existing one. Tweed, as chairman of the Senate committee on cities, had staged a large and spectacular hearing at the State Capitol at Albany. It was attended by a large body of representative citizens from the metropolis. Some spoke for civic and commercial bodies, and there were also other prominent men who were interested. Everybody interested in public affairs in Albany at the time attended. Not only was there a large gathering of legislators, but there were also in the audience judges, lawyers, and politicians from all parts of the State.

After hearing from the Chamber of Commerce and various reform organizations, Mr. Samuel J. Tilden came forward with a complete charter. It was soon evident that he was better prepared and informed on the subject than any one present. He knew intimately the weaknesses of the present charter, and had thought out with great care and wisdom what was needed in new legislation.

From the contemptuous way in which Senator Tweed treated Mr. Tilden, scouted his plans, and ridiculed his propositions, it was evident that the whole scheme had been staged as a State-wide spectacle to humiliate and end the political career of Samuel J. Tilden.

In answer to Tilden's protest against this treatment, Tweed loudly informed him that he represented no one but himself, that he had neither influence nor standing in the city, that he was an intermeddler with things that did not concern him, and a general nuisance.

Mr. Tilden turned ashy white, and showed evidences of suppressed rage and vindictiveness more intense than I ever saw in any one before, and abruptly left the hearing.

I knew Mr. Tilden very well, and from contact with him in railroad matters had formed a high opinion of his ability and acquirements. He had a keen, analytic mind, tireless industry, and a faculty for clarifying difficulties and untangling apparently impossible problems to a degree that amounted to genius.

In reference to what had happened, I said to a friend: "Mr. Tweed must be very confident of his position and of his record, for he has deliberately defied and invited the attacks of a relentless and merciless opponent by every insult which could wound the pride and incite the hatred of the man so ridiculed and abused. Mr. Tilden is a great lawyer. He has made a phenomenal success financially, he has powerful associates in financial and business circles, and is master of his time for any purpose to which he chooses to apply it."

It was not long before one of the most remarkable and exhaustive investigations ever conducted by an individual into public records, books, ledgers, bank-accounts, and contracts, revealed to the public the whole system of governing the city. This master mind solved the problems so that they were plain to the average citizen as the simplest sum in arithmetic, or that two and two make four.

The result was the destruction of the power of Tweed and his associates, of their prosecution and conviction, and of the elevation of Samuel J. Tilden to a State and national figure of the first importance. He not only became in the public mind a leader of reforms in government, municipal, State, and national, but embodied in the popular imagination *reform itself*.

Mr. Tilden carried this same indefatigable industry and power of organization into a canvass for governor. His agencies reached not only the counties and towns, but the election districts of the State. He called into existence a new power in politics—the young men. The old leaders were generally against him, but he discovered in every locality ambitious, resourceful, and courageous youngsters and made them his lieutenants. This unparalleled preparation made him the master of his party and the governor of the State.

After the election he invited me to come and see him at the Executive Mansion in Albany, and in the course of the conversation he said: "In your speeches in the campaign against me you were absolutely fair, and as a fair and open-minded opponent I want to have a frank talk. I am governor of the State, elected upon an issue which is purely local. The Democratic party is at present without principles or any definite issue on which to appeal to the public. If I am to continue in power we must find an issue. The Erie Canal is not only a State affair, but a national one. Its early construction opened the great Northwest, and it was for years the only outlet to the seaboard. The public not only in the State of New York, but in the West, believes that there has been, and is, corruption in the construction and management of the Canal. This great waterway requires continuing contracts for continuing repairs, and the people believe that these contracts are given to favorites, and that the work is either not performed at all or is badly done. I believe that matter ought to be looked into and the result will largely justify the suspicion prevalent in the public mind. I want your judgment on the question and what will be the effect upon me."

I then frankly answered him: "Governor, there is no doubt it will be a popular movement, but you know that the Canal contractors control the machinery of your party, and I cannot tell what the effect of that may be upon what you desire, which is a second term."

"Those contractors," he said, "are good Democrats, and their ability to secure the contracts depends upon Democratic supremacy. A prosecution against them has been tried so often that they have little fear of either civil or criminal actions, and I think they will accept the issue as the only one which will keep their party in power."

It is a part of the history of the time that he made the issue so interesting that he became a national figure of the first importance and afterwards the candidate of his party for President of the United States. Not only that, but he so impressed the people that popular judgment is still divided as to whether or not he was rightfully elected president.

Once I was coming from the West after a tour of inspection, and when we left Albany the conductor told me that Governor Tilden was on the train. I immediately called and found him very uncomfortable, because he said he was troubled with boils. I invited him into the larger compartment which I had, and made him as comfortable as possible. His conversation immediately turned upon the second term and he asked what I, as a Republican, thought of his prospects as the result of his administration. We had hardly entered upon the subject when a very excited gentleman burst into the compartment and said: "Governor, I have been looking for you everywhere. I went to your office at the Capitol and to the Executive Mansion, but learned you were here and barely caught the train. You know who I am." (The governor knew he was mayor of a city.) "I want to see you confidentially."

The governor said to him: "I have entire confidence in my Republican friend here. You can trust him. Go on."

I knew the mayor very well, and under ordinary conditions he would have insisted on the interview with the governor being private and personal. But he was so excited and bursting with rage that he went right on. The mayor fairly shouted: "It is the station agent of the New York Central Railroad in our city of whom I complain. He is active in politics and controls the Democratic organization in our county. He is working to prevent myself and my friends and even ex-Governor Seymour from being delegates to the national convention. It is to the interest of our party, in fact, I may say, the salvation of our party in our county that this New York Central agent be either removed or silenced, and I want you to see Mr. Vanderbilt on the subject."

The governor sympathized with the mayor and dismissed him. Then in a quizzical way he asked me: "Do you know this agent?"

"Yes," I answered.

"What do you think of him?"

"I know nothing about his political activities," I answered, "but he is one of the most efficient employees of the company in the State."

"Well," said the governor, "I am glad to hear you say so. He was down to see me the other night; in fact, I sent for him, and I formed a very high opinion of his judgment and ability."

As a matter of fact, the governor had selected him to accomplish this very result which the mayor had said would ruin the party in the county.

When the New York Democratic delegation left the city for the Democratic national convention they had engaged a special train to leave from the Grand Central Station. I went down to see that the arrangements were perfected for its movement. It was a hilarious crowd, and the sides of the cars were strung with Tilden banners.

Mr. Tilden was there also to see them off. After bidding good-by to the leaders, and with a whispered conference with each, the mass of delegates and especially reporters, of whom there was a crowd, wished to engage him in conversation. He spied me and immediately hurried me into one of the alcoves, apparently for a private conversation. The crowd, of course, gathered around, anxious to know what it was all about. He asked me a few questions about the health of my family and then added: "Don't leave me. I want to avoid all these people, and we will talk until the train is off and the crowd disperses."

Life was a burden for me the rest of the day and evening, made so by the newspaper men and Democratic politicians trying to find out what the mysterious chief had revealed to me in the alcove of the Grand Central.

I was very much gratified when meeting him after the fierce battles for the presidency were over, to have him grasp me by the hand and say: "You were about the only one who treated me absolutely fairly during the campaign."

I love little incidents about great men. Mr. Tilden was intensely human and a great man.

Doctor Buckley, who was at the head of the Methodist Book Concern in New York, and one of the most delightful of men, told me that there came into his office one day a Methodist preacher from one of the mining districts of Pennsylvania, who said to him: "My church burned down. We had no insurance. We are poor people, and, therefore, I have come to New York to raise money to rebuild it."

The doctor told him that New York was overrun from all parts of the country with applicants for help, and that he thought he would have great difficulty in his undertaking.

"Well," the preacher said, "I am going to see Mr. Tilden."

Doctor Buckley could not persuade him that his mission was next to impossible, and so this rural clergyman started for Gramercy Park. When he returned he told the doctor of his experience.

"I rang the bell," he said, "and when the door was opened I saw Governor Tilden coming down the stairs. I rushed in and told him hastily who I was before the man at the door could stop me, and he invited me into his library. I stated my mission, and he said he was so overwhelmed with applications that he did not think he could do anything. 'But, governor,' I said, 'my case differs from all others. My congregation is composed of miners, honest, hardworking people. They have hitherto been Republicans on the protection issue, but they were so impressed by you as a great reformer that they all voted for you in the last election.' The governor said: 'Tell that story again.' So I started again to tell him about my church, but he interrupted me, saying: 'Not that, but about the election.' So I told him again about their having, on account of their admiration for him as a reformer, turned from the Republican party and voted the Democratic ticket. Then the governor said: 'Well, I think you have a most meritorious case, and so I will give you all I have.'"

Doctor Buckley interrupted him hastily, saying: "Great heavens, are you going to build a cathedral?"

"No," answered the clergyman; "all he had in his pocket was two dollars and fifty cents."

Governor Tilden had many followers and friends whose admiration for him amounted almost to adoration. They believed him capable of everything, and they were among the most intelligent and able men of the country.

John Bigelow, journalist, author, and diplomat, was always sounding his greatness, both with tongue and pen. Abram S. Hewitt was an equally enthusiastic friend and admirer. Both of these gentlemen, the latter especially, were, I think, abler than Mr. Tilden, but did not have his hypnotic power.

I was dining one night with Mr. Hewitt, whose dinners were always events to be remembered, when Mr.

Tilden became the subject of discussion. After incidents illustrating his manifold distinctions had been narrated, Mr. Hewitt said that Mr. Tilden was the only one in America and outside of royalties in Europe who had some blue-labelled Johannisberger. This famous wine from the vineyards of Prince Metternich on the Rhine was at that time reported to be absorbed by the royal families of Europe.

Our host said: "The bouquet of this wonderful beverage is unusually penetrating and diffusing, and a proof is that one night at a dinner in the summer, with the windows all open, the guests noticed this peculiar aroma in the air. I said to them that Governor Tilden had opened a bottle of his Johannisberger."

The governor's residence was on the other side of Gramercy Park from Mr. Hewitt's. The matter was so extraordinary that everybody at the table went across the park, and when they were admitted they found the governor in his library enjoying his bottle of blue-labelled Johannisberger.

When Mr. Tilden was elected governor, my friend, General Husted, was speaker of the assembly, which was largely Republican. The governor asked General Husted to come down in the evening, because he wanted to consult him about the improvements and alterations necessary for the Executive Mansion, and to have the speaker secure the appropriation. During the discussion the governor placed before the speaker a bottle of rare whiskey, with the usual accompaniments. In front of the governor was a bottle of his Johannisberger and a small liqueur glass, a little larger than a thimble, from which the governor would from time to time taste a drop of this rare and exquisite fluid. The general, after a while, could not restrain his curiosity any longer and said: "Governor, what is that you are drinking?"

The governor explained its value and the almost utter impossibility of securing any.

"Well, governor," said Speaker Husted, "I never saw any before and I think I will try it." He seized the bottle, emptied it in his goblet and announced to the astonished executive that he was quite right in his estimate of its excellence.

The governor lost a bottle of his most cherished treasure but received from the Republican legislature all the appropriation he desired for the Executive Mansion.

It has been my good fortune to know well the governors of our State of New York, commencing with Edmund D. Morgan. With many of them I was on terms of close intimacy. I have already spoken of Governors Seymour, Fenton, Dix, Tilden, Cleveland, and Roosevelt. It might be better to confine my memory to those who have joined the majority.

Lucius Robinson was an excellent executive of the business type, as also were Alonzo B. Cornell and Levi P. Morton. Frank S. Black was in many ways original. He was an excellent governor, but very different from the usual routine. In the Spanish-American War he had a definite idea that the National Guard of our State should not go into the service of the United States as regiments, but as individual volunteers. The Seventh Regiment, which was the crack organization of the Guard, was severely criticised because they did not volunteer. They refused to go except as the Seventh Regiment, and their enemies continued to assail them as tin soldiers.

General Louis Fitzgerald and Colonel Appleton came

to me very much disturbed by this condition. General Russell A. Alger, secretary of war, was an intimate friend of mine, and I went to Washington and saw him and the president on the acute condition affecting the reputation of the Seventh Regiment.

General Alger said: "We are about to make a desperate assault upon the fortifications of Havana. Of course there will be many casualties and the fighting most severe. Will the Seventh join that expedition?"

The answer of General Fitzgerald and Colonel Appleton was emphatic that the Seventh would march with full ranks on the shortest possible notice. Governor Black would not change his view of how the National Guard should go, and so the Seventh was never called. It seems only proper that I should make a record of this patriotic proposition made by this organization.

Governor Black developed after he became governor, and especially after he had retired from office, into a very effective orator. He had a fine presence and an excellent delivery. He was fond of preparing epigrams, and became a master in this sort of literature. When he had occasion to deliver an address, it would be almost wholly made up of these detached gems, each perfect in itself. The only other of our American orators who cultivated successfully this style of speech was Senator John J. Ingalls, of Kansas. It is a style very difficult to attain or to make successful.

David B. Hill was an extraordinary man in many ways. He was governor for three terms and United States senator for one. His whole life was politics. He was a trained lawyer and an excellent one, but his heart and soul was in party control, winning popular elections, and the art of governing. He consolidated the rural elements of his party so effectively that he compelled Tammany Hall to submit to his leadership and to recognize him as its master.

For many years, and winning in every contest, Governor Hill controlled the organization and the policies of the Democratic party of the State of New York. In a plain way he was an effective speaker, but in no sense an orator. He contested with Cleveland for the presidency, but in that case ran against a stronger and bigger personality than he had ever encountered, and lost. He rose far above the average and made his mark upon the politics of his State and upon the United States Senate while he was a member.

Levi P. Morton brought to the governorship business ability which had made him one of the great merchants and foremost bankers. As Governor of the State of New York, United States Minister to France, Congressman. and Vice-President of the United States, he filled every position with grace, dignity, and ability. A lovable personality made him most popular.

Roswell P. Flower, after a successful career as a banker, developed political ambitions. He had a faculty of making friends, and had hosts of them. He was congressman and then governor. While the Democratic organization was hostile to him, he was of the Mark Hanna type and carried his successful business methods into the canvass for the nomination and the campaign for the election and was successful.

Passing through Albany while he was governor, I stopped over to pay my respects. I was very fond of him personally. When I rang the door-bell of the Executive Mansion and inquired for the governor, the servant said: "The governor is very ill and can see nobody."

Then I asked him to tell the governor, when he was able to receive a message, that Chauncey Depew called and expressed his deep regret for his illness. Suddenly the governor popped out from the parlor and seized me by the hand and said: "Chauncey, come in. I was never so glad to see anybody in my life."

He told me the legislature had adjourned and left on his hands several thousands of thirty-days bills—that is, bills on which he had thirty days to sign or veto, or let them become laws by not rejecting them. So he had to deny himself to everybody to get the leisure to read them over and form decisions.

"Do you know, Chauncey," he said, "this is a new business to me. Most of these bills are on subjects which I never have examined, studied, or thought about. It is very difficult to form a wise judgment, and I want to do in each case just what is right." For the moment he became silent, seemingly absorbed by anxious thoughts about these bills. Then suddenly he exclaimed: "By the way, Chauncey, you've done a great deal of thinking in your life, and I never have done any except on business. Does intense thinking affect you as it does me, by upsetting your stomach and making you throw up?"

"No, governor," I answered; "if it did I fear I would be in a chronic state of indigestion."

While he was governor he canvassed the State in a private car and made many speeches. In a plain, homely man-to-man talk he was very effective on the platform. His train stopped at a station in a Republican community where there were few Democrats, while I was addressing a Republican meeting in the village. When I had finished my speech I said to the crowd, which was a large one: "Governor Flower is at the station, and as I passed he had very few people listening to him. Let us all go over and give him an audience."

The proposition was received with cheers. I went ahead, got in at the other end of the governor's car from the one where he was speaking from the platform. As this Republican crowd began to pour in, it was evident as I stood behind him without his knowing of my presence, that he was highly delighted. He shouted: "Fellow citizens, I told you they were coming. They are coming from the mountains, from the hills, and from the valleys. It is the stampede from the Republican party and into our ranks and for our ticket. This is the happiest evidence I have received of the popularity of our cause and the success of our ticket."

Standing behind him, I made a signal for cheers, which was heartily responded to, and the governor, turning around, saw the joke, grasped me cordially by the hand, and the whole crowd, including the veteran and hardened Democrats on the car, joined in the hilarity of the occasion.

He came to me when he was running for the second time for Congress, and said that some of the people of his district were anxious for me to deliver an address for one of their pet charities, and that the meeting would be held in Harlem, naming the evening. I told him I would go. He came for me in his carriage, and I said: "Governor, please do not talk to me on the way up. I was so busy that I have had no time since I left my office this afternoon to prepare this address, and I want every minute while we are riding to the meeting."

The meeting was a large one. The governor took the chair and introduced me in this original way: "Ladies and gentlemen," he said, "I want to say about Chauncey

Depew, whom I am now going to introduce to you as the lecturer of the evening, that he is no Demosthenes, because he can beat Demosthenes out of sight. He prepared his speech in the carriage in which I was bringing him up here, and he don't have, like the old Greek, to chew pebble-stones in order to make a speech."

Governor Flower in a conservative way was a successful trader in the stock market. When he felt he had a sure point he would share it with a few friends. He took special delight in helping in this way men who had little means and no knowledge of the art of money-making. There were a great many benefited by his bounty.

I was dining one night with the Gridiron Club at Washington, and before me was a plate of radishes. The newspaper man next to me asked if I would object to having the radishes removed.

I said: "There is no odor or perfume from them. What is the matter with the radishes?"

After they were taken away he told me his story. "Governor Flower," he said, "was very kind to me, as he invariably was to all newspaper men. He asked me one day how much I had saved in my twenty years in journalism. I told him ten thousand dollars. He said: 'That is not enough for so long a period. Let me have the money.' So I handed over to him my bank-account. In a few weeks he told me that my ten thousand dollars had become twenty, and I could have them if I wished. I said: 'No, you are doing far better than I could. Keep it.' In about a month or more my account had grown to thirty thousand dollars. Then the governor on a very hot day went fishing somewhere off the Long Island coast. He was a very large, heavy man, became overheated, and on his return drank a lot of ice-water and ate a bunch of radishes. He died that afternoon. There was a panic in the stocks which were his favorites the next day, and they fell out of sight. The result was that I lost my fortune of ten thousand dollars and also my profit of twenty. Since then the sight of a radish makes me sick."

XVIII

FIFTY-SIX YEARS WITH THE NEW YORK CENTRAL RAILROAD COMPANY

Heredity has much to do with a man's career. The village of Peekskill-on-the-Hudson, about forty miles from New York, was in the early days the market-town of a large section of the surrounding country, extending over to the State of Connecticut. It was a farming region, and its products destined for New York City were shipped by sloops on the Hudson from the wharfs at Peekskill, and the return voyage brought back the merchandise required by the country.

My father and his brother owned the majority of the sloops engaged in this, at that time, almost the only transportation. The sloops were succeeded by steamboats in which my people were also interested. When Commodore Vanderbilt entered into active rivalry with the other steamboat lines between New York and Albany, the competition became very serious. Newer and faster boats were rapidly built. These racers would reach the Bay of Peekskill in the late afternoon, and the younger population of the village would be on the banks of the river, enthusiastically applauding their favorites. Among well-known boats whose names and achievements excited as much interest and aroused as much partisanship and sporting spirit as do now famous race-horses or baseball champions, were the following: *Mary Powell, Dean Richmond, The Alida,* and *The Hendrick Hudson.*

I remember as if it were yesterday when the Hudson River Railroad had reached Peekskill, and the event was locally celebrated. The people came in as to a county fair from fifty miles around. When the locomotive steamed into the station many of those present had never seen one. The engineer was continuously blowing his whistle to emphasize the great event. This produced much consternation and confusion among the horses, as all farmers were there with their families in carriages or wagons.

I recall one team of young horses which were driven to frenzy; their owner was unable to control them, but he kept them on the road while they ran away with a wild dash over the hills. In telling this story, as illustrating how recent is railway development in the United States, at a dinner abroad, I stated that as far as I knew and believed, those horses were so frightened that they could not be stopped and were still running. A very successful and serious-minded captain of industry among the guests sternly rebuked me by saying: "Sir, that is impossible; horses were never born that could run for twenty-five years without stopping." American exaggeration was not so well known among our friends on the other side then as it is now.

As we boys of the village were gathered on the banks of the Hudson cheering our favorite steamers, or watching with eager interest the movements of the trains, a frequent discussion would be about our ambitions in life. Every young fellow would state a dream which he hoped but never expected to be realized. I was charged by my companions with having the greatest imagination and with painting more pictures in the skies than any of them. This was because I stated that in politics, for I was a great admirer of William H. Seward, then senator from New York, I expected to be a United States senator, and in business, because then the largest figure in the business world was Commodore Vanderbilt, I hoped to become president of the Hudson River Railroad. It is one of the strangest incidents of what seemed the wild imaginings of a village boy that in the course of long years both these expectations were realized.

When I entered the service of the railroad on the first of January, 1866, the Vanderbilt system consisted of the Hudson River and Harlem Railroads, the Harlem ending at Chatham, 128 miles, and the Hudson River at Albany, 140 miles long. The Vanderbilt system now covers 20,000 miles. The total railway mileage of the whole United States at that time was 36,000, and now it is 261,000 miles.

My connection with the New York Central Railroad covers practically the whole period of railway construction, expansion, and development in the United States. It is a singular evidence of the rapidity of our country's growth and of the way which that growth has steadily followed the rails, that all this development of States, of villages growing into cities, of scattered communities becoming great manufacturing centres, of an internal commerce reaching proportions where it has greater volume than the foreign interchanges of the whole world, has come about during a period covered by the official career of a railroad man who is still in the service: an attorney in 1866, a vice-president in 1882, president in 1885, chairman of the board of directors in 1899, and still holds that office.

There is no such record in the country for continuous service with one company, which during the whole period has been controlled by one family. This service of more than half a century has been in every way satisfactory. It is a pleasure to see the fourth generation, inheriting the ability of the father, grandfather, and great-grandfather, still active in the management.

I want to say that in thus linking my long relationship with the railroads to this marvellous development, I do not claim to have been better than the railway officers who during this time have performed their duties to the best of their ability. I wish also to pay tribute to the men of original genius, of vision and daring, to whom so much is due in the expansion and improvement of the American railway systems.

Commodore Vanderbilt was one of the most remarkable men our country has produced. He was endowed with wonderful foresight, grasp of difficult situations, ability to see opportunities before others, to solve serious problems, and the courage of his convictions. He had little education or early advantages, but was eminently successful in everything he undertook. As a boy on Staten Island he foresaw that upon transportation depended the settlement, growth, and prosperity of this nation. He began with a small boat running across the harbor from Staten Island to New York. Very early in his career he acquired a steamboat and in a few years was master of Long Island Sound. He then extended his operations to the Hudson River and speedily acquired the dominating ownership in boats competing between New York and Albany.

When gold was discovered in California he started a line on the Atlantic side of the Isthmus of Darien and secured from the government of Nicaragua the privilege of crossing the Isthmus for a transportation system

WITH THE NEW YORK CENTRAL 229

through its territory, and then established a line of steamers on the Pacific to San Francisco. In a short time the old-established lines, both on the Atlantic and the Pacific, were compelled to sell out to him. Then he entered the transatlantic trade, with steamers to Europe.

With that vision which is a gift and cannot be accounted for, he decided that the transportation work of the future was on land and in railroads. He abandoned the sea, and his first enterprise was the purchase of the New York and Harlem Railroad, which was only one hundred and twenty-eight miles long. The road was bankrupt and its road-bed and equipment going from bad to worse. The commodore reconstructed the line, re-equipped it, and by making it serviceable to its territory increased its traffic and turned its business from deficiency into profit. This was in 1864. The commodore became president, and his son, William H. Vanderbilt, vice-president. He saw that the extension of the Harlem was not advisable, and so secured the Hudson River Railroad, running from New York to Albany, and became its president in 1865. It was a few months after this when he and his son invited me to become a member of their staff.

The station of the Harlem Railroad in the city of New York was at that time at Fourth Avenue and Twenty-sixth Street, and that of the Hudson River Railroad at Chambers Street, near the North River.

In a few years William H. Vanderbilt purchased the ground for the Harlem Railroad Company, where is now located the Grand Central Terminal, and by the acquisition by the New York Central and Hudson River Railroad of the Harlem Railroad the trains of the New York

Central were brought around into the Grand Central Station.

In 1867, two years after Mr. Vanderbilt had acquired the Hudson River Railroad, he secured the control of the New York Central, which ran from Albany to Buffalo. This control was continued through the Lake Shore on one side of the lakes and the Michigan Central on the other to Chicago. Subsequently the Vanderbilt System was extended to Cincinnati and St. Louis. It was thus in immediate connection with the West and Northwest centering in Chicago, and the Southwest at Cincinnati and St. Louis. By close connection and affiliation with the Chicago and Northwestern Railway Company, the Vanderbilt system was extended beyond to Mississippi. I became director in the New York Central in 1874 and in the Chicago and Northwestern in 1877.

It has been my good fortune to meet with more or less intimacy many of the remarkable men in every department of life, but I think Commodore Vanderbilt was the most original. I had been well acquainted for some years both with the commodore and his son, William H. When I became attorney my relations were more intimate than those usually existing. I was in daily consultation with the commodore during the ten years prior to his death, and with his son from 1866 to 1885, when he died.

The commodore was constantly, because of his wealth and power, importuned by people who wished to interest him in their schemes. Most of the great and progressive enterprises of his time were presented to him. He would listen patiently, ask a few questions, and in a short time grasp the whole subject. Then with wonderful quickness and unerring judgment he would render his decision. No one knew by what process he arrived at these conclusions. They seemed to be the results as much of inspiration as of insight.

The Civil War closed in 1865, and one of its lessons had been the necessity for more railroads. The country had discovered that without transportation its vast and fertile territories could neither be populated nor made productive. Every mile of railroad carried settlers, opened farms and increased the national resources and wealth. The economical and critical conditions of the country, owing to the expansion of the currency and banking conditions, facilitated and encouraged vast schemes of railroad construction. This and a wild speculation resulted in the panic of 1873. Nearly the whole country went bankrupt. The recovery was rapid, and the constructive talent of the Republic saw that the restoration of credit and prosperity must be led by railway solvency. In August, 1874, Commodore Vanderbilt invited the representatives of the other and competitive lines to a conference at Saratoga. Owing, however, to the jealousies and hostilities of the period, only the New York Central, the Pennsylvania, and the Erie railways were represented.

The eastern railway situation was then dominated by Commodore Vanderbilt, Colonel Thomas A. Scott, of the Pennsylvania, and John W. Garrett, of the Baltimore and Ohio. Both Scott and Garrett were original men and empire builders. There was neither governmental nor State regulation. The head of a railway system had practically unlimited power in the operation of his road. The people were so anxious for the construction of railways that they offered every possible inducement to capital. The result was a great deal of unprofitable construction and immense losses to the promoters.

These able men saw that there was no possibility of

railway construction, operation, and efficiency, with a continuance of unrestricted competition. It has taken from 1874 until 1920 to educate the railway men, the shippers, and the government to a realization of the fact that transportation facilities required for the public necessities can only be had by the freest operations and the strictest government regulations; that the solution of the problem is a system so automatic that public arbitration shall decide the justice of the demands of labor, and rates be advanced to meet the decision, and that public authority also shall take into consideration the other factors of increased expenses and adequate facilities for the railroads, and that maintenance and the highest efficiency must be preserved and also necessary extensions. To satisfy and attract capital there must be the assurance of a reasonable return upon the investment.

The meeting called by Commodore Vanderbilt in 1874, at Saratoga, was an epoch-making event. We must remember the railway management of the country was in the absolute control of about four men, two of whom were also largest owners of the lines they managed. Fierce competition and cutting of rates brought on utter demoralization among shippers, who could not calculate on the cost of transportation, and great favoritism to localities and individuals by irresponsible freight agents who controlled the rates. Under these influences railway earnings were fluctuating and uncertain. Improvements were delayed and the people on the weaker lines threatened with bankruptcy.

Public opinion, however, believed this wild competition to be the only remedy for admitted railway evils. As an illustration of the change of public opinion and the better understanding of the railway problems, this occurred in the month of October, 1920. A committee of shippers and producers representing the farmers, manufacturers, and business men along a great railway system came to see the manager of the railroad and said to him: "We have been all wrong in the past. Our effort has always been for lower rates, regardless of the necessities of the railways. We have tried to get them by seeking bids from competing lines for our shipments and by appealing to the Interstate Commerce Commission. The expenses of the railroads have been increased by demands of labor, by constantly rising prices and cost of rails, cars, terminals, and facilities, but we have been against allowing the railroads to meet this increased cost of operation by adequate advances in rates. We now see that this course was starving the railroads, and we are suffering for want of cars and locomotives to move our traffic and terminals to care for it. We are also suffering because the old treatment of the railroads has frightened capital so that the roads cannot get money to maintain their lines and make necessary improvements to meet the demands of business. We know now that rates make very little difference, because they can be absorbed in our business. What we must have is facilities to transport our products, and we want to help the railroads to get money and credit, and again we emphasize our whole trouble is want of cars, locomotives, and terminal facilities."

Happily, public opinion was reflected in the last Congress in the passage of the Cummins-Esch bill, which is the most enlightened and adaptable legislation of the last quarter of a century.

To return to the conference at Saratoga, the New York Central, the Pennsylvania, and the Erie came to the conclusion that they must have the co-operation of the Baltimore and Ohio. As Mr. Garrett, president and controlling owner of that road, would not come to the conference, the members decided that the emergency was so great that they must go to him. This was probably the most disagreeable thing Commodore Vanderbilt ever did. The marvellous success of his wonderful life had been won by fighting and defeating competitors. The peril was so great that they went as associates, and the visit interested the whole country and so enlarged Mr. Garrett's opinion of his power that he rejected their offer and said he would act independently. A railway war immediately followed, and in a short time bankruptcy threatened all lines, and none more than the Baltimore and Ohio.

The trunk lines then got together and entered into an agreement to stabilize rates and carry them into effect. They appointed as commissioner Mr. Albert Fink, one of the ablest railway men of that time. Mr. Fink's administration was successful, but the rivalries and jealousies of the lines and the frequent breaking of agreements were too much for one man.

The presidents and general managers of all the railroads east of Chicago then met and formed an association, and this association was a legislative body without any legal authority to enforce its decrees. It had, however, two effects: the disputes which arose were publicly discussed, and the merits of each side so completely demonstrated that the decision of the association came to be accepted as just and right. Then the verdict of the association had behind it the whole investment and banking community and the press. The weight of this was sufficient to compel obedience to its decisions by the most rebellious member. No executive could continue to hold his position while endeavoring to break up the association.

It is one of the most gratifying events of my life that my associates in this great and powerful association elected me their president, and I continued in office until the Supreme Court in a momentous decision declared that the railroads came under the provision of the Sherman Anti-Trust Law and dissolved these associations in the East, West, and South.

It was a liberal education of the railway problems to meet the men who became members of this association. Most of them left an indelible impression upon the railway conditions of the time and of the railway policies of the future. All were executives of great ability and several rare constructive geniuses.

In our system there was John Newell, president of the Lake Shore and Michigan Southern, a most capable and efficient manager. Henry B. Ledyard, president of the Michigan Central, was admirably trained for the great responsibilities which he administered so well. There was William Bliss, president of the Boston and Albany, who had built up a line to be one of the strongest of the New England group.

Melville E. Ingalls, president of the Cleveland, Cincinnati, Chicago and St. Louis, had combined various weak and bankrupt roads and made them an efficient organization. He had also rehabilitated and put in useful working and paying condition the Chesapeake and Ohio.

Ingalls told me a very good story of himself. He had left the village in Maine, where he was born, and after graduation from college and admission to the bar had settled in Boston. To protect the interests of his clients he had moved to Cincinnati, Ohio, and rescued railroad properties in which they were interested. When his success was complete and he had under his control a large and successfully working railway system, he made a visit to his birthplace.

One evening he went down to the store where the village congress was assembled, sitting on the barrels and the counter. They welcomed him very cordially, and then an inquisitive farmer said to him: "Melville, it is reported around here that you are getting a salary of nigh unto ten thousand dollars a year."

Mr. Ingalls, who was getting several times that amount, modestly admitted the ten, which was a prodigious sum in that rural neighborhood. Whereupon the old farmer voiced the local sentiment by saying: "Well, Melville, that shows what cheek and circumstances can do for a man."

I recall an incident connected with one of the ablest of the executives in our system. One day we had a conference of rival interests, and many executives were there in the effort to secure an adjustment. For this purpose we had an arbitrator. After a most exhausting day in the battle of wits and experience for advantages, I arrived home used up, but after a half-hour's sleep I awoke refreshed and, consulting my diary, found I was down for a speech at a banquet at Delmonico's that night.

I arrived late, the intervening time being devoted to intensive and rapid preparation. I was called early. The speech attracted attention and occupied a column in the morning's papers. I was in bed at eleven o'clock and had between seven and eight hours' refreshing sleep.

On arriving at our meeting-place the next morning, one of the best-known presidents took me aside and said: "Chauncey, by making speeches such as you did last night you are losing the confidence of the people. They say you cannot prepare such speeches and give proper attention to your business."

"Well," I said to him, "my friend, did I lose anything before the arbitrator yesterday?"

He answered very angrily: "No, you gained entirely too much."

"Well," I then said, "I am very fresh this morning. But what did you do last night?"

He answered that he was so exhausted that he went to Delmonico's and ordered the best dinner possible. Then he went on to say: "A friend told me a little game was going on up-stairs, and in a close room filled with tobacco smoke I played poker until two o'clock and drank several high-balls. The result is, I think we better postpone this meeting, for I do not feel like doing anything to-day."

"My dear friend," I said, "you will get the credit of giving your whole time to business, while I am by doing what refreshes my mind discredited, because it gets in the papers. I shall keep my method regardless of consequences."

He kept his, and although much younger than myself died years ago.

George B. Roberts, president of the Pennsylvania, was a very wise executive and of all-around ability. Frank Thompson, vice-president and afterwards president of the same road, was one of the ablest operating officers of his time and a most delightful personality. Mr. A. J. Cassatt was a great engineer and possessed rare foresight and vision. He brought the Pennsylvania into New York City through a tunnel under the Hudson River, continued the tunnel across the city to the East River and then under the river to connect with the Long Island, which he had acquired for his system.

D. W. Caldwell, president of the New York, Chicago, and St. Louis, added to railway ability wit and humor. He told a good story on Mr. George Roberts. Caldwell was at one time division superintendent under President Roberts. He had obtained permission to build a new station-house, in whose plan and equipment he was deeply interested. It was Mr. Roberts's habit, by way of showing his subordinates that he was fully aware of their doings, to either add or take away something from their projects.

Caldwell prepared a station-house according to his ideas, and, to prevent Roberts from making any essential changes he added an unnecessary bay window to the front of the passengers' room. Roberts carefully examined the plans and said: "Remove that bay window," and then approved the plan, and Caldwell had what he wanted.

Caldwell used to tell of another occasion when on a Western line he had over him a very severe and harsh disciplinarian as president. This president was a violent prohibitionist and had heard that Caldwell was a bonvivant. He sent for Caldwell to discipline or discharge him. After a long and tiresome journey Caldwell arrived at the president's house. His first greeting was: "Mr. Caldwell, do you drink?"

Caldwell, wholly unsuspicious, answered: "Thank you, Mr. President, I am awfully tired and will take a little rye."

Mr. E. B. Thomas, president of the Lehigh Valley, was a valuable member of the association. The Baltimore and Ohio, as usual, had its president, Mr. Charles F. Mayer, accompanied by an able staff. The Erie was represented by one of the most capable and genial of its many presidents, Mr. John King.

King was a capital story-teller, and among them I remember this one: At one time he was general manager of the Baltimore and Ohio under John W. Garrett. In order to raise money for his projected extensions, Garrett had gone to Europe. The times were financially very difficult. Johns Hopkins, the famous philanthropist, died. His immortal monument is the Johns Hopkins University and Medical School. Everybody in Baltimore attended the funeral. Among the leading persons present was another John King, a banker, who was Hopkins's executor. A messenger-boy rushed in with a cable for John King, and handed it to John King, the executor, who sat at the head of the mourners. He read it and then passed it along so that each one could read it until it reached John King, of the Baltimore and Ohio, who sat at the foot of the line. The cable read as follows: "Present my sympathies to the family and my high appreciation of Mr. Johns Hopkins, and borrow from the executor all you can at five per cent. Garrett."

Commodore Vanderbilt was succeeded in the presidency by his son, William H. Vanderbilt, who was then past forty years old and had been a successful farmer on Staten Island. He was active in neighborhood affairs and in politics. This brought him in close contact with the people and was of invaluable benefit to him when he became president of a great railroad corporation. He also acquired familiarity in railway management as a director of one on Staten Island.

Mr. William H. Vanderbilt was a man of great ability, and his education made him in many ways an abler man than his father for the new conditions he had to meet. But, like many a capable son of a famous father, he did not receive the credit which was due him because of the overshadowing reputation of the commodore. Nevertheless, on several occasions he exhibited the highest executive qualities.

One of the great questions of the time was the duty of railroads to the cities in which they terminated, and the decision of the roads south of New York to have lower rates to Philadelphia and Baltimore. New York felt so secure in the strength of its unrivalled harbor and superior shipping facilities that the merchants and financiers were not alarmed. Very soon, however, there was such a diversion of freight from New York as to threaten very seriously its export trade and the superiority of its port. The commercial leaders of the city called upon Mr. Vanderbilt, who after the conference said to them: "I will act in perfect harmony with you and will see that the New York Central Railroad protects New York City regardless of the effect upon its finances." The city representatives said: "That is very fine, and we will stand together."

Mr. Vanderbilt immediately issued a statement that the rates to the seaboard should be the same to all ports, and that the New York Central would meet the lowest rates to any port by putting the same in effect on its own lines. The result was the greatest railroad war since railroads began to compete. Rates fell fifty per cent, and it was a question of the survival of the fittest.

Commerce returned to New York, and the competing railroads, to avoid bankruptcy, got together and formed the Trunk Line Association.

New York City has not always remembered how intimately bound is its prosperity with that of the great railroad whose terminal is within its city limits. Mr. Vanderbilt found that the railroad and its management were fiercely assailed in the press, in the legislature, and in municipal councils. He became convinced that no matter how wise or just or fair the railroad might be in the interests of every community and every business which were so dependent upon its transportation, the public would not submit to any great line being owned by one man. The Vanderbilt promptness in arriving at a decision was immediately shown. He called upon Mr. Pierpont Morgan, and through him a syndicate, which Morgan formed, took and sold the greater part of Mr. Vanderbilt's New York Central stock. The result was that the New York Central from that time was owned by the public. It is a tribute to the justice and fairness of the Vanderbilt management that though the management has been submitted every year since to a stockholders' vote, there has practically never been any opposition to a continuance of the Vanderbilt policy and management.

Among the most important of the many problems during Mr. Vanderbilt's presidency was the question of railway commissions, both in national and State governments. In my professional capacity of general counsel, and in common with representatives of other railroads, I delivered argumentative addresses against them. The discussions converted me, and I became convinced of their necessity. The rapidly growing importance of railway transportation had created the public opinion that railway management should be under the control and supervision of some public body; that all passengers or shippers, or those whose land was taken for construction and development, should have an appeal from the decision of the railway managers to the government through a government commission.

As soon as I was convinced that commissions were necessary for the protection of both the public and the railroads, I presented this view to Mr. Vanderbilt. The idea was contrary to his education, training, and opinion. It seemed to me that it was either a commission or government ownership, and that the commission, if strengthened as a judicial body, would be as much of a protection to the bond and stock holders and the investing public as to the general public and the employees. Mr. Vanderbilt, always open-minded, adopted this view and supported the commission system and favored legislation in its behalf.

In 1883 Mr. Vanderbilt decided, on account of illness, to retire from the presidency, and Mr. James H. Rutter was elected his successor. Mr. Rutter was the ablest freight manager in the country, but his health gave way under the exactions of executive duties, and I acted largely for him during his years of service. He died early in 1885, and I was elected president.

The war with the West Shore had been on for several years, with disastrous results to both companies. The Ontario and Western, which had large terminal facilities near Jersey City on the west side of the Hudson, ran for fifty miles along the river before turning into the interior. At its reorganization it had ten millions of cash in the treasury. With this as a basis, its directors decided to

WITH THE NEW YORK CENTRAL

organize a new railroad, to be called the West Shore, and parallel the New York Central through its entire length to Buffalo. As the New York Central efficiently served this whole territory, the only business the West Shore could get must be taken away from the Central. To attract this business it offered at all stations lower rates. To retain and hold its business the New York Central met those rates at all points so that financially the West Shore went into the hands of a receiver.

The New York Central was sustained because of its superior facilities and connections and established roadway and equipment. But all new and necessary construction was abandoned, maintenance was neglected, and equipment run down under forced reduction of expenses.

I had very friendly personal relations with the managers and officers of the West Shore, and immediately presented to them a plan for the absorption of their line, instead of continuing the struggle until absolute exhaustion. Mr. Vanderbilt approved of the plan, as did the financial interests represented by Mr. Pierpont Morgan.

By the reorganization and consolidation of the two companies the New York Central began gradually to establish its efficiency and to work on necessary improvements. As evidence of the growth of the railway business of the country, the New York Central proper has added since the reorganization an enormous amount of increased trackage, and has practically rebuilt, as a necessary second line, the West Shore and used fully its very large terminal facilities on the Jersey side of the Hudson.

During his active life Mr. Vanderbilt was very often importuned to buy a New York daily newspaper. He was personally bitterly assailed and his property put in peril by attacks in the press. He always rejected the proposition to buy one. "If," he said, "I owned a newspaper, I would have all the others united in attacking me, and they would ruin me, but by being utterly out of the journalistic field, I find that taking the press as a whole I am fairly well treated. I do not believe any great interest dealing with the public can afford to have an organ."

Colonel Scott, of the Pennsylvania, thought otherwise, but the result of his experiment demonstrated the accuracy of Mr. Vanderbilt's judgment. Scott selected as editor of the *New York World* one of the most brilliant journalistic writers of his time, William H. Hurlburt. When it became known, however, that the *World* belonged to Colonel Scott, Hurlburt's genius could not save it. The circulation ran down to a minimum, the advertising followed suit, and the paper was losing enormously every month. Mr. Joseph Pulitzer, with the rare insight and foresight which distinguished him, saw what could be made of the *World*, with its privileges in the Associated Press, and so he paid Scott the amount he had originally invested, and took over and made a phenomenal success of this bankrupt and apparently hopeless enterprise.

I tried during my presidency to make the New York Central popular with the public without impairing its efficiency. The proof of the success of this was that without any effort on my part and against my published wishes the New York delegation in the national Republican convention in 1888, with unprecedented unanimity, presented me as New York's candidate for president. I retired from the contest because of the intense hostility to railroad men in the Western States. Those States could not understand how this hostility, which they had to railroads and everybody connected with them, had disappeared in the great State of New York.

During my presidency the labor question was very acute and strikes, one after another, common. The universal method of meeting the demands of labor at that time was to have a committee of employees or a leader present the grievances to the division superintendent or the superintendent of motive power. These officers were arbitrary and hostile, as the demands, if acceded to, led to an increase of expenses which would make them unpopular with the management. They had a difficult position. The employees often came to the conclusion that the only way for them to compel the attention of the higher officers and directors was to strike.

Against the judgment of my associates in the railway management I decided to open my doors to any individual or committee of the company. At first I was overwhelmed with petty grievances, but when the men understood that their cases would be immediately heard and acted upon, they decided among themselves not to bring to me any matters unless they regarded them of vital importance. In this way many of the former irritations, which led ultimately to serious results, no longer appeared.

I had no trouble with labor unions, and found their representatives in heart-to-heart talks very generally reasonable. Mr. Arthur, chief of the Brotherhood of Locomotive Engineers, had many of the qualities of a statesman. He built up his organization to be the strongest of its kind among the labor unions. I enjoyed his confidence and friendship for many years.

There never was but one strike on the New York Central during my administration, and that one occurred while I was absent in Europe. Its origin and sequel were somewhat dramatic. I had nearly broken down by overwork, and the directors advised me to take an absolute rest and a trip abroad.

I sent word over the line that I wanted everything settled before leaving, and to go without care. A large committee appeared in my office a few mornings after. To my surprise there was a representative from every branch of the service, passenger and freight conductors, brakemen, shopmen, yardmen, switchmen, and so forth. These had always come through their local unions. I rapidly took up and adjusted what each one of the representatives of his order claimed, and then a man said: "I represent the locomotive engineers."

My response was: "You have no business here, and I will have nothing to do with you. I will see no one of the locomotive engineers, except their accredited chief officer."

"Well," he said, "Mr. President, there is a new condition on the road, a new order of labor called the Knights of Labor. We are going to absorb all the other unions and have only one. The only obstacle in the way is the locomotive engineers, who refuse to give up their brotherhood and come in with us, but if you will recognize us only, that will force them to join. Now, the Brotherhood intends to present a demand very soon, and if you will recognize our order, the Knights of Labor, and not the Brotherhood of Locomotive Engineers, we will take care of what they demand and all others from every department for two years, and you can take your trip to Europe in perfect peace of mind. If you do not do this there will be trouble."

I declined to deal with them as representatives of the Brotherhood of Locomotive Engineers. Then their spokesman said: "As this is so serious to you, we will give you to-night to think it over and come back in the morning."

I immediately sent for the superintendent of motive power and directed him to have posted by telegraph in every roundhouse that the request of the Brotherhood of Locomotive Engineers, of which this committee had told me, had been granted. The next morning the committee returned, and their leader said: "Well, Mr. President, you have beaten us and we are going home."

Then I appealed to them, saying: "I am a pretty badly broken-up man. The doctors tell me that if I can have three months without care I will be as good as ever. You must admit that I have at all times been absolutely square with you and tried to adjust fairly the matters you have brought to me. Now, will you take care of me while I am absent?"

They answered unanimously: "Mr. President, we will, and you can be confident there will be no trouble on the New York Central while you are away."

I sailed with my mind free from anxiety, hopeful and happy, leaving word to send me no cables or letters. After a visit to the Passion Play at Ober-Ammergau in Upper Bavaria, I went into the Austrian Tyrol. One night, at a hotel in Innsbruck, Mr. Graves, a very enterprising reporter of a New York paper, suddenly burst into my room and said: "I have been chasing you all over Europe for an interview on the strike on the New York Central." This was my first information of the strike.

As soon as I had left New York and was on the ocean,

the young and ambitious officers who were at the head of the operations of the railroad and disapproved of my method of dealing with the employees, discharged every member of the committee who had called upon me. Of course, this was immediately followed by a sympathetic outburst in their behalf, and the sympathizers were also discharged. Then the whole road was tied up by a universal strike. After millions had been lost in revenue by the railroad and in wages by the men, the strike was settled, as usual, by a compromise, but it gave to the Knights of Labor the control, except as to the Brotherhood of Locomotive Engineers. The early settlement of the strike was largely due to the loyalty and courage of the Brotherhood.

During my presidency I was much criticised by the public, but never by the directors of the company, because of my activities in politics and on the platform. For some time, when the duties of my office became most onerous, and I was in the habit of working all day and far into the night, I discovered that this concentrated attention to my railroad problems and intense and continuous application to their solution was not only impairing my efficiency but my health. As I was not a sport, and never had time for games or horses, I decided to try a theory, which was that one's daily duties occupied certain cells of the brain while the others remained idle; that the active cells became tired by overwork while others lost their power in a measure by idleness; that if, after a reasonable use of the working cells, you would engage in some other intellectual occupation, it would furnish as much relief or recreation as outdoor exercise of any kind. I had a natural facility for quick and easy preparation for public speaking, and so adopted that as my recreation. The result proved entirely successful.

After a hard day's work, on coming home late in the afternoon, I accustomed myself to take a short nap of about fifteen minutes. Then I would look over my tablets to see if any engagement was on to speak in the evening, and, if so, the preparation of the speech might be easy, or, if difficult, cause me to be late at dinner. These speeches were made several times a week, and mainly at banquets on closing of the sessions of conventions of trade organizations of the country. The reciprocal favors and friendship of these delegates transferred to the New York Central a large amount of competitive business.

While I was active in politics I issued strict orders that every employee should have the same liberty, and that any attempt on the part of their superior officers to influence or direct the political action of a subordinate would be cause for dismissal. This became so well known that the following incident, which was not uncommon, will show the result.

As I was taking the train the morning after having made a political speech at Utica, the yardmaster, an Irishman, greeted me very cordially and then said: "We were all up to hear ye last night, boss, but this year we are agin ye."

The position which this activity gave me in my own party, and the fact that, unlike most employers, I protected the employees in their liberty and political action, gave me immense help in protecting the company from raids and raiders.

We had a restaurant in the station at Utica which had deteriorated. The situation was called to my attention in order to have the evils corrected by the receipt of the following letter from an indignant passenger: "Dear Mr. President: You are the finest after-dinner speaker in the world. I would give a great deal to hear the speech you would make after you had dined in the restaurant in your station at Utica."

After thirteen years of service as president I was elected chairman of the board of directors. Mr. Samuel R. Callaway succeeded me as president, and on his resignation was succeeded by Mr. William H. Newman, and upon his resignation Mr. W. C. Brown became president. Following Mr. Brown, Mr. Alfred H. Smith was elected and is still in office. All these officers were able and did excellent service, but I want to pay special tribute to Mr. Smith.

Mr. Smith is one of the ablest operating officers of his time. When the United States Government took over the railroads he was made regional director of the government for railroads in this territory. He received the highest commendation from the government and from the owners of the railroads for the admirable way in which he had maintained them and their efficiency during the government control.

On the surrender of the railroads by the government, Mr. Smith was welcomed back by his directors to the presidency of the New York Central. The splendid condition of the Central and its allied lines is largely due to him. During his service as regional director the difficult task of the presidency of the New York Central was very ably performed by Mr. William K. Vanderbilt, Jr. Though the youngest among the executive officers of the railroads of the country, he was at the same time one of the best.

WITH THE NEW YORK CENTRAL

Among the efficient officers who have served the New York Central during the time I have been with the company, I remember many on account of their worth and individuality. H. Walter Webb came into the railway service from an active business career. With rare intelligence and industry he rapidly rose in the organization and was a very capable and efficient officer. There was F. W. Voorhees, the general superintendent, an unusually young man for such a responsible position. He was a graduate of Troy Polytechnical School and a very able operating officer. Having gone directly from the college to a responsible position, he naturally did not understand or know how to handle men until after long experience. He showed that want of experience in a very drastic way in the strike of 1892 and its settlement. Being very arbitrary, he had his own standards. For instance, I was appealed to by many old brakemen and conductors whom he had discharged. I mention one particularly, who had been on the road for twenty-five years. Voorhees's answer to me was: "These old employees are devoted to Toucey, my predecessor, and for efficient work I must have loyalty to me."

I reversed his order and told him I would begin to discharge, if necessary, the latest appointments, including himself, keeping the older men in the service who had proved their loyalty to the company by the performance of their duties.

Mr. Voorhees became afterwards vice-president and then president of the Philadelphia and Reading. With experience added to his splendid equipment and unusual ability he became one of the best executives in the country.

Mr. John M. Toucey, who had come up from the bottom to be general superintendent and general manager, was a hard student. His close contact with his fellow employees gave him wonderful control over men. He supplemented his practical experience by hard study and was very well educated. Though self-taught, he had no confidence in the graduates of the professional schools.

In selecting an assistant, one of them told me that Toucey subjected him to a rigid examination and then said: "What is your railroad career?"

"I began at the bottom," answered the assistant, "and have filled every office on my old road up to division superintendent, which I have held for so many years."

"That is very fine," said Toucey, "but are you a graduate of the Troy Technical School?"

"No, sir."

"Of the Stevens Tech.?"

"No, sir."

"Of Massachusetts Tech.?"

"No, sir."

"Then you are engaged," said Toucey.

Mr. Toucey was well up-to-date, and differed from a superintendent on another road in which I was a director. The suburban business of that line had increased very rapidly, but there were not enough trains or cars to accommodate the passengers. The overcrowding caused many serious discomforts. I had the superintendent called before the board of directors, and said to him: "Why don't you immediately put on more trains and cars?"

"Why, Mr. Depew," he answered, "what would be the use? They are settling so fast along the line that the people would fill them up and overcrowd them just as before."

I was going over the line on an important tour at one time with John Burroughs, superintendent of the Western Division. We were on his pony engine, with seats at the front, alongside the boiler, so that we could look directly on the track. Burroughs sat on one side and I on the other. He kept on commenting aloud by way of dictating to his stenographer, who sat behind him, and praise and criticism followed rapidly. I heard him utter in his monotonous way: "Switch misplaced, we will all be in hell in a minute," and then a second afterwards continue: "We jumped the switch and are on the track again. Discharge that switchman."

Major Enos Priest was for fifty years a division superintendent. It was a delightful experience to go with him over his division. He knew everybody along the line, was general confidant in their family troubles and arbiter in neighborhood disputes. He knew personally every employee and his characteristics and domestic situation. The wives were generally helping him to keep their husbands from making trouble. To show his control and efficiency, he was always predicting labor troubles and demonstrating that the reason they did not occur was because of the way in which he handled the situation.

Mr. C. M. Bissell was a very efficient superintendent, and for a long time in charge of the Harlem Railroad. He told me this incident. We decided to put in effect as a check upon the conductors a system by which a conductor, when a fare was paid on the train, must tear from a book a receipt which he gave to the passenger, and mark the amount on the stub from which the receipt was torn. Soon after a committee of conductors called upon Mr. Bissell and asked for an increase of pay. "Why," Bissell asked, "boys, why do you ask for that now?"

After a rather embarrassing pause the oldest conductor said: "Mr. Bissell, you have been a conductor yourself."

This half-century and six years during which I have been in the service of the New York Central Railroad has been a time of unusual pleasure and remarkably free from friction or trouble. In this intimate association with the railroad managers of the United States I have found the choicest friendships and the most enduring. The railroad manager is rarely a large stockholder, but he is a most devoted and efficient officer of his company. He gives to its service, for the public, the employees, the investors, and the company, all that there is in him. In too many instances, because these officers do not get relief from their labor by variation of their work, they die exhausted before their time.

The story graphically told by one of the oldest and ablest of railroad men, Mr. Marvin Hughitt, for a long time president and now chairman of the Chicago and Northwestern Railway, illustrates what the railroad does for the country. Twenty-five years ago the Northwestern extended its lines through Northern Iowa. Mr. Hughitt drove over the proposed extension on a buckboard. The country was sparsely settled because the farmers could not get their products to market, and the land was selling at six dollars per acre.

In a quarter of a century prosperous villages and cities had grown up along the line, and farms were selling at over three hundred dollars per acre. While this enormous profit from six dollars per acre to over three hundred has come to the settlers who held on to their farms because of the possibilities produced by the railroad, the people whose capital built the road must remain satisfied with a moderate return by way of dividend and interest, and without any enhancement of their capital, but those investors should be protected by the State and the people to whom their capital expenditures have been such an enormous benefit.

XIX

RECOLLECTIONS FROM ABROAD

I know of nothing more delightful for a well-read American than to visit the scenes in Great Britain with which he has become familiar in his reading. No matter how rapidly he may travel, if he goes over the places made memorable by Sir Walter Scott in the "Waverley Novels," and in his poems, he will have had impressions, thrills, and educational results which will be a pleasure for the rest of his life. The same is true of an ardent admirer of Dickens or of Thackeray, in following the footsteps of their heroes and heroines. I gained a liberal education and lived over again the reading and studies of a lifetime in my visits to England, Ireland, Scotland, and Wales. I also had much the same experience of vivifying and spiritualizing my library in France, Italy, Germany, Belgium, and Holland.

London is always most hospitable and socially the most delightful of cities. While Mr. Gladstone was prime minister and more in the eyes of the world than any statesman of any country, a dinner was given to him with the special object of having me meet him. The ladies and gentlemen at the dinner were all people of note. Among them were two American bishops. The arrangement made by the host and hostess was that when the ladies left the dining-room I should take the place made vacant alongside Mr. Gladstone, but one of the American bishops, who in his younger days was a

RECOLLECTIONS FROM ABROAD 257

famous athlete, made a flying leap for that chair and no sooner landed than he at once proposed to Mr. Gladstone this startling question: "As the bishop of the old Catholic Church in Germany does not recognize the authority of the pope, how can he receive absolution?" —and some other abstruse theological questions. This at once aroused Mr. Gladstone, who, when once started, was stopped with difficulty, and there was no pause until the host announced that the gentlemen should join the ladies. I made it a point at the next dinner given for me to meet Mr. Gladstone that there should be no American bishops present.

At another time, upon arriving at my hotel in London from New York, I found a note from Lord Rosebery saying that Mr. Gladstone was dining with Lady Rosebery and himself that evening, and there would be no other guests, and inviting me to come. I arrived early and found Mr. Gladstone already there. While the custom in London society then was for the guests to be late, Mr. Gladstone was always from fifteen minutes to half an hour in advance of the time set by his invitation. He greeted me with great cordiality, and at once what were known as the Gladstone tentacles were fastened on me for information. It was a peculiarity with the grand old man that he extracted from a stranger practically all the man knew, and the information was immediately assimilated in his wonderful mind. He became undoubtedly the best-informed man on more subjects than anybody in the world.

Mr. Gladstone said to me: "It has been raining here for forty days. What is the average rainfall in the United States and in New York?" If there was any subject about which I knew less than another, it was the meteorological conditions in America. He then continued with great glee: "Our friend, Lord Rosebery, has everything and knows everything, so it is almost impossible to find for him something new. Great books are common, but I have succeeded in my explorations among antiquarian shops in discovering the most idiotic book that ever was written. It was by an old lord mayor of London, who filled a volume with his experiences in an excursion on the Thames, which is the daily experience of every Englishman." To the disappointment of Mr. Gladstone, Lord Rosebery also had that book. The evening was a memorable one for me.

After a most charming time and dinner, while Lord Rosebery went off to meet an engagement to speak at a meeting of colonial representatives, Lady Rosebery took Mr. Gladstone and myself to the opera at Covent Garden. There was a critical debate on in the House of Commons, and the whips were running in to inform him of the progress of the battle and to get instructions from the great leader.

During the entr'actes Mr. Gladstone most interestingly talked of his sixty years' experience of the opera. He knew all the great operas of that period, and criticised with wonderful skill the composers and their characteristics. He gave a word picture of all the great artists who had appeared on the English stage and the merits and demerits of each. A stranger listening to him would have said that a veteran musical critic, who had devoted his life to that and nothing else, was reminiscing. He said that thirty years before the manager of Covent Garden had raised the pitch, that this had become so difficult that most of the artists, to reach it, used the tremolo, and that the tremolo had taken away from him the exquisite pleasure which he formerly had in listening to an opera.

Mr. Gladstone was at that time the unquestionable master of the House of Commons and its foremost orator. I unfortunately never heard him at his best, but whether the question was of greater or lesser importance, the appearance of Mr. Gladstone at once lifted it above ordinary discussion to high debate.

Mr. Gladstone asked many questions about large fortunes in the United States, was curious about the methods of their accumulation, and whether they survived in succeeding generations. He wanted to know all about the reputed richest man among them. I told him I did not know the amount of his wealth, but that it was at least one hundred millions of dollars.

"How invested?" he asked.

I answered: "All in fluid securities which could be turned into cash in a short time."

He became excited at that and said: "Such a man is dangerous not only to his own country but to the world. With that amount of ready money he could upset the exchanges and paralyze the borrowing power of nations."

"But," I said, "you have enormous fortunes," and mentioned the Duke of Westminster.

"I know every pound of Westminster's wealth," he said. "It is in lands which he cannot sell, and burdened with settlements of generations and obligations which cannot be avoided."

"How about the Rothschilds?" I asked.

"Their fortunes," he answered, "are divided among the firms in London, Paris, Vienna, and Frankfort, and it would be impossible for them to be combined and used to unsettle the markets of the world. But

Mr. —— could do this and prevent governments from meeting their obligations."

Mr. Gladstone had no hostility to great fortunes, however large, unless so invested as to be immediately available by a single man for speculation. But fortunes larger than that of one hundred millions have since been acquired, and their management is so conservative that they are brakes and safeguards against unreasoning panics. The majority of them have been used for public benefit. The most conspicuous instances are the Rockefeller Foundation, the Carnegie Endowment, and the Frick Creation.

Henry Labouchère told me a delightful story of Mr. Gladstone's first meeting with Robert T. Lincoln, when he arrived in London as American minister. Mr. Lincoln became in a short time after his arrival one of the most popular of the distinguished list of American representatives to Great Britain. He was especially noted for the charm of his conversation. Labouchère said that Mr. Gladstone told him that he was very anxious to meet Mr. Lincoln, both because he was the new minister from the United States and because of his great father, President Lincoln. Labouchère arranged for a dinner at his house, which was an hour in the country from Mr. Gladstone's city residence. Mrs. Gladstone made Mr. Labouchère promise, as a condition for permitting her husband to go, that Mr. Gladstone should be back inside of his home at ten o'clock.

The dinner had no sooner started than some question arose which not only interested but excited Mr. Gladstone. He at once entered upon an eloquent monologue on the subject. There was no possibility of interruption by any one, and Mr. Lincoln had no chance whatever to interpose a remark. When the clock was nearing eleven Labouchère interrupted this torrent of talk by saying: "Mr. Gladstone, it is now eleven; it is an hour's ride to London, and I promised Mrs. Gladstone to have you back at ten." When they were seated in the carriage Labouchère said to Mr. Gladstone: "Well, you have passed an evening with Mr. Lincoln; what do you think of him?" He replied: "Mr. Lincoln is a charming personality, but he does not seem to have much conversation."

Among the very able men whom I met in London was Joseph Chamberlain. When I first met him he was one of Mr. Gladstone's trusted lieutenants. He was a capital speaker, a close and incisive debater, and a shrewd politician. When he broke with Mr. Gladstone, he retained his hold on his constituency and continued to be a leader in the opposite party.

Mr. Chamberlain told me that in a critical debate in the House of Commons, when the government was in danger, Mr. Gladstone, who alone could save the situation, suddenly disappeared. Every known resort of his was searched to find him. Mr. Chamberlain, recollecting Mr. Gladstone's interest in a certain subject, drove to the house of the lady whose authority on that subject Mr. Gladstone highly respected. He found him submitting to the lady for her criticism and correction some of Watts's hymns, which he had translated into Italian.

The British Government sent Mr. Chamberlain to America, and he had many public receptions given him by our mercantile and other bodies. On account of his separating from Mr. Gladstone on Home Rule, he met with a great deal of hostility here from the Irish. I was present at a public dinner where the interruptions and hostile demonstrations were very pronounced. But Mr. Chamberlain won his audience by his skill and fighting qualities.

I gave him a dinner at my house and had a number of representative men to meet him. He made the occasion exceedingly interesting by presenting views of domestic conditions in England and international ones with this country, which were quite new to us.

Mr. Chamberlain was a guest on the *Teutonic* at the famous review of the British navy celebrating Queen Victoria's jubilee, where I had the pleasure of again meeting him. He had recently married Miss Endicott, the charming daughter of our secretary of war, and everybody appreciated that it was a British statesman's honeymoon.

He gave me a dinner in London, at which were present a large company, and two subjects came under very acute discussion. There had been a recent marriage in high English society, where there were wonderful pedigree and relationships on both sides, but no money. It finally developed, however, that under family settlements the young couple might have fifteen hundred pounds a year, or seven thousand five hundred dollars. The decision was unanimous that they could get along very well and maintain their position on this sum and be able to reciprocate reasonably the attentions they would receive. Nothing could better illustrate the terrific increase in the cost of living than the contrast between then and now.

Some one of the guests at the dinner said that the Americans by the introduction of slang were ruining the English language. Mr. James Russell Lowell had come evidently prepared for this controversy. He said that

American slang was the common language of that part of England from which the Pilgrims sailed, and that it had been preserved in certain parts of the United States, notably northern New England. He then produced an old book, a sort of dictionary of that period, and proved his case. It was a surprise to everybody to know that American slang was really classic English, and still spoken in the remoter parts of Massachusetts and New Hampshire, though no longer in use in England.

The period of Mr. Gladstone's reign as prime minister was one of the most interesting for an American visitor who had the privilege of knowing him and the eminent men who formed his Cabinet. The ladies of the Cabinet entertained lavishly and superbly. A great favorite at these social gatherings was Miss Margot Tennant, afterwards Mrs. Asquith. Her youth, her wit, her originality and audacity made every function a success which was graced by her presence.

The bitterness towards Mr. Gladstone of the opposition party surpassed anything I have met in American politics, except during the Civil War. At dinners and receptions given me by my friends of the Tory party I was supposed as an American to be friendly to Mr. Gladstone and Home Rule. I do not know whether this was the reason or whether it was usual, but on such occasions the denunciation of Mr. Gladstone as a traitor and the hope of living to see him executed was very frequent.

I remember one important public man who was largely interested and a good deal of a power in Canadian and American railroads. He asked a friend of mine to arrange for me to meet him. I found him a most agreeable man and very accurately informed on the railway situation in Canada and the United States. He was preparing for a visit, and so wanted me to fill any gaps there might be in his knowledge of the situation.

Apropos of the political situation at the time, he suddenly asked me what was the attitude of the people of the United States towards Mr. Gladstone and his Home Rule bill. I told him they were practically unanimous in favor of the bill, and that Mr. Gladstone was the most popular Englishman in the United States. He at once flew into a violent rage, the rarest thing in the world for an Englishman, and lost control of his temper to such a degree that I thought the easiest way to dam the flood of his denunciation was to plead another engagement and retire from the field. I met him frequently afterwards, especially when he came to the United States, but carefully avoided his pet animosity.

One year, in the height of the crisis of Mr. Gladstone's effort to pass the Home Rule bill, a member of his Cabinet said to me: "We of the Cabinet are by no means unanimous in believing in Mr. Gladstone's effort, but he is the greatest power in our country. The people implicitly believe in him and we are helping all we can."

It is well known that one after another broke away from him in time. The same Cabinet minister continued: "Mr. Gladstone has gone to the extreme limit in concessions made in his Home Rule bill, and he can carry the English, Scotch, and Welsh members. But every time the Irish seem to be satisfied, they make a new demand and a greater one. Unless this stops and the present bill is accepted, the whole scheme will break down. Many of the Irish members are supported by contributions from America. Their occupation is politics. If Home Rule should be adopted the serious people of Ireland, whose economic interests are at stake,

RECOLLECTIONS FROM ABROAD

might come to the front and take all representative offices themselves. We have come to the conclusion that enough of the Irish members to defeat the bill do not want Home Rule on any conditions. I know it is a custom when you arrive home every year that your friends meet you down the Bay and give you a reception. Then you give an interview of your impressions over here, and that interview is printed as widely in this country as in the United States. Now I wish you would do this: At the reception put in your own way what I have told you, and especially emphasize that Mr. Gladstone is imperilling his political career and whole future for the sake of what he believes would be justice to Ireland. He cannot go any further and hold his English, Scotch, and Welsh constituencies. He believes that he can pass the present bill and start Ireland on a career of Home Rule if he can receive the support of the Irish members. The Americans who believe in Mr. Gladstone and are all honest Home Rulers will think this is an indirect message from himself, and it would be if it were prudent for Mr. Gladstone to send the message."

On my return to New York I did as requested. The story was published and commented on everywhere, and whether it was due to American insistence or not, I do not know, but shortly after Mr. Gladstone succeeded in carrying his Home Rule bill through the House of Commons, but it was defeated by the Conservatives in the House of Lords.

His Irish policy is a tribute to Mr. Gladstone's judgment and foresight, because in the light and conditions of to-day it is perfectly plain that if the Gladstone measure had been adopted at that time, the Irish question would not now be the most difficult and dangerous in British politics.

I had many talks with Mr. Parnell and made many speeches in his behalf and later for Mr. Redmond. I asked him on one occasion if the Irish desired complete independence and the formation of an independent government. He answered: "No, we want Home Rule, but to retain our connection in a way with the British Empire. The military, naval, and civil service of the British Empire gives great opportunities for our young men. Ireland in proportion to its population is more largely represented in these departments of the British Government than either England, Scotland, or Wales."

Incidental to the division in Mr. Gladstone's Cabinet, which had not at this time broken out, was the great vogue which a story of mine had. I was dining with Earl Spencer. He had been lord lieutenant of Ireland and was very popular. His wife especially had been as great a success as the vice-regent. He was called the Red Earl because of his flowing auburn beard. He was a very serious man, devoted to the public service and exceedingly capable. He almost adored Mr. Gladstone and grieved over the growing opposition in the Cabinet.

The guests at the dinner were all Gladstonians and lamenting these differences and full of apprehension that they might result in a split in the party. The earl asked me if we ever had such conditions in the United States. I answered: "Yes." Mr. Blaine, at that time at the head of President Harrison's Cabinet as secretary of state, had very serious differences with his chief, and the people wondered why he remained. Mr. Blaine told me this story apropos of the situation: The author of a play invited a friend of his to witness the first production and sent him a complimentary ticket. During the first act there were signs of disapproval, which during the second act broke out into a riot. An excited man sitting alongside the guest of the playwright said: "Stranger, are you blind or deaf, or do you approve of the play?" The guest replied: "My friend, my sentiments and opinion in regard to this play do not differ from yours and the rest, but I am here on a free ticket. If you will wait a little while till I go out and buy a ticket, I will come back and help you raise hell."

The most brilliant member of Mr. Gladstone's Cabinet and one of the most accomplished, versatile, and eloquent men in Great Britain was Lord Rosebery. I saw much of him when he was foreign minister and also after he became prime minister. Lord Rosebery was not only a great debater on political questions, he was also the most scholarly orator of his country on educational, literary, and patriotic subjects. He gathered about him always the people whom a stranger pre-eminently desired to meet.

I recall one of my week-end visits to his home at Mentmore, which is one of the most delightful of my reminiscences abroad. He had taken down there the leaders of his party. The dinner lasted, the guests all being men, except Lady Rosebery, who presided, until after twelve o'clock. Every one privileged to be there felt that those four hours had passed more quickly and entertainingly than any in their experience.

It was a beautiful moonlight night and the very best of English weather, and we adjourned to the terrace. There were recalled personal experiences, incidents of travel from men who had been all over the world and in critical situations in many lands, diplomatic secrets revealing crises seriously threatening European wars, and how these had been averted, alliances made and territories acquired, adventures of thrilling interest and personal episodes surpassing fiction. The company reluctantly separated when the rising sun admonished them that the night had passed.

It has been my good fortune to be the guest of eminent men in many lands and on occasions of memorable interest, but the rarest privilege for any one was to be the guest of Lord Rosebery, either at his city house or one of his country residences. The wonderful charm of the host, his tact with his guests, his talent for drawing people out and making them appear at their best, linger in their memories as red-letter days and nights of their lives.

All Americans took great interest in the career of Lord Randolph Churchill. His wife was one of the most beautiful and popular women in English society, and an American. I knew her father, Leonard Jerome, very well. He was a successful banker and a highly educated and cultured gentleman. His brother, William Jerome, was for a long time the best story-teller and one of the wittiest of New Yorkers.

Lord Randolph Churchill advanced very rapidly in British politics and became not only one of the most brilliant debaters but one of the leaders of the House of Commons. On one of my visits abroad I received an invitation from the Churchills to visit them at their country place. When I arrived I found that they occupied a castle built in the time of Queen Elizabeth, and in which few modern alterations had been made. It was historically a very unique and interesting structure.

Additions had been made to it by succeeding generations, each being another house with its own methods of ingress and egress. Lord Randolph said: "I welcome you to my ancestral home, which I have rented for three months."

Though this temporary residence was very ancient, yet its hospitalities were dispensed by one of the most up-to-date and progressive couples in the kingdom. In the intimacy of a house-party, not too large, one could enjoy the versatility, the charm, the wide information, the keen political acumen of this accomplished and magnetic British statesman. It was unfortunate for his country that from overwork he broke down so early in life.

No one during his period could surpass Baron Alfred Rothschild as host. His dinners in town, followed by exquisite musicales, were the social events of every season. He was, however, most attractive at his superb place in the country. A week-end with him there met the best traditions of English hospitality. In the party were sure to be men and women of distinction, and just the ones whom an American had read about and was anxious to meet.

Baron Rothschild was a famous musician and an ardent lover of music. He had at his country place a wonderfully trained orchestra of expert musicians. In the theatre he gave concerts for the enjoyment of his guests, and led the orchestra himself. Among the company was sure to be one or more of the most famous artists from the opera at Covent Garden, and from these experts his own leadership and the performance of his perfectly trained company received unstinted praise and applause. Baron Rothschild had the art so necessary for the enjoyment of his guests of getting together the right people. He never risked the harmony of his house by inviting antagonists.

Lord Rothschild, the head of the house, differed entirely from his amiable and accomplished brother. While he also entertained, his mind was engrossed in business and affairs. I had a conference with him at the time of the Spanish-American War, which might have been of historical importance. He asked me to come and see him in the Rothschild banking-house, where the traditions of a century are preserved and unchanged. He said to me: "We have been for a long time the bankers of Spain. We feel the responsibility for their securities, which we have placed upon the market. The United States is so all-powerful in its resources and spirit that it can crush Spain. This we desire to avert. Spain, though weak and poor compared to the United States, has nevertheless the proudest people in the world, and it is a question of Spanish pride we have to deal with."

In answering him I said: "Lord Rothschild, it seems to me that if you had any proposition you should take it to Mr. John Hay, our accomplished minister."

"No," he said; "then it would become a matter of diplomacy and publicity. Now the Spanish Government is willing to comply with every demand the United States can make. The government is willing to grant absolute independence to Cuba, or what it would prefer, a self-governing colony, with relations like that of Canada to Great Britain. Spain is willing to give to the United States Porto Rico and the Philippine Islands, but she must know beforehand if these terms will be accepted before making the offer, because if an offer so great as this and involving such a loss of territory and prestige should be rejected by the United States there would be a revolution in Spain which might overthrow not only the government but the monarchy. What would be regarded as an insult would be resented by every Spaniard to the bitter end. That is why I have asked you to come and wish you to submit this proposition to your president. Of course, I remain in a position, if there should be any publicity about it, to deny the whole thing."

The proposition unfortunately came too late, and Mr. McKinley could not stop the war. It was well known in Washington that he was exceedingly averse to hostilities and believed the difficulties could be satisfactorily settled by diplomacy, but the people were aroused to such an extent that they were determined not only to free Cuba but to punish those who were oppressing the Cubans.

One incident which received little publicity at the time was in all probability the match which fired the magazine. One of the ablest and most level-headed members of the Senate was Senator Redfield Proctor, of Vermont. The solidity of his character and acquirements and his known sense and conservatism made him a power in Congress, and he had the confidence of the people. He visited Cuba and wrote a report in which he detailed as an eyewitness the atrocities which the government and the soldiers were perpetrating. He read this report to Mr. McKinley and Senator Hanna. They both said: "Senator Proctor, if you read that to the Senate, our negotiations end and war is inevitable."

The president requested the senator to delay reporting to the Senate. The excitement and interest in that body were never more unanimous and intense. I doubt if any senator could have resisted this rare opportunity not only to be the centre of the stage but to occupy the whole platform. Senator Proctor made his report and the country was aflame.

One summer I arrived in London and was suffering from a fearful attack of muscular rheumatism. I knew perfectly well that I had brought it on myself by overwork. I had suffered several attacks before, but this one was so acute that I consulted Sir Henry Thompson, at that time the acknowledged head of the British medical profession. He made a thorough examination and with most satisfactory result as to every organ.

"With your perfect constitution," he said, "this attack is abnormal. Now tell me of your day and every day at home. Begin with breakfast."

"I breakfast at a quarter of eight," I said.

"Then," continued the doctor, "give me the whole day."

"I arrive at my office," I said, "at nine. Being president of a great railway company, there is a large correspondence to be disposed of. I see the heads of the different departments and get in touch with every branch of the business. Then I meet committees of chambers of commerce or shippers, or of employees who have a grievance, and all this will occupy me until five o'clock, when I go home. I take a very short lunch, often at my desk, to save time. On arriving home I take a nap of ten or fifteen minutes, and then look over my engagements for the evening. If it is a speech, which will probably happen four evenings in a week, I prepare in the next hour and then deliver it at some public banquet or hall. If I have accepted a formal address or, as we call them in America, orations, it is ground out on odd evenings, Sunday afternoon and night."

The doctor turned to me abruptly and said: "You ought to be dead. Now, you have the most perfect constitution and less impaired than any I have examined at your time of life. If you will follow the directions which I give you, you can be perfectly well and sound at the age of one hundred. If you continue your present life until seventy, you will have a nervous breakdown, and thereafter become a nuisance to yourself and everybody else. I advise absolute rest at a remote place in Switzerland. There you will receive no newspapers, and you will hear nothing from the outside world. You will meet there only English who are seeking health, and they will not speak to you. Devote your day to walking over the mountains, adding to your tramp as your strength increases, and lie for hours on the bank of a quiet stream there, and be intensely interested as you throw pebbles into it to see how wide you can make the circles from the spot where the pebble strikes the water."

I thought I understood my temperament better than the doctor, and that any rest for me was not solitude but entire change of occupation. So I remained in London and lunched and dined out every day for several weeks, with a week-end over every Sunday. In other ways, however, I adopted the doctor's directions and not only returned home cured, but have been free from rheumatism ever since.

I was in London at both the queen's fiftieth anniversary of her reign and her jubilee. The reverence and love the English people had for Queen Victoria was a wonderful exhibition of her wisdom as a sovereign and of her charm and character as a woman. The sixty years of her reign were a wonderful epoch in the growth of her empire and in its relations to the world.

Once I said to a member of the Cabinet, who, as minister of foreign affairs had been brought in close contact with the queen: "I am very much impressed with the regard which the people have for Queen Victoria. What is her special function in your scheme of government?"

"She is invaluable," he answered, "to every prime minister and the Cabinet. The prime minister, after the close of the debate in the House of Commons every night, writes the queen a full report of what has occurred at that session. This has been going on for more than half a century. The queen reads these accounts carefully and has a most retentive memory. If these communications of the prime ministers were ever available to the public, they would present a remarkable contrast of the minds and the methods of different prime ministers and especially those two extreme opposites, Gladstone and Disraeli. The queen did not like Gladstone, because she said he always preached, but she had an intense admiration for Disraeli, who threw into his nightly memoranda all his skill not only as a statesman but a novelist. The queen also has been consulted during all these years on every crisis, domestic or foreign, and every matter of Cabinet importance. The result is that she is an encyclopædia. Very often there will be a dispute with some of the great powers or lesser ones, which is rapidly growing to serious proportions. We can find no report of its beginning. The queen, however, will remember just when the difficulty began, and why it was pushed aside and not settled, and who were the principal actors in the negotiations. With that data we often arrive at a satisfactory settlement."

I remember one garden-party at Buckingham Palace. The day was perfect and the attendance phenomenally large and distinguished. While there were places on the grounds where a luncheon was served, the guests neglected these places and gathered about a large tent where the royalties had their refreshments. It was an intense curiosity, not so much to see their sovereign eat and drink, as to improve the opportunity to reverently gaze upon her at close range. The queen called various people whom she knew from this circle of onlookers for a familiar talk.

When the luncheon was served the attendant produced an immense napkin, which she spread over herself, almost from her neck to the bottom of her dress. A charming English lady, who stood beside me, said: "I know you are laughing at the economy of our Queen."

"On the contrary," I said, "I am admiring an example of carefulness and thrift which, if it could be universally known, would be of as great benefit in the United States as in Great Britain."

"Well," she continued, "I do wish that the dear old lady was not quite so careful."

At a period when the lives of the continental rulers were in great peril from revolutionists and assassins, the queen on both her fiftieth anniversary and her jubilee rode in an open carriage through many miles of London streets, with millions of spectators on either side pressing closely upon the procession, and there was never a thought that she was in the slightest danger. She was fearless herself, but she had on the triple armor of the overmastering love and veneration of the whole people.

Americans remembered that in the crisis of our Civil War it was the influence of the queen, more than any other, which prevented Great Britain recognizing the Southern Confederacy.

Among the incidents of her jubilee was the greatest naval demonstration ever known. The fleets of Great Britain were summoned from all parts of the globe and anchored in a long and imposing line in the English Channel. Mr. Ismay, at that time the head of the White Star Line, took the *Teutonic*, which had just been built and was not yet in regular commission, as his private yacht. He had on board a notable company, representing the best, both of men and women, of English life. He was the most generous of hosts, and every care taken for the individual comfort of his guests. In the intimacy for several days of such an excursion we all became very well acquainted. There were speeches at the dinners and dances afterwards on the deck for the younger people. The war-ships were illuminated at night by electric lights, and the launch of the *Teutonic* took us down one lane and up another through the long lines of these formidable defenders of Great Britain.

One day there was great excitement when a war-ship steamed into our midst and it was announced that it was the German emperor's. Even as early as that he excited in the English mind both curiosity and apprehension. One of the frequent questions put to me, both then and for years afterwards at English dinners, was: "What do you think of the German emperor?"

Shortly after his arrival he came on to the *Teutonic* with the Prince of Wales, afterwards King Edward VII. The prince knew many of the company and was most cordial all around. The emperor was absorbed in an investigation of this new ship and her possibilities both in the mercantile marine and as a cruiser. I heard him say to the captain: "How are you armed?" The captain told him that among his equipment he had a new invention, a quick-firing gun. The emperor was immediately greatly excited. He examined the gun and questioned its qualities and possibilities until he was master of every detail. Then he turned to one of his officers and gave a quick order that the gun should be immediately investigated and all that were required should be provided for Germany.

I heard a picturesque story from a member of the court, of Queen Victoria's interest in all public affairs. There was then, as there is generally in European relations, some talk of war. The queen was staying at her castle at Osborne on the Isle of Wight. He said she drove alone down to the shore one night and sat there a long time looking at this great fleet, which was the main protection of her empire and her people. It would be interesting if one could know what were her thoughts, her fears, and her hopes.

The queen was constantly assisting the government in the maintenance of friendly relations with foreign powers by entertaining their representatives at Windsor Castle. When General Grant, after he retired from the presidency, made his trip around the world, the question which disturbed our American minister, when General Grant arrived in London, was how he could be properly received and recognized. Of course, under our usage, he had become a private citizen, and was no more entitled to official recognition than any other citizen. This was well known in the diplomatic circles. When the ambassadors and ministers of foreign countries in London were appealed to, they unanimously said that as they represented their sovereigns they could not yield precedence to General Grant, but he must sit at the foot of the table. The Prince of Wales solved this question with his usual tact and wisdom. Under the recognized usage at any entertainment, the Prince of Wales can select some person as his special guest to sit at his right, and, therefore, precede everybody else. The prince made this suggestion to our minister and performed this courteous act at all functions given to General Grant. Queen Victoria supplemented this by extending the same invitation to General and Mrs. Grant to dine and spend the night with her at Windsor Castle, which was extended only to visiting royalty.

I remember that the Army of the Potomac was holding its annual meeting and commemoration at one of our cities when the cable announced that General Grant was being entertained by Queen Victoria at Windsor Castle. The conventions of diplomacy, which requires all communications to pass through the ambassador of one's country to the foreign minister of another country before it can reach the sovereign were not known to these old soldiers, so they cabled a warm message to General Grant, care of Queen Victoria, Windsor Castle, England.

One of the most delightful bits of humor in my recollections of journalistic enterprise was an editorial by a Mr. Alden, one of the editors of the *New York Times*. Mr. Alden described with great particularity, as if giving the details of the occurrence, that the messenger-boy arrived at Windsor Castle during the night and rang the front door-bell; that Her Majesty called out of the window in quite American style, "Who is there?" and the messenger-boy shouted, "Cable for General Grant. Is he staying at this house?" I can only give a suggestion of Alden's fun, which shook the whole country.

One of the court officers said to me during the jubilee: "Royalties are here from every country, and among those who have come over is Liliuokalani, Queen of the Hawaiian Islands. She is as insistent of her royal rights as the Emperor of Germany. We have consented that she should be a guest at a dinner of our queen and spend the night at Windsor Castle. We have settled her place among the royalties in the procession through London and offered her the hussars as her guard of honor. She insists, however, that she shall have the same as the other kings, a company of the guards. Having recognized her, we are obliged to yield." The same officer told me that at the dinner the dusky queen said to Queen Victoria: "Your Majesty, I am a blood relative of yours."

"How so?" was the queen's astonished answer.

"Why," said Liliuokalani, "my grandfather ate your Captain Cook."

One of the most interesting of the many distinguished men who were either guests on the *Teutonic* or visited us was Admiral Lord Charles Beresford. He was a typical sailor of the highest class and very versatile. He made a good speech, either social or political, and was a delightful companion on all occasions. He had remarkable adventures all over the world, and was a word painter of artistic power. He knew America well and was very sympathetic with our ideals. I met him many times in many relations and always with increasing regard and esteem.

I was entertained by Lord Beresford once in the most original way. He had a country place about an hour from London and invited me to come down on a Sunday afternoon and meet some friends. It was a delightful garden-party on an ideal English summer day. He pressed me to stay for dinner, saying: "There will be a few friends coming, whom I am anxious for you to know."

The friends kept coming, and after a while Lady Beresford said to him: "We have set all the tables we have and the dining-room and the adjoining room can hold. How many have you invited?"

The admiral answered: "I cannot remember, but if we delay the dinner until a quarter of nine, I am sure they will all be here."

When we sat down we numbered over fifty. Lord Charles's abounding and irresistible hospitality had included everybody whom he had met the day before.

The butler came to Lord Charles shortly after we sat down and said: "My lord, it is Sunday night, and the shops are all closed. We can add nothing to what we have in the house, and the soup has given out."

"Well," said this admirable strategist, "commence with those for whom you have no soup with the fish. When the fish gives out, start right on with the next course, and so to the close of the dinner. In that way everybody will get something."

After a while the butler again approached the admiral and said: "My lord, the champagne is all gone."

"Well," said Lord Charles, "start in on cider."

It was a merry company, and they all caught on to the situation. The result was one of the most hilarious, enjoyable, and original entertainments of my life. It lasted late, and everybody with absolute sincerity declared he or she had had the best time ever.

I was asked to meet Lord John Fisher, in a way a rival of Lord Beresford. Both were exceedingly able and brilliant officers and men of achievement, but they were absolutely unlike; one had all the characteristics of the Celt and the other of the Saxon.

One of the most interesting things in Lord Fisher's talk, especially in view of later developments, was his description of the discoveries and annexations to the British Empire, made by the British navy. In regard to this he said: "The British navy had been acquiring positions of strategic importance to the safety and growth of the empire from time immemorial, and some fool of a prime minister on a pure matter of sentiment is always giving away to our possible enemies one or the other of these advantageous positions." He referred especially to Heligoland, the gift of which to Germany had taken place not long before. If Heligoland, fortified like Gibraltar, had remained in the possession of the British Government, Germany would not have ventured upon the late war.

Lord Fisher exemplified what I have often met with in men who have won eminent distinction in some career, whose great desire was to have fame in another and entirely different one. Apparently he wished his friends and those he met to believe that he was the best storyteller in the world; that he had the largest stock of original anecdotes and told them better than anybody else. I found that he was exceedingly impatient and irritable when any one else started the inevitable "that reminds me," and he was intolerant with the story the other was trying to tell. But I discovered, also, that most of his stories, though told with great enthusiasm, were very familiar, or, as we Americans would say, "chestnuts."

During my summer vacations I spent two weeks or more at Homburg, the German watering-place. It was at that time the most interesting resort on the continent. The Prince of Wales, afterwards King Edward VII, was always there, and his sister, the Dowager Empress of Germany, had her castle within a few miles. It was said that there was a quorum of both Houses of Parliament in Homburg while the prince was there, but his presence also drew representatives from every department of English life, the bench and the bar, writers of eminence of both sexes, distinguished artists, and people famous on both the dramatic and the operatic stage. The prince, with keen discrimination, had these interesting people always about him. There were also social leaders, whose entertainments were famous in London, who did their best to add to the pleasure of the visit of the prince. I met him frequently and was often his guest at his luncheons and dinners. He fell in at once in the Homburg way.

The routine of the cure was to be at the springs every morning at seven o'clock, to take a glass of water, walk half an hour with some agreeable companion, and repeat this until three glasses had been consumed. Then breakfast, and after that the great bathing-house at eleven o'clock. The bathing-house was a meeting-place for everybody. Another meeting-place was the open-air concerts in the afternoon. In the evening came the formal dinners and some entertainment afterwards.

Both for luncheon and dinner the prince always had quite a large company. He was a host of great charm, tact, and character. He had a talent of drawing out the best there was in those about his table, and especially of making the occasion very agreeable for a stranger. Any one at his entertainments always carried away either in the people he met or the things that were said, or both, permanent recollections.

I do not think the prince bothered about domestic questions. He was very observant of the limitations and restrictions which the English Government imposes upon royalty. He was, however, very keen upon his country's foreign relations. In the peace of Europe he was an important factor, being so closely allied with the imperial houses of Germany and Russia. There is no doubt that he prevented the German Emperor from acquiring a dangerous control over the Czar. He was very fixed and determined to maintain and increase friendly relations between the United States and Great Britain. He succeeded, after many varied and long-continued efforts, in doing away with the prejudices and hostilities of the French towards the English, an accomplishment of infinite value to his country in these later years.

I was told that the prince required very little sleep, that he retired to bed late and was an early riser. I was awakened one night by his equerry calling me up, saying the prince was on the terrace of the Kursaal and wanted to see me. The lights were all out, everybody had gone, and he was sitting alone at a table illuminated by a single candle. What he desired was to discuss American affairs and become more familiar with our public men, our ideals, our policies, and especially any causes which could possibly be removed of irritation between his own country and ours. This discussion lasted till daylight.

Meeting him on the street one day, he stopped and

asked me to step aside into an opening there was in the hedge. He seemed laboring under considerable excitement, and said: "Why do the people in the United States want to break up the British Empire?"

I knew he referred to the Home Rule bill for Ireland, which was then agitating Parliament and the country, and also the frequent demonstrations in its favor which were occurring in the United States.

I said to him: "Sir, I do not believe there is a single American who has any thought of breaking up the British Empire. We are wedded to the federal principle of independent States, which are sovereign in their local affairs and home matters, but on everything you call imperial the United States is supreme. To vindicate this principle we fought a Civil War, in which we lost more lives, spent more money, destroyed more property, and incurred more debt than any contest of modern time. The success of the government has been so complete that the States which were in rebellion and their people are quite as loyal to the general government as those who fought to preserve it. The prosperity of the country, with this question settled, has exceeded the bounds of imagination. So Americans think of your trouble with Ireland in terms of our federated States, and believe that all your difficulties could be adjusted in the same way."

We had a long discussion in which he asked innumerable questions, and never referred to the subject again. I heard afterwards among my English friends that he who had been most hostile was becoming a Home Ruler.

At another time he wanted to know why our government had treated the British ambassador, Lord Sackville West, so badly and ruined his career. The Sackville West incident was already forgotten, though it was the liveliest question of its time.

Cleveland was president and a candidate for re-election. Sackville West was the British ambassador. A little company of shrewd Republican politicians in California thought if they could get an admission that the British Government was interfering in our election in favor of Cleveland, it would be a fine asset in the campaign, and so they wrote to Lord Sackville West, telling him they were Englishmen who had become naturalized American citizens. In voting they were anxious to vote for the side which would be best for their native land; would he kindly and very confidentially advise them whether to support the Democratic or the Republican ticket. Sackville West swallowed the bait without investigation, and wrote them a letter advising them to vote the Democratic ticket.

There never had been such consternation in diplomatic circles in Washington. Of course, Mr. Cleveland and his supporters had to get out from under the situation as quickly and gracefully as possible.

The administration instantly demanded that the British Government should recall Lord Sackville West, which was done, and he was repudiated for his activity in American politics. It was curious that the prince had apparently never been fully informed of the facts, but had been misled by Sackville West's explanation, and the prince was always loyal to a friend.

One year Mr. James G. Blaine visited Homburg, and the prince at once invited him to luncheon. Blaine's retort to a question delighted every American in the place. One of the guests was the then Duke of Manchester, an old man and a great Tory. When the duke grasped that Blaine was a leading American and had been a candidate for the presidency of the United States, all his old Toryism was aroused, and he was back in the days of George III. To the horror of the prince, the duke said to Mr. Blaine: "The most outrageous thing in all history was your rebellion and separation from the best government on earth." He said much more before the prince could stop him.

Blaine, with that grace and tact for which he was so famous, smilingly said: "Well, your Grace, if George III had had the sense, tact, and winning qualities of his great-grandson, our host, it is just possible that we might now be a self-governing colony in the British Empire."

The answer relieved the situation and immensely pleased the host. Lord Rosebery once said in a speech that, with the tremendous growth in every element of greatness of the United States, if the American colonies had remained in the British Empire, with their preponderating influence and prestige, the capital of Great Britain might have been moved to New York and Buckingham Palace rebuilt in Central Park.

At another dinner one of the guests of the prince suddenly shot at me across the table the startling question: "Do you know certain American heiresses"—naming them—"now visiting London?"

I answered "Yes"—naming one especially, a very beautiful and accomplished girl who was quite the most popular débutante of the London season.

"How much has she?" he asked.

I named the millions which she would probably inherit. "But," I added, "before you marry an American heiress, you better be sure that she can say the Lord's Prayer."

He said with great indignation that he would be astonished if any American girl could be recognized in English society who had been so badly brought up that she was not familiar with the Lord's Prayer.

"All of them are," I replied, "but few heiresses, unless they have come into their inheritance and can say 'Our Father, who art in heaven,' will inherit much, because American fathers are very speculative."

He continued to express his astonishment at this lack of religious training in an American family, while the prince enjoyed the joke so much that I was fearful in his convulsive laughter he would have a fit of apoplexy.

Once, at a dinner given by the prince, an old lady of very high rank and leading position said suddenly to me, and in a way which aroused the attention of the whole company: "Is it true that divorces are very common in America?"

I knew that a denial by me would not convince her or any others who shared in this belief, then very common in Europe. Of course, the prince knew better. I saw from his expression that he wished me to take advantage of the opportunity. I made up my mind quickly that the best way to meet this belief was by an exaggeration which would show its absurdity.

Having once started, the imaginative situation grew beyond my anticipation. I answered: "Yes, divorces are so common with us that the government has set aside one of our forty-odd States for this special purpose. It is the principal business of the authorities. Most of these actions for divorce take place at the capital, which is always crowded with great numbers of people from all parts of the country seeking relief from their marital obligations."

"Did you ever visit that capital?" asked the prince.

"Yes, several times," I answered, "but not for divorce. My domestic relations have always been very happy, but it is also a famous health resort, and I went there for the cure."

"Tell us about your visit," said the prince.

"Well," I continued, "it was out of season when I was first there, so the only amusement or public occasions of interest were prayer-meetings."

The old lady asked excitedly: "Share meetings?" She had been a large and unfortunate investor in American stocks.

I relieved her by saying: "No, not share meetings, but religious prayer-meetings. I remember one evening that the gentleman who sat beside me turned suddenly to his wife and said: 'We must get out of here at once; the air is too close.' 'Why, no,' she said; 'the windows are all open and the breeze is fresh.' 'Yes,' he quickly remarked, 'but next to you are your two predecessors from whom I was divorced, and that makes the air too close for me.'"

The old lady exclaimed: "What a frightful condition!"

"Tell us more," said the prince.

"Well," I continued, "one day the mayor of the city invited me to accompany him to the station, as the divorce train was about to arrive. I found at the station a judge and one of the court attendants. The attendant had a large package of divorce decrees to which the seal of the court had been attached, and also the signature of the judge. They only required to have the name of the party desiring divorce inserted. Alongside the judge stood a clergyman of the Established Church in full robes of his sacred office. When the passengers had all left the cars, the conductor jumped on to one of the car platforms and shouted to the crowd: 'All those who desire divorce will go before the judge and make their application.'

"When they had all been released by the court the conductor again called out: 'All those who have been accompanied by their partners, or where both have been to-day released from their former husbands and wives to be remarried, will go before the rector.' He married them in a body, whereupon they all resumed their places on the train. The blowing of the whistle and the ringing of the bell on the locomotive was the music of their first, second, or third honeymoon journey."

The old lady threw up her hands in horror and cried: "Such an impious civilization must come speedily not only to spiritual and moral destruction, but chaos."

Most of the company saw what an amazing caricature the whole story was and received it with great hilarity. The effect of it was to end, for that circle, at least, and their friends, a serious discussion of the universality of American divorces.

The prince was always an eager sportsman and a very chivalric one. At the time of one of the races at Cowes he became very indignant at the conduct of an American yachtsman who had entered his boat. It was charged by the other competitors that this American yachtsman violated all the unwritten laws of the contest.

After the race the prince said to me: "A yacht is a gentleman's home, whether it is racing or sailing about for pleasure. The owner of this yacht, to make her lighter and give her a better chance, removed all the furniture and stripped her bare. He even went so far, I am told, that when he found the steward had left in his stateroom a tooth-brush, he threw it out of the port window."

It will be seen from these few anecdotes how intensely human was the Prince of Wales. He did much for his country, both as prince and king, and filled in a wise and able way the functions of his office. Certainly no official did quite so much for the peace of Europe during his time, and no royalty ever did more to make the throne popular with the people. I heard him speak at both formal and informal occasions, and his addresses were always tactful and wise.

While at Homburg we used to enjoy the delightful excursions to Nauheim, the famous nerve-cure place. I met there at one time a peculiar type of Americans, quite common in former years. They were young men who, having inherited fortunes sufficient for their needs, had no ambitions. After a strenuous social life at home and in Europe, they became hypochondriacs and were chasing cures for their imaginary ills from one resort to another.

One of them, who had reached middle life, had, of course, become in his own opinion a confirmed invalid. I asked him: "What brought you here? You look very well."

"That is just my trouble," he answered. "I look very well and so get no sympathy, but my nervous system is so out of order that it only takes a slight shock to completely disarrange it. For instance, the cause of my present trouble. I was dining in Paris at the house of a famous hostess, and a distinguished company was present. The only three Americans were two ladies and myself. I was placed between them. You know one of these ladies, while a great leader at home, uses very emphatic language when she is irritated. The dinner, like most French dinners, with many courses, was unusually long. Suddenly this lady, leaning over me, said to her sister: 'Damn it, Fan, will this dinner never end?' The whole table was shocked and my nerves were completely shattered." The great war, as I think, exterminated this entire tribe.

I was delighted to find at Nauheim my old friends, Mark Twain and the Reverend Doctor Joseph Twichell, of Hartford, Conn. Doctor Twichell was Mark Twain's pastor at home. He was in college with me at Yale, and I was also associated with him in the governing corporation of Yale University. He was one of the finest wits and remarkable humorists of his time. Wit and humor were with him spontaneous, and he bubbled over with them. Mark Twain's faculties in that line were more labored and had to be worked out. Doctor Twichell often furnished in the rough the jewels which afterwards in Mark Twain's workshop became perfect gems.

I invited them to come over and spend the day and dine with me in the evening at Homburg. Mark Twain at that time had the reputation in England of being the greatest living wit and humorist. It soon spread over Homburg that he was in town and was to dine with me in the evening, and requests came pouring in to be invited. I kept enlarging my table at the Kursaal, with these requests, until the management said they could go no farther. I placed Mark Twain alongside Lady Cork, one of the most brilliant women in England. In the course of years of acquaintance I had met Mark Twain under many conditions. He was very uncertain in a social gathering. Sometimes he would be the life of the occasion and make it one to be long remembered, but generally he contributed nothing. At this dinner, whenever he showed the slightest sign of making a remark, there was dead silence, but the remark did not come. He had a charming time, and so did Lady Cork, but the rest of the company heard nothing from the great humorist, and they were greatly disappointed.

The next morning Mark Twain came down to the springs in his tramping-suit, which had fairly covered the continent. I introduced him to the Prince of Wales, and he was charmed with him in their hour of walk and talk. At dinner that evening the prince said to me: "I would have invited Mark Twain this evening, if I thought he had with him any dinner clothes."

"At my dinner last night," I said, "he met every conventional requirement."

"Then," continued the prince, "I would be much obliged if you would get him for dinner with me tomorrow evening."

It was very much the same company as had dined with the prince the night before. Again Twain was for a long time a complete disappointment. I knew scores of good things of his and tried my best to start him off, but without success. The prince, who was unusually adroit and tactful in drawing a distinguished guest out, also failed. When the dinner was over, however, and we had reached the cigars, Mark Twain started in telling a story in his most captivating way. His peculiar drawl, his habit in emphasizing the points by shaking his bushy hair, made him a dramatic narrator. He never had greater success. Even the veteran Mark himself was astonished at the uproarious laughter which greeted almost every sentence and was overwhelming when he closed.

There are millions of stories in the world, and several hundred of them good ones. No one knew more of them than Mark Twain, and yet out of this vast collection he selected the one which I had told the night before to the same company. The laughter and enjoyment were not at the story, but because the English had, as they thought, caught me in retailing to them from Mark Twain's repertoire one of his stories. It so happened that it was a story which I had heard as happening upon our railroad in one of my tours of inspection. I had told it in a speech, and it had been generally copied in the American newspapers. Mark Twain's reputation as the greatest living humorist caused that crowd to doubt the originality of my stories.

Mark had declined the cigars, but the prince was so delighted that he offered him one of the highly prized selection from his own case. This drew from him a story, which I have not seen in any of his books. I have read Mark Twain always with the greatest pleasure. His books of travel have been to me a source of endless interest, and his "Personal Recollections of Joan of Arc" is the best representation of the saint and heroine that I know.

When the prince offered him the cigar, Mark said: "No, prince, I never smoke. I have the reputation in Hartford, Conn., of furnishing at my entertainments the worst of cigars. When I was going abroad, and as I would be away for several years, I gave a reception and invited all my friends. I had the governor of the State of Connecticut and the judges of the highest courts, and the most distinguished members of the legislature. I had the leading clergymen and other citizens, and also the president and faculty of Yale University and Trinity College.

"At three o'clock in the afternoon my butler, who is a colored man, Pompey by name, came to me and said: 'Mr. Clemens, we have no cigars.' Just then a pedler's wagon stopped at the gate. In England they call them cheap jacks. I hailed the merchant and said: 'What have you in your wagon?' 'Well,' he answered, 'I have some Gobelin tapestries, Sèvres china, and Japanese cloisonné vases, and a few old masters.' Then I said to him: 'I do not want any of those, but have you cigars, and how much?' The pedler answered: 'Yes, sir, I have some excellent cigars, which I will sell you at seventeen cents a barrel.' I have to explain that a cent is an English farthing. Then I told him to roll a barrel in."

"It was a great occasion, one of the greatest we ever had in the old State of Connecticut," continued Mark, "but I noticed that the guests left unusually early after supper. The next morning I asked the butler why they left so early. 'Well,' he said, 'Mr. Clemens, everybody enjoyed the supper, and they were all having a good time until I gave them the cigars. After the gentleman had taken three puffs, he said: "Pomp, you infernal nigger, get me my hat and coat quick." When I went out, my stone walk, which was one hundred yards long from the front door to the gate, was just paved with those cigars.'" This specimen of American exaggeration told in Mark Twain's original way made a great hit.

I met Mark Twain at a theatrical supper in London given by Sir Henry Irving. It was just after his publishing firm had failed so disastrously. It was a notable company of men of letters, playwrights, and artists. Poor Mark was broken in health and spirits. He tried to make a speech, and a humorous one, but it saddened the whole company.

I met him again after he had made the money on his remarkable lecture tour around the world, with which he met and paid all his debts. It was an achievement worthy of the famous effort of Sir Walter Scott. Jubilant, triumphant, and free, Mark Twain that night was the hero never forgotten by any one privileged to be present.

One year, after strenuous work and unusual difficulties, which, however, had been successfully met, I was completely exhausted. I was advised to take a short trip to Europe, and, as usual, the four weeks' change of air and occupation was a complete cure. I decided to include Rome in my itinerary, though I felt that my visit would be something like the experience of Phineas Fogg, who did the whole of Europe and saw all there was of it in ten days.

When I arrived in the Eternal City, my itinerary gave me four days there. I wanted to see everything and also to meet, if possible, one of the greatest of popes, Leo XIII. I was armed only with a letter from my accomplished and distinguished friend, Archbishop Corrigan. I secured the best-known guide, who informed me that my efforts to see the sights within my limited time would be impossible. Nevertheless, the incentive of an extra large commission dependent upon distances covered and sights seen, led to my going through the streets behind the best team of horses in Rome and pursued by policemen and dogs, and the horses urged on by a driver frantic for reward, and a guide who professionally and financially was doing the stunt of his life. It was astounding how much ground was really covered in the city of antiquities and art by this devotion to speed and under competent guidance.

When I asked to see the pope, I was informed that his health was not good and audiences had been suspended. I wrote a letter to the cardinal-secretary, enclosing Archbishop Corrigan's letter, and stated my anxiety to meet His Holiness and the limited time I had. A few hours afterwards I received a letter from the cardinal, stating that the Holy Father appreciated the circumstances, and would be very glad to welcome me in private audience at eleven o'clock the next morning.

When I arrived at the Vatican I was received as a distinguished visitor. The papal guards were turned out, and I was finally ushered into the room of Cardinal Merry del Val. He was a young man then and an accomplished diplomat, and most intimately informed on all questions of current interest. Literature, music, drama, political conditions in Europe were among his accomplishments. He said the usual formula when a stranger is presented to the pope is for the guest to kneel and kiss his ring. The pope has decided that all this will be omitted in your case. He will receive you exactly as an eminent foreigner calling by appointment upon the President of the United States.

When I was ushered into the presence of the pope he left his throne, came forward, grasped me cordially by the hand, and welcomed me in a very charming way. He was not a well man, and his bloodless countenance was as white and pallid as his robes. This was all relieved, however, by the brilliancy of his wonderful eyes.

After a few preliminary remarks he plunged into the questions in which he was deeply interested. He feared the spread of communism and vividly described its efforts to destroy the church, ruin religion, extirpate faith, and predicted that if successful it would destroy civilization.

I told him that I was deeply interested in the encyclical he had recently issued to reconcile or make more harmonious the relations between capital and labor. He commenced speaking upon that subject, and in a few minutes I saw that I was to be privileged to hear an address from one who as priest and bishop had been one of the most eloquent orators of the age. In his excitement he leaned forward, grasping the arms of the throne, the color returned to his cheeks, his eyes flashed, his voice was vibrant, and I was the audience, the entranced audience of the best speech I ever heard upon the question of labor and capital.

I was fearful on account of his health, that the exertion might be too great, and so arose to leave. He again said to me, and taking my hand: "I know all about you and am very grateful to you that in your official capacity as president of the New York Central Railroad you are treating so fairly the Catholics. I know that among your employees twenty-eight thousand are of the Catholic faith, and not one of them has ever known any discrimination because of their belief, but all of them have equal opportunities with the others for the rewards of their profession and protection in their employment."

The next day he sent a special messenger for a renewal of the conversation, but unhappily I had left Rome the night before.

During my stay in Rome of four days I had visited

most of its antiquities, its famous churches, and spent several hours in the Vatican gallery. Our American minister, one of the most accomplished of our diplomats, Mr. William Potter, had also given me a dinner, where I was privileged to meet many celebrities of the time.

Among English statesmen I found in Lord Salisbury an impressive figure. In a long conversation I had with him at the Foreign Office he talked with great freedom on the relations between the United States and Great Britain. He was exceedingly anxious that friendly conditions should continue and became most cordial.

The frequent disposition on the part of American politicians to issue a challenge or create eruptions disturbed him. I think he was in doubt when President Cleveland made his peremptory demands on the Venezuela boundary question if the president recognized their serious importance both for the present and the future. He, however, reluctantly yielded to the arbitration, won a complete victory, and was satisfied that such irritating questions were mainly political and for election purposes, and had better be met in a conciliatory spirit.

I remember a garden-party at Hatfield House, the historical home of the Cecils, given in honor of King Victor Emmanuel III, who had recently come to the throne. Lord Salisbury was of gigantic proportions physically, while the king was undersized. The contrast between the two was very striking, especially when they were in animated conversation—the giant prime minister talking down to His Majesty, and he with animated gestures talking up to the premier.

It is not too great a stretch of imagination, when one knows how traditional interviews and conversations between European rulers affect their relations, present and future, to find in that entertainment and conference that the seed there was sown for the entrance of Italy, at one of the crises of the Great War, on the side of the Allies and against Germany, to whom she was bound by the Triple Alliance.

Mr. Gladstone said to me at one time: "I have recently met a most interesting countryman of yours. He is one of the best-informed and able men of any country whom I have had the pleasure of talking with for a long time, and he is in London now. I wish you would tell me all about him."

Mr. Gladstone could not recall his name. As there were a number of American congressmen in London, I asked: "Was he a congressman?"

"No," he answered; "he had a more important office."

I then remembered that DeWitt Clinton, when a United States senator, resigned to become mayor of the City of New York. On that inspiration I asked: "Mayor of the City of New York?"

"Yes, that is it," Mr. Gladstone answered.

I then told him that it was Abram S. Hewitt, and gave him a description of Mr. Hewitt's career. Mr. Gladstone was most enthusiastic about him.

It was my fortune to know Mr. Hewitt very well for many years. He richly merited Mr. Gladstone's encomium. He was one of the most versatile and able Americans in public or private life during his time. His father was an English tenant-farmer who moved with his family to the United States. Mr. Hewitt received a liberal education and became a great success both in business and public life. He was much more than a business man, mayor of New York, or a congressman—he was public-spirited and a wise reformer.

Mr. Hewitt told me two interesting incidents in his career. When he visited England he was received with many and flattering attentions. Among his invitations was a week-end to the home of the nobleman upon whose estates his father had been a tenant-farmer. When Mr. Hewitt told the nobleman, who was entertaining him as a distinguished American, about his father's former relations as one of his tenants, the nobleman said: "Your father made a great mistake in giving up his farm and emigrating to the United States. He should have remained here."

Mr. Hewitt said: "But, my lord, so far as I am concerned I do not think so."

"Why?" asked his lordship.

"Because," answered Mr. Hewitt, "then I could never have been a guest on equal terms in your house."

Mr. Hewitt was one of the foremost iron founders and steel manufacturers of the country. At the time of our Civil War our government was very short of guns, and we were unable to manufacture them because we did not know the secret of gun-metal.

The government sent Mr. Hewitt abroad to purchase guns. The English gunmakers at once saw the trouble he was in and took advantage of it. They demanded prices several times greater than they were asking from other customers, and refused to give him any information about the manufacture of gun-metal.

After he had made the contract, with all its exorbitant conditions, he went to his hotel and invited the foreman of each department of the factory to meet him. They all came. Mr. Hewitt explained to them his mission, and found that they were sympathetic with Mr. Lincoln and his administration and the Union cause. Then he told them of the trouble he had had with their employers, and the hard terms which they had imposed. He asked them then all about the manufacture of gun-metal. Each one of the foremen was very clear and explicit as to his part, and so when they had all spoken, Mr. Hewitt, with his expert knowledge of the business, knew all the secrets of the manufacture of gun-metal, which he, of course, gave to the government at Washington for use in their several arsenals and shops.

"Now," he said to his guests, "you have done me a great favor. I will return it. Your company is obliged by the contract to deliver this immense order within a limited time. They are going to make an enormous amount of money out of it. You strike and demand what you think is right, and you will get it immediately."

The gun company made a huge profit but had to share some of it with their workers. It was an early instance of the introduction of profit-sharing, which has now become common all over the world.

One of the most interesting Englishmen, whom I saw much of both in London and in the United States, was Sir Henry Irving. The world of art, drama, and history owes much to him for his revival of Shakespeare. Irving was a genius in his profession, and in private life perfectly delightful.

He gave me a dinner and it was, like everything he did, original. Instead of the usual formal entertainment, he had the dinner at one of the old royal castles in the country, which had become a very exclusive hotel. He carried us out there in coaches.

The company of authors, playwrights, and men of affairs made the entertainment late and the evening memorable. Returning home on the top of the coach, the full moon would appear and reappear, but was generally under a cloud. Irving remarked: "I do much better with that old moon in my theatre. I make it shine or obscure it with clouds, as the occasion requires."

I received a note from him at the time of his last visit to the United States, in which he said that a friend from the western part of the country was giving him a dinner at Delmonico's to precede his sailing in the early morning on his voyage home. The company was to be large and all good friends, and he had the positive assurance that there would be no speaking, and wished I would come.

The dinner was everything that could be desired. The company was a wonderful one of distinguished representatives of American life. The hours passed along rapidly and joyously, as many of these original men contributed story, racy adventure, or song.

Suddenly the host arose and said: "Gentlemen, we have with us to-night—" Of course, that meant an introductory speech about Irving and a reply from the guest. Irving turned to me, and in his deepest and most tragic Macbeth voice said: "God damn his soul to hell!" However, he rose to the occasion, and an hour or so afterwards, when everybody else had spoken, not satisfied with his first effort, he arose and made a much better and longer speech. He was an admirable after-dinner speaker as well as an unusual actor. His wonderful presentations, not only of Shakespeare's but of other dramas, did very much for the stage both in his own country and in ours.

Those who heard him only in his last year had no

conception of him in his prime. In his later years he fell into the fault, so common with public speakers and actors, of running words together and failing to articulate clearly. I have known a fine speech and a superior sermon and a great part in a play ruined because of the failure to articulate clearly. The audience could not follow the speaker and so lost interest.

Sir Henry told me a delightful story about Disraeli. A young relative of Irving's took orders and became a clergyman in the Established Church. At the request of Irving, Disraeli appointed this young man one of the curates at Windsor.

One day the clergyman came to Irving in great distress and said: "The unexpected has happened. Every one has dropped out, and I have been ordered to preach on Sunday."

Irving took him to see Disraeli for advice. The prime minister said to the young clergyman: "If you preach thirty minutes, Her Majesty will be bored. If you preach fifteen minutes, Her Majesty will be pleased. If you preach ten minutes, Her Majesty will be delighted."

"But," said the young clergyman, "my lord, what can a preacher possibly say in only ten minutes?"

"That," answered the statesman, "will be a matter of indifference to Her Majesty."

Sir Frederick Leighton, the eminent English artist, and at one time president of the Royal Academy, was one of the most charming men of his time. His reminiscences were delightful and told with rare dramatic effect. I remember a vivid description which he gave me of the wedding of one of the British royalties with a

German princess. Sir Frederick was one of the large and distinguished delegation which accompanied the prince.

The principality of the bride's father had been shorn of territory, power, and revenue during the centuries. Nevertheless, at the time of the wedding he maintained a ministry, the same as in the Middle Ages, and a miniature army. Palaces, built centuries before, housed the Cabinet.

The minister of foreign affairs came to Sir Frederick and unbosomed himself of his troubles. He said: "According to the usual procedure I ought to give a ball in honor of the union of our house with the royal family of England. My palace is large enough, but my salary is only eight hundred a year, and the expense would eat up the whole of it."

Sir Frederick said: "Your Excellency can overcome the difficulty in an original way. The state band can furnish the music, and that will cost nothing. When the time comes for the banquet, usher the guests with due ceremony to a repast of beer and pretzels."

The minister followed the instructions. The whole party appreciated the situation, and the minister was accredited with the most brilliant and successful ball the old capital had known for a century.

For several years one of the most interesting men in Europe was the Duke d'Aumale, son of Louis Philippe. He was a statesman and a soldier of ability and a social factor of the first rank. He alone of the French royalty was relieved from the decree of perpetual banishment and permitted to return to France and enjoy his estates. In recognition of this he gave his famous château and property at Chantilly to the French Academy. The gift was valued at ten millions of dollars. In the château at Chantilly is a wonderful collection of works of art.

I remember at one dinner, where the duke was the guest of honor, those present, including the host, were mostly new creations in the British peerage. After the conversation had continued for some time upon the fact that a majority of the House of Lords had been raised to the peerage during the reign of Queen Victoria, those present began to try and prove that on account of their ancient lineage they were exempt from the rule of parvenu peers. The duke was very tolerant with this discussion and, as always, the soul of politeness.

The host said: "Your Royal Highness, could you oblige us with a sketch of your ancestry?"

"Oh, certainly," answered the duke; "it is very brief. My family, the Philippes, are descendants from Æneas of Troy, and Æneas was the son of Venus." The mushrooms seemed smaller than even the garden variety.

The duke was talking to me at one time very interestingly about the visit of his father to America. At the time of the French Revolution his father had to flee for his life and came to the United States. He was entertained at Mount Vernon by Washington. He told me that after his father became King of France, he would often hesitate, or refuse to do something or write something which his ministers desired. The king's answer always was: "When I visited that greatest man of all the world, General Washington, at his home, I asked him at one time: 'General, is it not possible that in your long and wonderful career as a soldier and statesman that you have made mistakes?' The general answered: 'I have never done anything which I cared to recall or said anything which I would not repeat,' and the king would say: 'I cannot do that or sign that, because if I do I cannot say for myself what General Washington said of himself.'"

The duke asked me to spend a week-end with him at Chantilly, and it is one of the regrets of my life that I was unable to accept.

I happened to be in London on two successive Sundays. On the first I went to Westminster Abbey to hear Canon Farrar preach. The sermon was worthy of its wonderful setting. Westminster Abbey is one of the most inspiring edifices in the world. The orator has to reach a high plane to be worthy of its pulpit. I have heard many dull discourses there because the surroundings refuse to harmonize with mediocrity. The sermon of Canon Farrar was classic. It could easily have taken a place among the gems of English literature. It seemed to me to meet whatever criticism the eminent dead, buried in that old mausoleum, might have of these modern utterances. I left the Abbey spiritually and mentally elated.

The next Sunday I went to hear Charles Spurgeon. It was a wonderful contrast. Spurgeon's Metropolitan Tabernacle was a very plain structure of immense proportions but with admirable acoustics. There was none of the historic enshrining the church, which is the glory of Westminster Abbey, no church vestments or ceremonials.

Mr. Spurgeon, a plain, stocky-looking man, came out on the platform dressed in an ordinary garb of black coat, vest, and trousers. It was a vast audience of what might be called middle-class people. Mr. Spurgeon's sermon was a plain, direct, and exceedingly forcible appeal to their judgment and emotions. There was no attempt at rhetoric, but hard, hammerlike blows. As he rose in his indignation and denunciation of some current evils, and illustrated his argument with the Old Testament examples of the punishment of sinners, the audience became greatly excited. One of the officers of the church, in whose pew I sat, groaned aloud and gripped his hands so that the nails left their mark. Others around him were in the same frame of mind and spirit.

I saw there and then that the men who fought with Cromwell and won the battle of Naseby had in modern England plenty of descendants. They had changed only in outward deference to modern usages and conditions. If there had been occasion, Mr. Spurgeon could have led them for any sacrifice to what they believed to be right. I felt the power of that suppressed feeling—I would not say fanaticism, but intense conscientiousness —which occasionally in elections greatly surprises English politicians.

Canon Farrar's sermon easily takes its place among the selected books of the library. Spurgeon's address was straight from the shoulder, blow for blow, for the needs of the hour.

One of the novel incidents of the generous hospitality which I enjoyed every year in London was a dinner at the Athenæum Club given to me by one of the members of the government at that time. He was a gentleman of high rank and political importance. There were twenty-six at the dinner, and it was a representative gathering.

At the conclusion our host made a very cordial speech on more intimate relations between the United States and Great Britain, and then in a complimentary phrase introduced me, saying: "I hope you will speak freely and without limit."

I was encouraged by a most sympathetic audience and had a good time during my effort. No one else was called upon. My host was complimentary and said: "Your speech was so satisfactory that I thought best not to have any more."

Some time afterwards he said to me: "Many of my friends had heard of you but never heard you, so I made up my mind to give them the opportunity, and what was really a purely social affair for every other guest, I turned into an international occasion just to draw you out. However, the fraud, if it was a fraud, was an eminent success."

No one in England did more for Americans than Sir Henry Lucy. Every American knew all about him, because of his reputation, and particularly because he was the author of that most interesting column in *Punch* called the "Essence of Parliament."

At his luncheons he gathered eminent men in public life and in the literary and journalistic activities of Great Britain. These luncheons were most informal, and under the hospitable genius of Lucy the guests became on intimate terms. There was no table in London where so many racy stories and sometimes valuable historical reminiscences could be heard.

To be a guest at one of Sir Lucy's luncheons was for an American to meet on familiar terms with distinguished men whom he knew all about and was most anxious to see and hear.

At a large dinner I had a pleasant encounter with Sir

Henry. In order to meet another engagement, he tried to slip quietly out while I was speaking. I caught sight of his retreating figure and called loudly the refrain of the familiar song, "Linger longer, Lucy." The shout of the crowd brought Sir Henry back, and the other entertainment lost a guest.

In several of my visits to London I went to see not only places of interest but also houses and streets made famous in English literature. In one of my many trips to St. Paul's Cathedral I was looking at the tomb of the Duke of Wellington in the crypt and also at the modest tomb of Cruikshank, the artist, near by.

The superintendent asked me who I was and many questions about America, and then said: "Many Americans come here, but the most remarkable of them all was Colonel Robert G. Ingersoll. He was very inquisitive and wanted to know all about Wellington's tomb. I told him that the duke's body was first put in a wooden coffin, and this was incased in steel; that this had made for it a position in a stone weighing twenty tons and over that was a huge stone weighing forty tons. He gave me a slap on the back which sent me flying quite a distance and exclaimed: 'Old man, you have got him safe. If he ever escapes cable at my expense to Robert G. Ingersoll, Peoria, Illinois, U. S. A.'"

I had an opportunity to know that the war by Germany against France and England was a surprise to both countries. While in London during part of June, 1914, I met Cabinet ministers and members of Parliament, and their whole thought and anxiety were concentrated on the threatened revolution in Ireland.

The Cabinet had asked the king to intervene and he had called representatives of all parties to meet him at Buckingham Palace. After many consultations he declared settlement or compromise were impossible. The situation was so critical that it absorbed the attention of the government, the press, and the public.

About the first of July I was in Paris and found the French worried about their finances and the increase in their military expenses which were reaching threatening figures. The syndicate of French bankers were seriously alarmed. There was no suspicion of German purpose and preparations for attack.

While in Geneva a few weeks afterwards I became alarmed by letters from relatives in Germany who were socially intimate with people holding very important positions in the government and the army, and their apprehensions from what their German friends told them and what they saw led to their joining us in Switzerland.

One day the Swiss refused to take foreign money or to make exchange for Swiss, or to cash letters of credit or bank checks. I immediately concluded that the Swiss bankers knew of or suspected Germany's hostile intentions, and with only two hours, and two families with their trunks to pack, we managed to reach and secure accommodations on the regular train for Paris. There was nothing unusual either at the railroad station or in the city.

One of the amusing incidents which are my life-preservers occurred at the station. Two elderly English spinsters were excitedly discussing the currency trouble. One of them smoothed out a bank of England note and said to her sister: "There, Sarah, is a bank of England note which has been good as gold all over the world since Christ came to earth, and these Swiss pigs won't take it."

I told this incident afterwards to a banker in London. He said they were very ignorant women, there were no bank of England notes at that time.

German hostility developed so rapidly that our train was the last which left Switzerland for France for nearly two months. We were due in Paris at ten o'clock in the evening, but did not arrive until the next morning because of the mobilization of French recruits.

The excitement in Paris was intense. A French statesman said to me: "We are doing our best to avoid war. Our troops are kept ten kilometres from the frontier, but the Germans have crossed and seized strategic points. They will hear nothing and accept nothing and are determined to crush us if they can."

From all ranks of the people was heard: "We will fight to the last man, but we are outnumbered and will be destroyed unless England helps. Will England help? Will England help?" I have been through several crises but never witnessed nor felt such a reaction to ecstatic joy as occurred when Great Britain joined France.

The restrictions on leaving Paris required time, patience, and all the resources of our Embassy to get us out of France. The helpfulness, resourcefulness, and untiring efforts of our Ambassador, Myron T. Herrick, won the gratitude of all Americans whom the war had interned on the continent and who must get home.

There was a remarkable change in England. When we left in July there was almost hysteria over the threatening civil war. In October the people were calm though involved in the greatest war in their history. They did not minimize the magnitude of the struggle, or the sacrifices it would require. There was a characteristic grim determination to see the crisis through, regardless of cost. Cabinet ministers whom I met thought the war would last three years.

The constant appeal to me, as to other Americans, was, "When will you join us? If we fail it is your turn next. It is autocracy and militarism against civilization, liberty, and representative government for the whole world."

We had a perilous and anxious voyage home and found few grasping the situation or working to be prepared for the inevitable, except Theodore Roosevelt and General Wood.

XX

ORATORS AND CAMPAIGN SPEAKERS

During my college days at Yale Wendell Phillips, William Lloyd Garrison, and Henry Ward Beecher were frequent lecturers, and generally on the slavery question. I have heard most of the great orators of the world, but none of them produced such an immediate and lasting effect upon their audience as Wendell Phillips. He was the finest type of a cultured New Englander. He was the recipient of the best education possible in his time and with independent means which enabled him to pursue his studies and career. Besides, he was one of the handsomest men I ever saw upon the platform, and in his inspired moments met one's imaginative conception of a Greek god.

Phillips rarely made a gesture or spoke above the conversational, but his musical voice reached the remotest corners of the hall. The eager audience, fearful of losing a word, would bend forward with open mouths as well as attentive ears. It was always a hostile audience at the beginning of Mr. Phillips's address, but before the end he swayed them to applause, tears, or laughter, as a skilled performer upon a perfect instrument. His subject was nearly always slavery, his views very extreme and for immediate abolition, but at that time he had a very small following. Nevertheless, his speeches, especially because of the riots and controversies they caused, set people thinking, and largely increased the hostility to slavery, especially to its extension.

I met Mr. Phillips one evening, after a lecture, at the house of Professor Goodrich. He was most courtly and considerate to students and invited questions. While I was charmed, even captivated, by his eloquence, I had at that time very little sympathy with his views. I said to him: "Mr. Phillips, your attack to-night upon Caleb Cushing, one of the most eminent and able public men in the country, was very vitriolic and most destructive of character and reputation. It seems so foreign to all I know of you that, if you will pardon me, I would like to know why you did it." He answered: "I have found that people, as a rule, are not interested in principles or their discussions. They are so absorbed in their personal affairs that they do very little thinking upon matters outside their business or vocation. They embody a principle in some public man in whom they have faith, and so that man stands for a great body of truth or falsehood, and may be exceedingly dangerous because a large following connects the measure with the man, and, therefore, if I can destroy the man who represents a vicious principle I have destroyed the principle." It did not strike me favorably at the time, nor does it now. Nevertheless, in politics and in the battles of politics it represents a dynamic truth.

The perfect preparation of a speech was, in Wendell Phillip's view, that one in which the mental operations were assisted in no way by outside aid. Only two or three times in his life did he prepare with pen and paper an address, and he felt that these speeches were the poorest of his efforts. He was constantly studying the art of oratory. In his daily walks or in his library metaphors and similes were suggested, which he tucked away in his memory, and he even studied action as he watched the muscular movements of men whom he saw in public places. He believed that a perfect speech could be prepared only after intense mental concentration. Of course the mind must first be fortified by such reading as provided facts. Having thus saturated his mind with information, he would frequently lie extended for hours upon his sofa, with eyes closed, making mental arrangements for the address. In fact, he used to write his speeches mentally, as Victor Hugo is said to have written some of his poems. A speech thus prepared, Phillips thought, was always at the command of the speaker. It might vary upon every delivery, and could be altered to meet emergencies with the audience, but would always be practically the same.

This method of preparation explains what has been a mystery to many persons. The several reports of Phillips's lecture on "The Lost Arts" differ in phraseology and even in arrangement. Mr. Phillips did not read his speeches in print, and, therefore, never revised one. He was firmly of the belief that the printed thought and the spoken thought should be expressed in different form, and that the master of one form could not be the master of the other.

I met many young men like myself in the canvass of 1856, and also made many acquaintances of great value in after-life. It was difficult for the older stump speakers to change the addresses they had been delivering for years, so that the young orators, with their fresh enthusiasm, their intense earnestness and undoubting faith, were more popular with the audiences, who were keenly alive to the issues raised then by the new Republican party.

The Republican party was composed of Whigs and

anti-slavery Democrats. In this first campaign the old-timers among the Whigs and the Democrats could not get over their long antagonism and distrusted each other. The young men, whether their ancestry was Democratic or Whig, were the amalgam which rapidly fused all elements, so that the party presented a united front in the campaign four years afterwards when Mr. Lincoln was elected.

In the course of that campaign I had as fellow speakers many times on the platform statesmen of national reputation. These gentlemen, with few exceptions, made heavy, ponderous, and platitudinous speeches. If they ever had possessed humor they were afraid of it. The crowd, however, would invariably desert the statesman for the speaker who could give them amusement with instruction. The elder statesmen said by way of advice: "While the people want to be amused, they have no faith in a man or woman with wit or anecdote. When it comes to the election of men to conduct public affairs, they invariably prefer serious men." There is no doubt that a reputation for wit has seriously impaired the prospects of many of the ablest men in the country.

The only exception to this rule was Abraham Lincoln. But when he ran for president the first time he was comparatively unknown outside his State of Illinois. The campaign managers in their literature put forward only his serious speeches, which were very remarkable, especially the one he delivered in Cooper Union, New York, which deeply impressed the thoughtful men of the East. He could safely tell stories and jokes after he had demonstrated his greatness as president. Then the people regarded his story-telling as the necessary relief and relaxation of an overburdened and overworked public servant. But before he had demonstrated his genius as an executive, they would probably have regarded these same traits as evidences of frivolity, unfitting the possessor for great and grave responsibilities.

I had a very interesting talk on the subject with General Garfield, when he was running for president. He very kindly said to me: "You have every qualification for success in public life; you might get anywhere and to the highest places except for your humor. I know its great value to a speaker before an audience, but it is dangerous at the polls. When I began in politics, soon after graduation, I found I had a keen sense of humor, and that made me the most sought-after of all our neighborhood speakers, but I also soon discovered it was seriously impairing the public opinion of me for responsible positions, so I decided to cut it out. It was very difficult, but I have succeeded so thoroughly that I can no longer tell a story or appreciate the point of one when it is told to me. Had I followed my natural bent I should not now be the candidate of my party for President of the United States."

The reason so few men are humorists is that they are very shy of humor. My own observations in studying the lives and works of our public men demonstrate how thoroughly committed to this idea they have been. There is not a joke, nor a mot, nor a scintilla of humor irradiating the Revolutionary statesmen. There is a stilted dignity about their utterances which shows that they were always posing in heroic attitudes. If they lived and moved in family, social, and club life, as we understand it, the gloom of their companionship accounts for the enjoyment which their contemporaries took in the three hours' sermons then common from the pulpit.

As we leave the period of Washington, Hamilton, Jefferson, and the Adamses, we find no humor in the next generation. The only relief from the tedium of argument and exhaustless logic is found in the savage sarcasm of John Randolph, which was neither wit nor humor.

A witty illustration or an apt story will accomplish more than columns of argument. The old-time audience demanded a speech of not less than two hours' duration and expected three. The audience of to-day grows restive after the first hour, and is better pleased with forty minutes. It prefers epigrams to arguments and humor to rhetoric. It is still true, however, that the press presents to readers from a speaker who indulges in humor only the funny part of his effort, and he is in serious danger of receiving no credit for ability in the discussion of great questions, no matter how conspicuous that ability may be. The question is always presented to a frequent speaker whether he shall win the applause of the audience and lose the flattering opinion of the critics, or bore his audience and be complimented by readers for wisdom.

When I look back over sixty-five years on the platform in public speaking, and the success of different methods before audiences, political, literary, business, or a legislative committee, or a legislature itself, and especially when I consider my own pleasure in the efforts, the results and compensations have been far greater than the attainment of any office. For, after all, a man might be dull and a bore to himself and others for a lifetime and have the reputation of being a serious thinker and a solid citizen, and yet never reach the presidency.

It was always a delight to listen to George W. Curtis. He was a finished orator of the classic type, but not of the Demosthenian order. His fine personal appearance,

ORATORS AND CAMPAIGN SPEAKERS

his well-modulated and far-reaching voice, and his refined manner at once won the favor of his audience. He was a splendid type of the scholar in politics. In preparing a speech he took as much pains as he did with a volume which he was about to publish.

I accepted under great pressure the invitation to deliver the oration at the unveiling of the Bartholdi Statue of Liberty in New York harbor, because the time was so short, only a few days. Mr. Curtis said to me afterwards: "I was very much surprised that you accepted that invitation. I declined it because there was only a month left before the unveiling. I invariably refuse an invitation for an important address unless I can have three months. I take one month to look up authorities and carefully prepare it and then lay it on the shelf for a month. During that period, while you are paying no attention to the matter, your mind is unconsciously at work upon it. When you resume correcting your manuscript you find that in many things about which you thought well you have changed your mind. Leisurely corrections and additions will perfect the address."

As my orations and speeches have always been the by-product of spare evenings and Sundays taken from an intensely active and busy life, if I had followed any of these examples my twelve volumes of speeches would never have seen the light of day.

One of the greatest orators of his generation, and I might say of ours, was Robert G. Ingersoll. I was privileged to meet Colonel Ingersoll many times, and on several occasions to be a speaker on the same platform. The zenith of his fame was reached by his "plumed-knight" speech, nominating James G. Blaine for president at the national Republican convention in 1876. It was the testimony of all the delegates that if the vote could have been taken immediately at the conclusion of the speech, Mr. Blaine would have been elected.

Colonel Ingersoll carried off the oratorical honors of that campaign in a series of speeches, covering the whole country. I say a series of speeches; he really had but one, which was the most effective campaign address I ever heard, but which he delivered over and over again, and every time with phenomenal success, a success the like of which I have never known. He delivered it to an immense audience in New York, and swept them off their feet. He repeated this triumph the next day at an open-air meeting in Wall Street, and again the next day at a great gathering in New Jersey. The newspapers printed the speech in full every day after its delivery, as if it had been a new and first utterance of the great orator.

I spoke with him several times when he was one of the speakers after an important dinner. It was a rare treat to hear him. The effort apparently was impromptu, and that added to its effect upon his auditors. That it was thoroughly prepared I found by hearing it several times, always unchanged and always producing the same thrilling effect.

He spoke one night at Cooper Institute at a celebration by the colored people of Mr. Lincoln's proclamation emancipating them from slavery. As usual he was master of the occasion and of his audience. He was then delivering a series of addresses attacking the Bible. His mind was full of that subject, and apparently he could not help assailing the faith of the negroes by asking, if there was a God of justice and mercy, why did he leave

ORATORS AND CAMPAIGN SPEAKERS

them so long in slavery or permit them ever to be slaves.

To an emotional audience like the one before him it was a most dangerous attack upon faith. I was so fond of the colonel and such an intense admirer of him, I hated to controvert him, but felt it was necessary to do so. The religious fervor which is so intense with the colored people, made it comparatively easy to restore their faith, if it had been weakened, and to bring them to a recognition of the fact that their blessings had all come from God.

Probably the most brilliant speaker of the period immediately preceding the Civil War was Thomas Corwin, of Ohio. We have on the platform in these times no speaker of his type. He had remarkable influence whenever he participated in debate in the House of Representatives. On the stump or hustings he would draw audiences away from Henry Clay or any of the famous speakers of the time. I sometimes wonder if our more experienced and more generally educated audiences of to-day would be swayed by Corwin's methods. He had to the highest degree every element of effective speech. He could put his audience in tears or hilarious laughter, or arouse cheers. He told more stories and told them better than any one else, and indulged freely in what is called Fourth of July exaggeration. He would relieve a logical presentation which was superb and unanswerable by a rhetorical flight of fancy, or by infectious humor. Near the close of his life he spoke near New York, and his great reputation drew to the meeting the representatives of the metropolitan press. He swept the audience off their feet, but the comment of the journals was very critical and unfavorable, both of the speech and the orator. It was an illustration of what I have often met with: of a speech which was exactly the right thing for the occasion and crowd, but lost its effect in publication. Corwin's humor barred his path to great office, and he saw many ordinary men advance ahead of him.

The most potent factor in the destruction of his enemies and buttressing his own cause was his inimitable wit and humor. In broad statesmanship, solid requirements, and effective eloquence, he stood above the successful mediocrity of his time—the Buchanans and the Polks, the Franklin Pierces and the Winfield Scotts—like a star of the first magnitude above the Milky Way. But in later years he thought the failure to reach the supreme recognition to which he was entitled was due to his humor having created the impression in the minds of his countrymen that he was not a serious person.

Wayne MacVeagh was a very interesting and original speaker. He had a finished and cultured style and a very attractive delivery. He was past master of sarcasm as well as of burning eloquence on patriotic themes. When I was a freshman at Yale he was a senior. I heard him very often at our debating society, the Linonian, where he gave promise of his future success. His father-in-law was Simon Cameron, secretary of war, and he was one of the party which went with Mr. Lincoln to Gettysburg and heard Lincoln's famous address. He told me that it did not produce much impression at the time, and it was long after before the country woke up to its surpassing excellence, and he did not believe the story still current that Mr. Lincoln wrote it on an envelope while on the train to Gettysburg.

MacVeagh became one of the leaders of the American bar and was at one time attorney-general of the United

ORATORS AND CAMPAIGN SPEAKERS

States. He was successful as a diplomat as minister to Turkey and to Italy.

I heard him on many occasions and spoke with him on many after-dinner platforms. As an after-dinner speaker he was always at his best if some one attacked him, because he had a very quick temper. He got off on me a witticism which had considerable vogue at the time. When I was elected president of the New York Central Railroad, the Yale Association of New York gave me a dinner. It was largely attended by distinguished Yale graduates from different parts of the country. MacVeagh was one of the speakers. In the course of his speech he said: "I was alarmed when I found that our friend Chauncey had been elected president of the most unpopular railroad there is in the country. But rest assured, my friends, that he will change the situation, and before his administration is closed make it the most popular of our railroad corporations, because he will bring the stock within the reach of the poorest citizen of the land." The stock was then at the lowest point in its history on account of its life-and-death fight with the West Shore Railroad, and so, of course, the reverse of my friend MacVeagh's prediction was not difficult.

One of the greatest and most remarkable orators of his time was Henry Ward Beecher. I never met his equal in readiness and versatility. His vitality was infectious. He was a big, healthy, vigorous man with the physique of an athlete, and his intellectual fire and vigor corresponded with his physical strength. There seemed to be no limit to his ideas, anecdotes, illustrations, and incidents. He had a fervid imagination and wonderful power of assimilation and reproduction and the most observant of eyes. He was drawing material constantly from the forests, the flowers, the gardens, and the domestic animals in the fields and in the house, and using them most effectively in his sermons and speeches. An intimate friend of mine, a country doctor and great admirer of Mr. Beecher, became a subscriber to the weekly paper in which was printed his Sunday sermon, and carefully guarded a file of them which he made. He not only wanted to read the sermons of his favorite preacher, but he believed him to have infinite variety, and was constantly examining the efforts of his idol to see if he could not find an illustration, anecdote, or idea repeated.

Mr. Beecher seemed to be teeming with ideas all the time, almost to the point of bursting. While most orators are relying upon their libraries and their commonplace book, and their friends for material, he apparently found more in every twenty-four hours than he could use. His sermons every Sunday appeared in the press. He lectured frequently; several times a week he delivered after-dinner speeches, and during such intervals as he had he made popular addresses, spoke at meetings on municipal and general reform, and on patriotic occasions. One of the most effective, and for the time one of the most eloquent addresses I ever heard in my life was the one he delivered at the funeral of Horace Greeley.

When the sentiment in England in favor of the South in our Civil War seemed to be growing to a point where Great Britain might recognize the Southern Confederacy, Mr. Lincoln asked Mr. Beecher to go over and present the Union side. Those speeches of Mr. Beecher, a stranger in a strange country, to hostile audiences, were probably as extraordinary an evidence of oratorical power as was ever known. He captured audiences, he overcame the hostility of persistent disturbers of the

ORATORS AND CAMPAIGN SPEAKERS 325

meetings, and with his ready wit overwhelmed the heckler.

At one of the great meetings, when the sentiment was rapidly changing from hostility to favor, a man arose and asked Mr. Beecher: "If you people of the North are so strong and your cause is so good, why after all these years of fighting have you not licked the South?" Mr. Beecher's instant and most audacious reply was: "If the Southerners were Englishmen we would have licked them." With the English love of fair play, the retort was accepted with cheers.

While other orators were preparing, he seemed to be seeking occasions for talking and drawing from an overflowing reservoir. Frequently he would spend an hour with a crowd of admirers, just talking to them on any subject which might be uppermost in his mind. I knew an authoress who was always present at these gatherings, who took copious notes and reproduced them with great fidelity. There were circles of Beecher worshippers in many towns and in many States. This authoress used to come to New Haven in my senior year at Yale, and in a circle of Beecher admirers, which I was permitted to attend, would reproduce these informal talks of Mr. Beecher. He was the most ready orator, and with his almost feminine sympathies and emotional nature would add immensely to his formal speech by ideas which would occur to him in the heat of delivery, or with comment upon conversations which he had heard on the way to church or meeting.

I happened to be on a train with him on an all-day journey, and he never ceased talking in the most interesting and effective way, and pouring out from his rich and inexhaustible stores with remarkable lucidity and eloquence his views upon current topics, as well as upon recent literature, art, and world movements.

Beecher's famous trial on charges made by Theodore Tilton against him on relations with Tilton's wife engrossed the attention of the world. The charge was a shock to the religious and moral sense of countless millions of people. When the trial was over the public was practically convinced of Mr. Beecher's innocence. The jury, however, disagreed, a few holding out against him. The case was never again brought to trial. The trial lasted six months.

One evening when I was in Peekskill I went from our old homestead into the crowded part of the village, to be with old friends. I saw there a large crowd and also the village military and fire companies. I asked what it was all about, and was informed that the whole town was going out to Mr. Beecher's house, which was about one and one-half miles from the village, to join in a demonstration for his vindication. I took step with one of the companies to which I belonged when I was a boy, and marched out with the crowd.

The president of the village and leading citizens, one after another, mounted the platform, which was the piazza of Mr. Beecher's house, and expressed their confidence in him and the confidence of his neighbors, the villagers. Then Mr. Beecher said to me: "You were born in this town and are known all over the country. If you feel like saying something it would travel far." Of course, I was very glad of the opportunity because I believed in him. In the course of my speech I told a story which had wonderful vogue. I said: "Mr. Lincoln told me of an experience he had in his early practice when he was defending a man who had been accused of a vicious assault upon a neighbor. There were no witnesses, and under the laws of evidence at that time the accused could not testify. So the complainant had it all his own way. The only opportunity Mr. Lincoln had to help his client was to break down the accuser on a cross-examination. Mr. Lincoln said he saw that the accuser was a boastful and bumptious man, and so asked him: 'How much ground was there over which you and my client fought?' The witness answered proudly: 'Six acres, Mr. Lincoln.' 'Well,' said Lincoln, 'don't you think this was a mighty small crop of fight to raise on such a large farm?' Mr. Lincoln said the judge laughed and so did the district attorney and the jury, and his client was acquitted."

The appositeness was in the six acres of ground of the Lincoln trial and of the six months of the Beecher trial. As this was a new story of Lincoln's, which had never been printed, and as it related to the trial of the most famous of preachers on the worst of charges that could be made against a preacher, the story was printed all over the country, and from friends and consular agents who sent me clippings I found was copied in almost every country in the world.

Mr. Beecher was one of the few preachers who was both most effective in the pulpit and, if possible, more eloquent upon the platform. When there was a moral issue involved he would address political audiences. In one campaign his speeches were more widely printed than those of any of the senators, members of the House, or governors who spoke. I remember one illustration of his about his dog, Noble, barking for hours at the hole from which a squirrel had departed, and was enjoying the music sitting calmly in the crotch of a tree. The illustration caught the fancy of the country and turned the laugh upon the opposition.

Hugh J. Hastings, at one time editor and proprietor of the *Albany Knickerbocker*, and subsequently of the *New York Commercial Advertiser*, was full of valuable reminiscences. He began life in journalism as a very young man under Thurlow Weed. This association made him a Whig. Very few Irishmen belonged to that party. Hastings was a born politician and organized an Irish Whig club. He told me that he worshipped Daniel Webster.

Webster, he said, once stopped over at Albany while passing through the State, and became a guest of one of Albany's leading citizens and its most generous host and entertainer. The gentleman gave in Webster's honor a large dinner at which were present all the notables of the capital.

Hastings organized a procession which grew to enormous proportions by the time it reached the residence where Mr. Webster was dining. When the guests came out, it was evident, according to Hastings, that they had been dining too well. This was not singular, because then no dinner was perfect in Albany unless there were thirteen courses and thirteen different kinds of wine, and the whole closed up with the famous Regency rum, which had been secured by Albany bon-vivants before the insurrection in the West Indies had stopped its manufacture. There was a kick in it which, if there had been no other brands preceding, was fatal to all except the strongest heads. I tested its powers myself when I was in office in Albany fifty-odd years ago.

Hastings said that when Webster began his speech he was as near his idol as possible and stood right in front of him. When the statesman made a gesture to emphasize a sentence he lost his hold on the balustrade and pitched forward. The young Irishman was equal to the occasion, and interposed an athletic arm, which prevented Mr. Webster from falling, and held him until he had finished his address. The fact that he could continue his address under such conditions increased, if that was possible, the admiration of young Hastings. Webster was one of the few men who, when drunk all over, had a sober head.

The speech was very effective, not only to that audience, but, as reported, all over the country. Hastings was sent for and escorted to the dining-room, where the guests had reassembled. Webster grasped him by the hand, and in his most Jovian way exclaimed: "Young man, you prevented me from disgracing myself. I thank you and will never forget you." Hastings reported his feelings as such that if he had died that night he had received of life all it had which was worth living for.

I do not know what were Mr. Webster's drinking habits, but the popular reports in regard to them had a very injurious effect upon young men and especially young lawyers. It was the universal conversation that Webster was unable to do his best work and have his mind at its highest efficiency except under the influence of copious drafts of brandy. Many a young lawyer believing this drank to excess, not because he loved alcohol, but because he believed its use might make him a second Webster.

Having lived in that atmosphere, I tried the experiment myself. Happily for me, I discovered how utterly false it is. I tried the hard liquors, brandy, whiskey, and gin, and then the wines. I found that all had a depressing and deadening effect upon the mind, but that there was a certain exhilaration, though not a healthy one, in champagne. I also discovered, and found the same was true with every one else, that the mind works best and produces the more satisfactory results without any alcohol whatever.

I doubt if any speaker, unless he has become dependent upon stimulants, can use them before making an important effort without having his mental machinery more or less clogged. I know it is reported that Addison, whose English has been the model of succeeding generations, in writing his best essays wore the carpet out while walking between sentences from the sideboard where the brandy was to his writing-table. But they had heroic constitutions and iron-clad digestive apparatus in those times, which have not been transmitted to their descendants.

I heard another story of Webster from Horace F. Clarke, a famous lawyer of New York, and a great friend of his. Mr. Clarke said that he had a case involving very large interests before the chancellor. He discovered that Mr. Webster was at the Astor House, and called upon him. Mr. Webster told him that his public and professional engagements were overwhelming, and that it was impossible for him to take up anything new. Clarke put a thousand dollars on the table and pleaded with Mr. Webster to accept a retainer. Clarke said that Webster looked longingly at the money, saying: "Young man, you cannot imagine, and I have no words which can express how much I need that money, but it is impossible. However, let me see your brief." Webster read it over and then said to Clarke: "You will not win on that brief, but if you will incorporate this, I think your case is all right." Clarke said that when he presented the brief and made his argument before the chancellor, the chancellor decided in his favor, wholly on the suggestion made by Mr. Webster. An eminent lawyer told me that studying Mr. Webster's arguments before the Supreme Court and the decisions made in those cases, he discovered very often that the opinion of the court followed the reasoning of this marvellous advocate.

Henry J. Raymond told me the following story of Mr. William H. Seward. He said that one morning a messenger came to his office (Raymond at that time was editor of the *New York Times*) and said that Mr. Seward was at the Astor House and wanted to see me. When I arrived Mr. Seward said: "I am on my way to my home at Auburn, where I am expected to deliver a speech for the whole country in explanation and defense of our administration. [Johnson was president.] When I am ready I will wire you, and then send me one of your best reporters." About two weeks afterwards Mr. Raymond received this cryptic telegram from Mr. Seward: "Send me the man of whom I spoke."

When the reporter returned he said to Mr. Raymond: "When I arrived at Auburn I expected that a great meeting had been advertised, but there were no handbills, notices, or anything in the local papers, so I went up to Mr. Seward's house. He said to me: 'I am very glad to see you. Have you your pencil and note-book? if so, we will make a speech.' After the dictation Mr. Seward said: 'Please write that out on every third line, so as to leave room for corrections, and bring it back to me in the morning.' When I gave the copy to Mr. Seward, he took it and kept it during the day, and when I returned in the evening the vacant space had been filled with corrections and new matter. Mr. Seward said to me: 'Now make me a clean copy as corrected.' When I returned with the corrected copy he remarked: 'I think you and I made a very poor speech. Let us try it again.' The same process was repeated a second time, and this corrected copy of the speech was delivered in part to a few friends who were called into Mr. Seward's library for the occasion. The next morning these headlines appeared in all the leading papers in the country: 'GREAT SPEECH ON BEHALF OF THE ADMINISTRATION BY THE SECRETARY OF STATE AT A BIG MASS MEETING AT AUBURN, N. Y.'"

In the career of a statesman a phrase will often make or unmake his future. In the height of the slavery excitement and while the enforcement of the fugitive-slave law was arousing the greatest indignation in the North, Mr. Seward delivered a speech at Rochester, N. Y., which stirred the country. In that speech, while paying due deference to the Constitution and the laws, he very solemnly declared that "there is a higher law." Mr. Seward sometimes called attention to his position by an oracular utterance which he left the people to interpret. This phrase, "the higher law," became of first-class importance, both in Congress, in the press, and on the platform. On the one side, it was denounced as treason and anarchy. On the other side, it was the call of conscience and of the New Testament's teaching of the rights of man. It was one of the causes of his defeat for the presidency.

Senator Henry Wilson, of Massachusetts, afterwards vice-president, was in great demand. He was clear in his historical statements and emphatic in his expression of views. If he had any apprehension of humor he never showed it in his speeches. His career had been very picturesque—from unskilled laborer to the Senate and the vice-presidency. The impression he gave was of an example of American opportunity, and he was more impressive and influential by his personality and history than by what he said.

One of the most picturesque and popular stump speakers was Daniel S. Dickinson. He had been a United States senator and party leader, and was a national figure. His venerable appearance gave force to his oratory. He seemed to be of great age, but was remarkably vigorous. His speeches were made up of epigrams which were quotable and effective. He jumped rapidly from argument to anecdote and was vitriolic in attack.

I had an interesting experience with Mr. Dickinson when running for secretary of state in 1863. The drawing card for that year, and the most sought-after and popular for campaign speaking, was Governor Andrew, of Massachusetts. He had a series of appointments in New York State, but on account of some emergency cancelled them all. The national and State committees selected me to fill his appointments. The most unsatisfactory and disagreeable job in the world is to meet the appointments of a popular speaker. The expectations of the audience have been aroused to a degree by propaganda advertising the genius and accomplishments of the expected speaker. The substitute cannot meet those expectations, and an angry crowd holds him responsible for their disappointment.

When I left the train at the station I was in the midst of a mass-meeting of several counties at Deposit, N. Y. A large committee, profusely decorated with campaign badges, were on the platform to welcome the distinguished war governor of Massachusetts. I did not meet physically their expectations of an impressive statesman of dignified presence, wearing a Prince Albert suit and a top hat. I had been long campaigning, my soft hat was disreputable, and I had added a large shawl to my campaigning equipment. Besides that, I was only twenty-eight and looked much younger. The committee expected at least sixty. Finally the chairman rushed up to me and said: "You were on the train. Did you see Governor Andrew, of Massachusetts?" I answered him: "Governor Andrew is not coming; he has cancelled all his engagements, and I have been sent to take his place." The chairman gasped and then exclaimed: "My God!" He very excitedly summoned his fellow members of the committee and said to them: "Gentlemen, Governor Andrew is not coming, but the State committee has sent *this*," pointing to me. I was the party candidate as secretary of state, and at the head of the ticket, but nobody asked me who I was, nor did I tell them. I was left severely alone.

Some time after, the chairman of the committee came to me and said: "Young fellow, we won't be hard on you, but the State committee has done this once before. We were promised a very popular speaker well known among us, but in his place they sent the damnedest fool who ever stood before an audience. However, we have sent to Binghamton for Daniel S. Dickinson, and he will be here in a short time and save our big mass-meeting."

Mr. Dickinson came and delivered a typical speech; every sentence was a bombshell and its explosion very effective. He had the privilege of age, and told a story which I would not have dared to tell, the audience being half women. He said: "Those constitutional lawyers, who are proclaiming that all Mr. Lincoln's acts are unconstitutional, don't know any law. They remind me of a doctor we have up in Binghamton, who has a large practice because of his fine appearance, his big words, and gold-headed cane. He was called to see a young lad who was sitting on his grandmother's lap. After looking at the boy's tongue and feeling his pulse, he rested his head in deep thought for a while on his gold-headed cane and then said: 'Madam, this boy has such difficulties with the epiglottis and such inflamed larynx that we will have to apply phlebotomy.' The old lady clasped the boy frantically to her bosom and cried: 'For heaven's sake, doctor, what on earth can ail the boy that you are going to put all that on his bottom?'"

Mr. Dickinson introduced me as the head of the State ticket. My speech proved a success, and the chairman paid me the handsome compliment of saying: "We are glad they sent you instead of Governor Andrew."

One of the most effective of our campaign speakers was General Bruce, of Syracuse, N. Y. The general had practically only one speech, which was full of picturesque illustrations, striking anecdotes, and highly wrought-up periods of patriotic exaltation. He delivered this speech, with necessary variations, through many campaigns. I was with the general, who was Canal commissioner when I was secretary of state, on our official tour on the Canal.

One night the general said to me: "Mr. Blank, who has a great reputation, is speaking in a neighboring town, and I am going to hear him." He came back enraged and unhappy. In telling me about it, he said: "That infernal thief delivered my speech word for word, and better than I can do it myself. I am too old to get up another one, and, as I love to speak, I am very unhappy."

This illustrated one of the accidents to which a campaign speaker is liable. The man who stole the general's speech afterwards played the same trick on me. He came into our State from New England with a great reputation. He was a very fine elocutionist, of excellent presence and manner, but utterly incapable of original thought. He could not prepare a speech of any kind. However, he had a phenomenal memory. He could listen to a speech made by another and repeat it perfectly. His attractive appearance, good voice, and fine elocution made the speech a great success. Several orators told me that when they found their efforts a failure they asked for the cause, and discovered that this man had delivered their speeches a few nights before, and the audience, of course, thought the last speaker was a fraud and a thief.

General Bruce told me a good campaign story of Senator James W. Nye, of Nevada. Nye was a prominent lawyer of western New York, and the most eloquent and witty member of the bar of that section, and also the most popular campaign speaker. He moved to Nevada and so impressed the people of that young State that he was elected United States senator. In the Senate he became a notable figure.

Nye and General Bruce were sent by the national committee to canvass New England. Nye had become senatorial in his oratory, with much more dignity and elevation of style than before. He began his first speech at Bridgeport, Conn., in this way: "Fellow citizens, I have come three thousand miles from my mountain home, three thousand feet above the level of the sea, to discuss with you these vital questions for the safety of our republic." The next night, at New Haven, he said: "I have come from my mountain home, five thousand feet above the level of the sea, to discuss with you these vital questions of the safety of our republic." Bruce interrupted him, saying: "Why, senator, it was only three thousand feet last night." Nye turned savagely on Bruce: "Bruce, you go to the devil!" Resuming with the audience, he remarked very impressively: "As I was saying, fellow citizens, I have come from my mountain home, ten thousand feet above the level of the sea, to, etc."

A story which illustrates and enforces the argument helps a political speech, and it is often the only part of the speech which is remembered. I have often heard people say to me: "I heard you speak thirty, forty, or fifty years ago, and this is the story you told." Sometimes, however, the story may prove a boomerang in the most unexpected way.

For many years, when I spoke in northern New York I was always met at the Syracuse station by a superintendent of the Lackawanna Railroad with a special train filled with friends. He carried me up to my destination and brought me back in the morning. It was his great day of the year, and during the trip he was full of reminiscences, and mainly of the confidences reposed in him by the president of the road, my old and valued friend, Samuel Sloan.

One fall he failed to appear, and there was no special train to meet me. I was told by friends that the reason was his wife had died and he was in mourning. The morning after the meeting I started to call upon him, but was informed that he was very hostile and would not see me. I was not going to lose an old friend like that and went up to his office. As soon as I entered, he said: "Go away, I don't want to see you again." I appealed to him, saying: "I cannot lose so good a friend as you. If there is anything I have done or said, I will do everything in my power to make it right." He turned on me sharply and with great emotion told this story: "My wife and I lived in loving harmony for over thirty years, and when she died recently I was heartbroken. The whole town was sympathetic; most of the business houses closed during the hour of the funeral. I had arranged to have ministers whom my wife admired, and with them selected passages of scriptures and hymns to which she was devoted. A new minister in town was invited by the others to participate, and without my knowledge. I looked over the congregation, all Mary's friends. I listened to the services, which Mary herself would have chosen, and said to Mary's spirit, which I knew to be hovering about: 'We are all paying you a loving tribute.' Then the new minister had for his part the announcement and reading of a hymn. At the last Republican convention at Saratoga, in order to illustrate the condition of the Democratic party, you told a story about a boy walking among the children's graves in the old cemetery at Peekskill, eating green apples and whistling 'Nearer, my God, to Thee.' The new minister gave that hymn, 'Nearer, my God, to Thee.' Your story came up in my mind, and I burst out laughing. I disgraced myself, insulted the memory of Mary, and I never want to see you again."

XXI

NATIONAL REPUBLICAN CONVENTIONS

When the Republican convention met in 1912 I was again a delegate. In my fifty-six years of national conventions I never had such an intensely disagreeable experience. I felt it my duty to support President Taft for renomination. I thought he had earned it by his excellent administration. I had many ties with him, beginning with our associations as graduates of Yale, and held for him a most cordial regard. I was swayed by my old and unabated love for Roosevelt. In that compromise and harmony were impossible. I saw that, with the control of the organization and of the convention on the side of Mr. Taft, and with the wild support for Roosevelt of the delegates from the States which could be relied upon to give Republican majorities, the nomination of either would be sure defeat.

I was again a delegate to the Republican convention of 1916. The party was united. Progressives and conservatives were acting together, and the convention was in the happiest of moods. It was generally understood that Justice Hughes would be nominated if he could be induced to resign from the Supreme Court and accept. The presiding officer of the convention was Senator Warren G. Harding. He made a very acceptable keynote speech. His fine appearance, his fairness, justice, and good temper as presiding officer captured the convention. There was a universal sentiment that if Hughes declined the party could do no better than to nominate Senator Harding. It was this impression among the delegates, many of whom were also members of the convention of 1920, which led to the selection as the convention's candidate for president of Warren G. Harding.

My good mother was a Presbyterian and a good Calvinist. She believed and impressed upon me the certainty of special Providence. It is hard for a Republican to think that the election of Woodrow Wilson was a special Providence, but if our candidate, Mr. Hughes, had been elected he would have had a hostile Democratic majority in Congress.

When the United States went into the war, as it must have done, the president would have been handicapped by this pacifist Congress. The draft would have been refused, without which our army of four millions could not have been raised. The autocratic measures necessary for the conduct of the war would have been denied. With the conflict between the executive and Congress, our position would have been impossible and indefensible.

I had a personal experience in the convention. Chairman Harding sent one of the secretaries to me with a message that there was an interval of about an hour when the convention would have nothing to do. It was during such a period the crank had his opportunity and the situation was dangerous, and he wished me to come to the platform and fill as much of that hour as possible. I refused on the ground that I was wholly unprepared, and it would be madness to attempt to speak to fourteen thousand people in the hall and a hundred million outside.

A few minutes afterwards Governor Whitman, chairman of the New York delegation, came to me and said:

"You must be drafted. The chairman will create some business to give you fifteen minutes to think up your speech." I spurred my gray matter as never before, and was then introduced and spoke for forty-five minutes. I was past eighty-two. The speech was a success, but when I returned to my seat I remembered what General Garfield had so earnestly said to me: "You are the only man of national reputation who will speak without preparation. Unless you peremptorily and decisively stop yielding you will some day make such a failure as to destroy the reputation of a lifetime."

In a letter President Harding has this to say in reference to the occasion: "Just about a year ago (1916) it was my privilege as chairman of the Republican convention at Chicago to call upon you for an address. There was a hiatus which called for a speech, and you so wonderfully met the difficult requirements that I sat in fascinated admiration and have been ready ever since to pay you unstinted tribute. You were ever eloquent in your more active years, but I count you the old man eloquent and incomparable in your eighties. May many more helpful and happy years be yours."

I was again a delegate to the convention in June, 1920. The Republicans had been for eight years out of office during Mr. Wilson's two terms. The delegates were exceedingly anxious to make no mistake and have no friction in the campaign.

The two leading candidates, General Wood and Governor Lowden, had nearly equal strength and were supported by most enthusiastic admirers and advocates. As the balloting continued the rivalry and feeling grew between their friends. It became necessary to harmonize the situation, and it was generally believed that this could be best done by selecting Senator Warren G. Harding.

Very few conventions have a dramatic surprise, but the nomination of Governor Coolidge, of Massachusetts, for vice-president came about in a very picturesque way. He had been named for president among the others, and the speech in his behalf by Speaker Frederick H. Gillett was an excellent one. Somehow the convention did not seem to grasp all that the governor stood for and how strong he was with each delegate. When the nominations for vice-president were called for, Senator Medill McCormick presented Senator Lenroot, of Wisconsin, in an excellent speech. There were also very good addresses on behalf of the Governor of Kansas and others.

When the balloting was about to start, a delegate from Oregon who was in the rear of the hall arose and said: "Mr. Chairman." The chairman said: "The gentleman from Oregon." The Oregon delegate, in a far-reaching voice, shouted: "Mr. Chairman, I nominate for vice-president Calvin Coolidge, a one-hundred-per-cent American." The convention went off its feet with a whoop and Coolidge was nominated hands down.

I again had a personal experience. The committee on resolutions, not being prepared to report, there was that interval of no business which is the despair of presiding officers of conventions. The crowd suddenly began calling for me. While, of course, I had thought much on the subject, I had not expected to be called upon and had no prepared speech. Happily, fifteen thousand faces and fifteen thousand voices giving uproarious welcome both steadied and inspired me. Though I was past eighty-six years of age, my voice was in as good condition as at forty, and was practically the only one which did fill that vast auditorium. The press of the country featured the effort next day in a way which was most gratifying.

Among the thousands who greeted me on the streets and in the hotel lobbies with congratulations and efforts to say something agreeable and complimentary, I selected one compliment as unique. He was an enthusiast. "Chauncey Depew," he said, "I have for over twenty years wanted to shake hands with you. Your speech was a wonder. I was half a mile off, way up under the roof, and heard every word of it, and it was the only one I was able to hear. That you should do this in your eighty-seventh year is a miracle. But then my father was a miracle. On his eighty-fifth birthday he was in just as good shape as you are to-day, and a week afterwards he was dead."

XXII

JOURNALISTS AND FINANCIERS

In reminiscences of my journalistic friends I do not include many of the most valued who are still living. Of those who have passed away one of the most faithful and devoted was Edward H. Butler, editor and proprietor of the *Buffalo Evening News*.

Mr. Butler began at the bottom as a newspaper man, and very early and rapidly climbed to the top. He secured control of the *Evening News* and soon made it one of the most, if not the most, widely circulated, influential, and prosperous papers of western New York. Personally and through his paper he was for many years my devoted friend. To those he loved he had an unbounded fidelity and generosity. He possessed keen insight and kept thoroughly abreast of public affairs, and was a journalist of high order.

It was my privilege to know Charles A. Dana very well. I first met him when he was on the *New York Tribune* and closely allied with Horace Greeley. He made the *New York Sun* one of the brightest, most original, and most quoted newspapers in the United States. His high culture, wonderful command of English, and refined taste gave to the *Sun* a high literary position, and at the same time his audacity and criticism made him a terror to those with whom he differed, and his editorials the delight of a reader.

Personally Mr. Dana was one of the most attractive and charming of men. As assistant secretary of war during Lincoln's administration he came in intimate contact with all the public men of that period, and as a journalist his study was invaded and he received most graciously men and women famous in every department of intellectual activity. His reminiscences were wonderful and his characterizations remarkable. He might have published an autobiography of rare value and interest.

When the elder James Gordon Bennett died the newspaper world recognized the loss of one of the most remarkable and successful of journalists and publishers. His son had won reputation in the field of sport, but his contemporaries doubted his ability to maintain, much less increase, the sphere of the *New York Herald*. But young Bennett soon displayed rare originality and enterprise. He made his newspaper one of national and international importance. By bringing out an edition in Paris he conferred a boon upon Americans abroad. For many years there was little news from the United States in foreign newspapers, but Americans crazy for news from home found it in the Paris edition of the *New York Herald*.

Mr. Bennett was a good friend of mine for half a century. He was delightful company, with his grasp of world affairs and picturesque presentation of them. A President of the United States who wished to change the hostile attitude of the *Herald* towards his administration and himself asked me to interview Mr. Bennett. The editor was courteous, frank, but implacable. But some time afterwards the *Herald* became a cordial supporter of the president. The interview and its subsequent result displayed a characteristic of Bennett. He would not recognize that his judgment or action could be influenced, but his mind was so open and fair that when convinced that he was wrong he would in his own way and at his own time do the right thing.

Mr. Bennett did me once an essential service. It was at the time when I was a candidate for re-election to the United States Senate. I cabled him in Paris and asked that he would look into the situation through his confidential friends, reporters, and employees, and if he found the situation warranted his taking a position to do so. Of course the *Herald* was an independent and not a party journal and rarely took sides. But not long afterwards, editorially and reportorially, the emphatic endorsement of the *Herald* came, and positive prediction of success, and were of great help. He was one of my groomsmen at my wedding in 1901.

Among the thousands of stories which appear and disappear like butterflies, it is a curious question what vogue and circulation one can have over others. By an accident I broke one of the tendons of my heel and was laid up in my house for some time, unable to walk. The surgeon fixed the bandage in place by a liquid cement, which soon solidified like glass.

Julian Ralph, a brilliant young newspaper reporter, wrote a long story in the *New York Sun* about a wonderful glass leg, which had been substituted for the natural one and did better work. The story had universal publication not only in the United States but abroad, and interested scientists and surgeons. My mail grew to enormous proportions with letters from eager inquirers wanting to know all the particulars. The multitude of unfortunates who had lost their legs or were dissatisfied with artificial ones wrote to me to find out where these wonderful glass legs could be obtained.

JOURNALISTS AND FINANCIERS

The glass-leg story nearly killed me, but it gave Ralph such a reputation that he was advanced to positions both at home and abroad, where his literary genius and imagination won him many honors, but he never repeated his success with my glass leg.

I suppose, having been more than half a century in close contact with matters of interest to the public, or officially in positions where I was a party to corporate activities or movements which might affect the market, I have been more interviewed than any one living and seen more reporters. No reporter has ever abused the confidence I reposed in him. He always appreciated what I told him, even to the verge of indiscretion, and knew what was proper for him to reveal and what was not for publication. In the critical situations which often occurred in railway controversies, this cordial relationship with reporters was of great value in getting our side before the public.

One reporter especially, a space writer, managed for a long time to get from me one-half to a column nearly every day, sometimes appearing as interviews and at other times under the general phrase: "It has been learned from a reliable source."

I recall a personal incident out of the ordinary. I was awakened one stormy winter night by a reporter who was well known to me, a young man of unusual promise. I met him in dressing gown and slippers in my library. There he told me that his wife was ill, and to save her life the doctor informed him that he must send her West to a sanitarium.

"I have no money," he continued, "and will not borrow nor beg, but you must give me a story I can sell."

We discussed various matters which a paper would

like to have, and finally I gave him a veiled but still intelligible story, which we both knew the papers were anxious to get. He told me afterwards that he sold the interview for enough to meet his present needs and his wife's journey. Some time after he entered Wall Street and made a success.

I have known well nearly all the phenomenally successful business men of my time. It is a popular idea that luck or chance had much to do with their careers. This is a mistake. All of them had vision not possessed by their fellows. They could see opportunities where others took the opposite view, and they had the courage of their convictions. They had standards of their own which they lived up to, and these standards differed widely from the ethical ideas of the majority.

Russell Sage, who died in the eighties, had to his credit an estate which amounted to a million dollars for every year of his life. He was not always a money-maker, but he was educated in the art as a banker, was diverted into politics, elected to Congress, and became a very useful member of that body. When politics changed and he was defeated, he came to New York and speedily found his place among the survival of the fittest. Mr. Sage could see before others when bad times would be followed by better ones and securities rise in value, and he also saw before others when disasters would follow prosperity. Relying upon his own judgment, he became a winner, whether the market went up or down.

I met Mr. Sage frequently and enjoyed his quick and keen appreciation of men and things. Of course, I knew that he cultivated me because he thought that from my official position he might possibly gain information which he could use in the market. I never received any points from him, or acted upon any of his suggestions. I think the reason why I am in excellent health and vigor in my eighty-eighth year is largely due to the fact that the points or suggestions of great financiers never interested me. I have known thousands who were ruined by them. The financier who gives advice may mean well as to the securities which he confidentially tells about, but an unexpected financial storm may make all prophecies worthless, except for those who have capital to tide it over.

One of the most certain opportunities for fortune was to buy Erie after Commodore Vanderbilt had secured every share and the shorts were selling wildly what they did not have and could not get. An issue of fraudulent and unauthorized stock suddenly flooded the market and thousands were ruined.

As Mr. Sage's wealth increased, the generous and public-spirited impulses which were his underlying characteristics, became entirely obscured by the craze for accumulation. His wife, to whom he was devotedly attached, was, fortunately for him, one of the most generous, philanthropic, and open-minded of women. She was most loyal to the Emma Willard School at Troy, N. Y., from which she graduated. Mrs. Sage wrote me a note at one time, saying: "Mr. Sage has promised to build and give to the Willard School a building which will cost one hundred and fifty thousand dollars, and he wants you to deliver the address at the laying of the corner-stone." I wrote back that I was so overwhelmed with business that it was impossible for me to accept. She replied: "Russell vows he will not give a dollar unless you promise to deliver the address. This is the first effort in his life at liberal giving. Don't you think he ought to be encouraged?" I immediately accepted.

Mrs. Sage was a *Mayflower* descendant. At one of the anniversaries of the society she invited me to be her guest and to make a speech. She had quite a large company at her table. When the champagne corks began to explode all around us, she asked what I thought she ought to do. I answered: "As the rest are doing." Mr. Sage vigorously protested that it was a useless and wasteful expense. However, Mrs. Sage gave the order, and Mr. Sage and two objecting gentlemen at the table were the most liberal participants of her hospitality. The inspiration of the phizz brought Sage to his feet, though not on the programme. He talked until the committee of arrangements succeeded in persuading him that the company was entirely satisfied.

Jay Gould told me a story of Sage. The market had gone against him and left him under great obligations. The shock sent Sage to bed, and he declared that he was ruined. Mr. Gould and Mr. Cyrus W. Field became alarmed for his life and went to see him. They found him broken-hearted and in a serious condition. Gould said to him: "Sage, I will assume all your obligations and give you so many millions of dollars if you will transfer to me the cash you have in banks, trust, and safe-deposit companies, and you keep all your securities and all your real estate." The proposition proved to be the shock necessary to counteract Sage's panic and save his life. He shouted, "I won't do it!" jumped out of bed, met all his obligations, and turned defeat into a victory.

Sage could not personally give away his fortune, so he left it all, without reservations, to his wife. The world is better and happier by her wise distribution of his accumulations.

One of Mr. Sage's lawyers was an intimate friend of mine, and he told me this story. Sage had been persuaded by his fellow directors in the Western Union Telegraph Company to make a will. As he was attorney for the company, Sage came to him to draw it. The lawyer began to write: "I, Russell Sage, of the City of New York, being of sound mind" . . . (Sage interrupted him in his quick way by saying, "Nobody will dispute that") "do publish and devise this to be my last will and testament as follows: First, I direct that all my just debts will be paid." . . . ("That's easy," said Sage, "because I haven't any.") "Also my funeral expenses and testamentary expenses." ("Make the funeral simple. I dislike display and ostentation, and especially at funerals," said Sage.) "Next," said the lawyer, "I give, devise, and bequeath" . . . (Sage shouted: "I won't do it! I won't do it!" and left the office.)

Nothing is so absorbing as the life of Wall Street. It is more abused, misunderstood, and envied than any place in the country. Wall Street means that the sharpest wits from every State in the Union, and many from South America and Europe, are competing with each other for the great prizes of development, exploitation, and speculation.

I remember a Wall Street man who was of wide reading and high culture, and yet devoted to both the operation and romance of the Street. He rushed into my room one night at Lucerne in Switzerland and said: "I have just arrived from Greece and have been out of touch with everything for six weeks. I am starving for news of the market."

I enlightened him as well as I could, and then he remarked: "Do you know, while in Athens our little party stood on the Acropolis admiring the Parthenon, and one enthusiastic Grecian exclaimed: 'There is the wonder of the world. For three thousand years its perfection has baffled and taught the genius of every generation. It can be copied, but never yet has been equalled. Surely, notwithstanding your love of New York and devotion to the ticker, you must admire the Parthenon.' I answered him, if I could be transported at this minute to Fifth Avenue and Broadway and could look up at the Flatiron Building, I would give the money to rebuild that old ruin."

While conditions in the United States because of the World War are serious, they are so much better than in the years following the close of the Civil War, that we who have had the double experience can be greatly encouraged. Then one-half of our country was devastated, its industries destroyed or paralyzed; now we are united and stronger in every way. Then we had a paper currency and dangerous inflation, now we are on a gold standard and with an excellent banking and credit system. The development of our resources and wonderful inventions and discoveries since the Civil War place us in the foremost position to enter upon world commerce when all other nations have come as they must to co-operation and co-ordination upon lines for the preservation of peace and the promotion of international prosperity.

Many incidents personal to me occur which illustrate conditions following the close of the war between the States. I knew very rich men who became paupers, and strong institutions and corporations which went into bankruptcy. I was in the Union Trust Company of New York when our financial circles were stunned by the closing of its doors following the closing of the New York Stock Exchange.

One of my clients was Mr. Augustus Schell, one of the ablest and most successful of financiers and public-spirited citizens. The panic had ruined him. As we left the Union Trust Company he had his hat over his eyes, and his head was buried in the upturned collar of his coat. When opposite Trinity Church he said: "Mr. Depew, after being a rich man for over forty years, it is hard to walk under a poor man's hat." When we reached the Astor House a complete reaction had occurred. His collar was turned down, his head came out confident and aggressive, his hat had shifted to the back of his head and on a rakish angle. The hopeful citizen fairly shouted: "Mr. Depew, the world has always gone around, it always will go around." He managed with the aid of Commodore Vanderbilt to save his assets from sacrifice. In a few years they recovered normal value, and Mr. Schell with his fortune intact found "the world had gone around" and he was on top again.

I have often felt the inspiration of Mr. Schell's confidence and hope and have frequently lifted others out of the depths of despair by narrating the story and emphasizing the motto "The world always has gone around, the world always will go around."

Illustrating the wild speculative spirit of one financial period, and the eagerness with which speculators grasped at what they thought points, the following is one of my many experiences.

Running down Wall Street one day because I was late for an important meeting, a well-known speculator stopped me and shouted: "What about Erie?" I threw him off impatiently, saying, "Damn Erie!" and rushed on. I knew nothing about Erie speculatively and was irritated at being still further delayed for my meeting.

Sometime afterwards I received a note from him in which he said: "I never can be grateful enough for the point you gave me on Erie. I made on it the biggest kill of my life."

I have often had quoted to me that sentence about "fortune comes to one but once, and if rejected never returns." When I declined President Harrison's offer of the position of secretary of state in his Cabinet, I had on my desk a large number of telegrams signed by distinguished names and having only that quotation. There are many instances in the lives of successful men where they have repeatedly declined Dame Fortune's gift, and yet she has finally rewarded them according to their desires. I am inclined to think that the fickle lady is not always mortally offended by a refusal. I believe that there come in the life of almost everybody several opportunities, and few have the judgment to wisely decide what to decline and what to accept.

In 1876 Gardner Hubbard was an officer in the United States railway mail service. As this connection with the government was one of my duties in the New York Central, we met frequently. One day he said to me: "My son-in-law, Professor Bell, has made what I think a wonderful invention. It is a talking telegraph. We need ten thousand dollars, and I will give you one-sixth interest for that amount of money."

I was very much impressed with Mr. Hubbard's description of the possibilities of Professor Bell's invention. Before accepting, however, I called upon my friend, Mr.

William Orton, president of the Western Union Telegraph Company. Orton had the reputation of being the best-informed and most accomplished electrical expert in the country. He said to me: "There is nothing in this patent whatever, nor is there anything in the scheme itself, except as a toy. If the device has any value, the Western Union owns a prior patent called the Gray's patent, which makes the Bell device worthless."

When I returned to Mr. Hubbard he again convinced me, and I would have made the investment, except that Mr. Orton called at my house that night and said to me: "I know you cannot afford to lose ten thousand dollars, which you certainly will if you put it in the Bell patent. I have been so worried about it that contrary to my usual custom I have come, if possible, to make you promise to drop it." This I did.

The Bell patent was sustained in the courts against the Gray, and the telephone system became immediately popular and profitable. It spread rapidly all over the country, and innumerable local companies were organized, and with large interests for the privilege to the parent company.

I rarely ever part with anything, and I may say that principle has brought me so many losses and so many gains that I am as yet, in my eighty-eighth year, undecided whether it is a good rule or not. However, if I had accepted my friend Mr. Hubbard's offer, it would have changed my whole course of life. With the dividends, year after year, and the increasing capital, I would have netted by to-day at least one hundred million dollars. I have no regrets. I know my make-up, with its love for the social side of life and its good things, and for good times with good fellows. I also know the necessity of activity and work. I am quite sure that with this necessity removed and ambition smothered, I should long ago have been in my grave and lost many years of a life which has been full of happiness and satisfaction.

My great weakness has been indorsing notes. A friend comes and appeals to you. If you are of a sympathetic nature and very fond of him, if you have no money to loan him, it is so easy to put your name on the back of a note. Of course, it is rarely paid at maturity, because your friend's judgment was wrong, and so the note is renewed and the amount increased. When finally you wake up to the fact that if you do not stop you are certain to be ruined, your friend fails when the notes mature, and you have lost the results of many years of thrift and saving, and also your friend.

I declined to marry until I had fifty thousand dollars. The happy day arrived, and I felt the fortunes of my family secure. My father-in-law and his son became embarrassed in their business, and, naturally, I indorsed their notes. A few years afterwards my father-in-law died, his business went bankrupt, I lost my fifty thousand dollars and found myself considerably in debt. As an illustration of my dear mother's belief that all misfortunes are sent for one's good, it so happened that the necessity of meeting and recovering from this disaster led to extraordinary exertions, which probably, except under the necessity, I never would have made. The efforts were successful.

Horace Greeley never could resist an appeal to indorse a note. They were hardly ever paid, and Mr. Greeley was the loser. I met him one time, soon after he had been a very severe sufferer from his mistaken kindness. He said to me with great emphasis: "Chauncey, I want you to do me a great favor. I want you to have a bill put through the legislature, and see that it becomes a law, making it a felony and punishable with imprisonment for life for any man to put his name by way of indorsement on the back of another man's paper."

Dear old Greeley kept the practice up until he died, and the law was never passed. There was one instance, which I had something to do with, where the father of a young man, through whom Mr. Greeley lost a great deal of money by indorsing notes, arranged after Mr. Greeley's death to have the full amount of the loss paid to Mr. Greeley's heirs.

XXIII

ACTORS AND MEN OF LETTERS

One cannot speak of Sir Henry Irving without recalling the wonderful charm and genius of his leading lady, Ellen Terry. She never failed to be worthy of sharing in Irving's triumphs. Her remarkable adaptability to the different characters and grasp of their characteristics made her one of the best exemplifiers of Shakespeare of her time. She was equally good in the great characters of other playwrights. Her effectiveness was increased by an unusual ability to shed tears and natural tears. I was invited behind the scenes one evening when she had produced a great impression upon the audience in a very pathetic part. I asked her how she did what no one else was ever able to do.

"Why," she answered, "it is so simple when you are portraying ——" (mentioning the character), "and such a crisis arises in your life, that naturally and immediately the tears begin to flow." So they did when she was illustrating the part for me.

It was a privilege to hear Edwin Booth as Richelieu and Hamlet. I have witnessed all the great actors of my time in those characters. None of them equalled Edwin Booth. For a number of years he was exiled from the stage because his brother, Wilkes Booth, was the assassin of President Lincoln. His admirers in New York felt that it was a misfortune for dramatic art that so consummate an artist should be compelled to remain in private life. In order to break the spell they united and invited Mr. Booth to give a performance at one of the larger theatres. The house, of course, was carefully ticketed with selected guests.

The older Mrs. John Jacob Astor, a most accomplished and cultured lady and one of the acknowledged leaders of New York society, gave Mr. Booth a dinner in honor of the event. The gathering represented the most eminent talent of New York in every department of the great city's activities. Of course, Mr. Booth had the seat of honor at the right of the hostess. On the left was a distinguished man who had been a Cabinet minister and a diplomat. During the dinner Mr. Evarts said to me: "I have known so and so all our active lives. He has been a great success in everything he has undertaken, and the wonder of it is that if there was ever an opportunity for him to say or do the wrong thing he never failed."

Curiously enough, the conversation at the dinner ran upon men outliving their usefulness and reputations. Several instances were cited where a man from the height of his fame gradually lived on and lived out his reputation. Whereupon our diplomat, with his fatal facility for saying the wrong thing, broke in by remarking in a strident voice: "The most remarkable instance of a man dying at the right time for his reputation was Abraham Lincoln." Then he went on to explain how he would have probably lost his place in history through the mistakes of his second term. Nobody heard anything beyond the words "Abraham Lincoln." Fortunately for the evening and the great embarrassment of Mr. Booth, the tact of Mrs. Astor changed the subject and saved the occasion.

Of all my actor friends none was more delightful either

on the stage or in private life than Joseph Jefferson. He early appealed to me because of his Rip Van Winkle. I was always devoted to Washington Irving and to the Hudson River. All the traditions which have given a romantic touch to different points on that river came from Irving's pen. In the days of my youth the influence of Irving upon those who were fortunate enough to have been born upon the banks of the Hudson was very great in every way.

As I met Jefferson quite frequently, I recall two of his many charming stories. He said he thought at one time that it would be a fine idea to play Rip Van Winkle at the village of Catskill, around which place was located the story of his hero. His manager selected the supernumeraries from among the farmer boys of the neighborhood. At the point of the play where Rip wakes up and finds the lively ghosts of the *Hendrick Hudson* crew playing bowls in the mountains, he says to each one of them, who all look and are dressed alike: "Are you his brother?"

"No," answered the young farmer who impersonated one of the ghosts, "Mr. Jefferson, I never saw one of these people before." As ghosts are supposed to be silent, this interruption nearly broke up the performance.

During the Spanish-American War I came on the same train with Mr. Jefferson from Washington. The interest all over the country at that time was the remarkable victory of Admiral Dewey over the Spanish fleet in the harbor of Manila. People wondered how Dewey could sink every Spanish ship and never be hit once himself. Jefferson said in his quaint way: "Everybody, including the secretary of the navy and several admirals, asked me how that could have happened. I told them the problem might be one which naval officers could not solve, but it was very simple for an actor. The failure of the Spanish admiral was entirely due to his not having rehearsed. Success is impossible without frequent rehearsals."

Returning for a moment to Washington Irving, one of the most interesting spots near New York is his old home, Wolfert's Roost, and also the old church at Tarrytown where he worshipped, and of which he was an officer for many years. The ivy which partially covers the church was given to Mr. Irving by Sir Walter Scott, from Abbotsford. At the time when the most famous of British reviewers wrote, "Whoever read or reads an American book?" Sir Walter Scott announced the merit and coming fame of Washington Irving. But, as Rip Van Winkle says, when he returns after twenty years to his native village, "how soon we are forgot."

There was a dinner given in New York to celebrate the hundredth anniversary of Washington Irving's birth. I was one of the speakers. In an adjoining room was a company of young and very successful brokers, whose triumphs in the market were the envy of speculative America. While I was speaking they came into the room. When I had finished, the host at the brokers' dinner called me out and said: "We were much interested in your speech. This Irving you talked about must be a remarkable man. What is the dinner about?"

I answered him that it was in celebration of the hundredth anniversary of the birth of Washington Irving.

"Well," he said, pointing to an old gentleman who had sat beside me on the speakers' platform, "it is astonishing how vigorous he looks at that advanced age."

It was my good fortune to hear often and know personally Richard Mansfield. He was very successful in many parts, but his presentation of Doctor Jekyll and Mr. Hyde was wonderful. At one time he came to me with a well-thought-out scheme for a national theatre in New York, which would be amply endowed and be the home of the highest art in the dramatic profession, and at the same time the finest school in the world. He wanted me to draw together a committee of the leading financiers of the country and, if possible, to impress them so that they would subscribe the millions necessary for carrying out his ideas. I was too busy a man to undertake so difficult a project.

One of the colored porters in the Wagner Palace Car service, who was always with me on my tours of inspection over the railroad, told me an amusing story of Mr. Mansfield's devotion to his art. He was acting as porter on Mansfield's car, when he was making a tour of the country. This porter was an exceedingly intelligent man. He appreciated Mansfield's achievements and played up to his humor in using him as a foil while always acting. When they were in a station William never left the car, but remained on guard for the protection of its valuable contents.

After a play at Kansas City Mansfield came into the car very late and said: "William, where is my manager?"

"Gone to bed, sir, and so have the other members of the company," answered William.

Then in his most impressive way Mansfield said: "William, they fear me. By the way, were you down at the depot to-night when the audience from the suburbs were returning to take their trains home?"

"Yes, sir," answered William, though he had not been out of the car.

"Did you hear any remarks made about my play?"

"Yes, sir."

"Can you give me an instance?"

"Certainly," replied William; "one gentleman remarked that he had been to the theatre all his life, but that your acting to-night was the most rotten thing he had ever heard or seen."

"William," shouted Mansfield, "get my Winchester and find that man."

So Mansfield and William went out among the crowds, and when William saw a big, aggressive-looking fellow whom he thought would stand up and fight, he said: "There he is."

Mansfield immediately walked up to the man, covered him with his rifle, and shouted: "Hold up your hands, you wretch, and take back immediately the insulting remark you made about my play and acting and apologize."

The man said: "Why, Mr. Mansfield, somebody has been lying to you about me. Your performance to-night was the best thing I ever saw in my life."

"Thank you," said Mansfield, shouldering his rifle, and added in the most tragic tone: "William, lead the way back to the car."

Among the most interesting memories of old New Yorkers are the suppers which Mr. Augustin Daly gave on the one hundredth performance of a play. Like everything which Daly did, the entertainment was perfect. A frequent and honored guest on these occasions was General Sherman, who was then retired from the army and living in New York. Sherman was a military genius but a great deal more. He was one of the most sensitive men in the world. Of course, the attraction at these suppers was Miss Rehan, Daly's leading lady. Her personal charm, her velvet voice, and her inimitable coquetry made every guest anxious to be her escort. She would pretend to be in doubt whether to accept the attentions of General Sherman or myself, but when the general began to display considerable irritation, the brow of Mars was smoothed and the warrior made happy by a gracious acceptance of his arm.

On one of these occasions I heard the best after-dinner speech of my life. The speaker was one of the most beautiful women in the country, Miss Fanny Davenport. That night she seemed to be inspired, and her eloquence, her wit, her humor, her sparkling genius, together with the impression of her amazing beauty were very effective.

P. T. Barnum, the showman, was a many-sided and interesting character. I saw much of him as he rented from the Harlem Railroad Company the Madison Square Garden, year after year. Barnum never has had an equal in his profession and was an excellent business man. In a broad way he was a man of affairs, and with his vast fund of anecdotes and reminiscences very entertaining socially.

An Englishman of note came to me with a letter of introduction, and I asked him whom he would like to meet. He said: "I think principally Mr. P. T. Barnum." I told this to Barnum, who knew all about him, and said: "As a gentleman, he knows how to meet me." When I informed my English friend, he expressed his regret and at once sent Barnum his card and an invitation for dinner. At the dinner Barnum easily carried off the honors with his wonderful fund of unusual adventures.

My first contact with Mr. Barnum occurred many years before, when I was a boy up in Peekskill. At that time he had a museum and a show in a building at the corner of Ann Street and Broadway, opposite the old Astor House. By skilful advertising he kept people all over the country expecting something new and wonderful and anxious to visit his show.

There had been an Indian massacre on the Western plains. The particulars filled the newspapers and led to action by the government in retaliation. Barnum advertised that he had succeeded in securing the Sioux warriors whom the government had captured, and who would re-enact every day the bloody battle in which they were victorious.

It was one of the hottest afternoons in August when I appeared there from the country. The Indians were on the top floor, under the roof. The performance was sufficiently blood-curdling to satisfy the most exacting reader of a penny-dreadful. After the performance, when the audience left, I was too fascinated to go, and remained in the rear of the hall, gazing at these dreadful savages. One of them took off his head-gear, dropped his tomahawk and scalping-knife, and said in the broadest Irish to his neighbor: "Moike, if this weather don't cool off, I will be nothing but a grease spot." This was among the many illusions which have been dissipated for me in a long life. Notwithstanding that, I still have faith, and dearly love to be fooled, but not to have the fraud exposed.

Wyndham, the celebrated English actor, was playing one night in New York. He saw me in the audience and sent a messenger inviting me to meet him at supper at the Hoffman House. After the theatre I went to the hotel, asked at the desk in what room the theatrical supper was, and found there Bronson Howard, the playwright, and some others. I told them the object of my search, and Mr. Howard said: "You are just in the right place."

The English actor came later, and also a large number of other guests. I was very much surprised and flattered at being made practically the guest of honor. In the usual and inevitable after-dinner speeches I joined enthusiastically in the prospects of American contributions to drama and especially the genius of Bronson Howard.

It developed afterwards that the actors' dinner was set for several nights later, and that I was not invited or expected to this entertainment, which was given by Mr. Howard to my actor friend, but by concert of action between the playwright and the actor, the whole affair was turned into a dinner to me. Broadway was delighted at the joke, but did not have a better time over it than I did.

The supper parties after the play which Wyndham gave were among the most enjoyable entertainments in London. His guests represented the best in society, government, art, literature, and drama. His dining-room was built and furnished like the cabin of a yacht and the illusion was so complete that sensitive guests said they felt the rolling of the sea.

One evening he said to me: "I expect a countryman of yours, a charming fellow, but, poor devil, he has only one hundred and fifty thousand pounds a year. He is still young, and all the managing mothers are after him for their daughters."

When the prosperous American with an income of

three-quarters of a million arrived, I needed no introduction. I knew him very well and about his affairs. He had culture, was widely travelled, was both musical and artistic, and his fad was intimacy with prominent people. His dinners were perfection and invitations were eagerly sought. On the plea of delicate health he remained a brief period in the height of the season in London and Paris. But during those few weeks he gave all that could be done by lavish wealth and perfect taste, and did it on an income of twenty thousand dollars a year.

Most of the year he lived modestly in the mountains of Switzerland or in Eastern travel, but was a welcome guest of the most important people in many lands. The only deceit about it, if it was a deceit, was that he never went out of his way to deny his vast wealth, and as he never asked for anything there was no occasion to publish his inventory. The pursuing mothers and daughters never succeeded, before his flight, in leading him far enough to ask for a show-down.

Many times during my visits to Europe I have been besieged to know the income of a countryman. On account of the belief over there in the generality of enormous American fortunes, it is not difficult to create the impression of immense wealth. While the man would have to make a statement and give references, the lady's story is seldom questioned. I have known some hundreds and thousands of dollars become in the credulous eyes of suitors as many millions, and a few millions become multimillions. In several instances the statements of the lady were accepted as she achieved her ambition.

For a tired man who has grown stale with years of unremitting work I know of no relief and recuperation equal to taking a steamer and crossing the ocean to Europe. I did this for a few weeks in midsummer many times and always with splendid and most refreshing results. With fortunate introductions, I became acquainted with many of the leading men of other countries, and this was a liberal education.

There is invariably a concert for charities to help the sailors on every ship. I had many amusing experiences in presiding on these occasions. I remember once we were having a rough night of it, and one of our artists, a famous singer, who had made a successful tour of the United States, was a little woman and her husband a giant. He came to me during the performance and said: "My wife is awfully seasick, but she wants to sing, and I want her to. In the intervals of her illness she is in pretty good shape for a little while. If you will stop everything when you see me coming in with her, she will do her part."

I saw him rushing into the saloon with his wife in his arms, and immediately announced her for the next number. She made a great triumph, but at the proper moment was caught up by her husband and carried again to the deck. He said to me afterwards: "My wife was not at her best last night, because there is a peculiarity about seasickness and singers; the lower notes in which she is most effective are not at such times available or in working order."

Augustin Daly did a great service to the theatre by his wonderful genius as a manager. He discovered talent everywhere and encouraged it. He trained his company with the skill of a master, and produced in his theatres here and in London a series of wonderful plays. He did not permit his artists to take part, as a rule, in these concerts on the ship, but it so happened that on one occasion we celebrated the Fourth of July. I went to Mr. Daly and asked him if he would not as an American take the management of the whole celebration. This appealed to him, and he selected the best talent from his company. Among them was Ada Rehan. I knew Miss Rehan when she was in the stock company at Albany in her early days. With Mr. Daly, who discovered her, she soon developed into a star of the first magnitude.

Mr. Daly persisted on my presiding and introducing the artists, and also delivering the Fourth of July oration. The celebration was so successful in the saloon that Mr. Daly had it repeated the next night in the second cabin, and the night after that in the steerage. The steerage did its best, and was clothed in the finest things which it was carrying back to astonish the old folks in the old country, and its enthusiasm was greater, if possible, than the welcome which had greeted the artists among the first and second cabin passengers.

After Miss Rehan had recited her part and been encored and encored, I found her in tears. I said: "Miss Rehan, your triumph has been so great that it should be laughter."

"Yes," she said, "but it is so pathetic to see these people who probably never before met with the highest art."

Among the many eminent English men of letters who at one time came to the United States was Matthew Arnold. The American lecture promoters were active in securing these gentlemen, and the American audiences were most appreciative. Many came with letters of introduction to me.

Mr. Arnold was a great poet, critic, and writer, and

an eminent professor at Oxford University and well known to our people. His first address was at Chickering Hall to a crowded house. Beyond the first few rows no one could hear him. Explaining this he said to me: "My trouble is that my lectures at the university are given in small halls and to limited audiences." I advised him that before going any farther he should secure an elocutionist and accustom himself to large halls, otherwise his tour would be a disappointment.

He gave me an amusing account of his instructor selecting Chickering Hall, where he had failed, and making him repeat his lecture, while the instructor kept a progressive movement farther and farther from the stage until he reached the rear seats, when he said he was satisfied. It is a tribute to the versatility of this great author that he learned his lesson so well that his subsequent lectures in different parts of the country were very successful.

Once Mr. Arnold said to me: "The lectures which I have prepared are for university audiences, to which I am accustomed. I have asked my American manager to put me only in university towns, but I wish you would look over my engagements."

Having done this, I remarked: "Managers are looking for large and profitable audiences. There is no university or college in any of these towns, though one of them has an inebriate home and another an insane asylum. However, both of these cities have a cultured population. Your noisiest and probably most appreciative audience will be at the one which is a large railroad terminal. Our railroad people are up-to-date."

I saw Mr. Arnold on his return from his tour. The description he gave of his adventures was very picturesque and the income had been exceedingly satisfactory and beyond expectation.

Describing the peculiarities of the chairmen who introduced him, he mentioned one of them who said: "Ladies and gentlemen, next week we will have in our course the most famous magician there is in the world, and the week after, I am happy to say, we shall be honored by the presence of a great opera-singer, a wonderful artist. For this evening it is my pleasure to introduce to you that distinguished English journalist, Mr. Edwin Arnold." Mr. Arnold began his lecture with a vigorous denial that he was Edwin Arnold, whom I judged he did not consider in his class.

Mr. Arnold received in New York and in the larger cities which he visited the highest social attention from the leading families. I met him several times and found that he never could be reconciled to our two most famous dishes—terrapin and canvasback duck—the duck nearly raw. He said indignantly to one hostess, who chided him for his neglect of the canvasback: "Madam, when your ancestors left England two hundred and fifty years ago, the English of that time were accustomed to eat their meat raw; now they cook it." To which the lady answered: "I am not familiar with the customs of my ancestors, but I know that I pay my chef, who cooked the duck, three hundred dollars a month."

We were all very fond of Thackeray. He did not have the general popularity of Charles Dickens, nor did he possess Dickens's dramatic power, but he had a large and enthusiastic following among our people. It was an intellectual treat and revelation to listen to him. That wonderful head of his seemed to be an enormous and perennial fountain of wit and wisdom.

They had a good story of him at the Century Club, which is our Athenæum, that when taken there after a lecture by his friends they gave him the usual Centurion supper of those days: saddlerock oysters. The saddlerock of that time was nearly as large as a dinner-plate. Thackeray said to his host: "What do I do with this animal?"

The host answered: "We Americans swallow them whole."

Thackeray, always equal to the demand of American hospitality, closed his eyes and swallowed the oyster, and the oyster went down. When he had recovered he remarked: "I feel as if I had swallowed a live baby."

We have been excited at different times to an absorbing extent by the stories of explorers. None were more generally read than the adventures of the famous missionary, David Livingstone, in Africa. When Livingstone was lost the whole world saluted Henry M. Stanley as he started upon his famous journey to find him. Stanley's adventures, his perils and escapes, had their final success in finding Livingstone. The story enraptured and thrilled every one. The British Government knighted him, and when he returned to the United States he was Sir Henry Stanley. He was accompanied by his wife, a beautiful and accomplished woman, and received with open arms.

I met Sir Henry many times at private and public entertainments and found him always most interesting. The Lotos Club gave him one of its most famous dinners, famous to those invited and to those who spoke.

It was arranged that he should begin his lecture tour of the United States in New York. At the request of Sir Henry and his committee I presided and introduced him at the Metropolitan Opera House. The great auditorium was crowded to suffocation and the audience one of the finest and most sympathetic.

We knew little at that time of Central Africa and its people, and the curiosity was intense to hear from Sir Henry a personal and intimate account of his wonderful discoveries and experiences. He thought that as his African life was so familiar to him, it must be the same to everybody else. As a result, instead of a thriller he gave a commonplace talk on some literary subject which bored the audience and cast a cloud over a lecture tour which promised to be one of the most successful. Of course Sir Henry's effort disappointed his audience the more because their indifference and indignation depressed him, and he did not do justice to himself or the uninteresting subject which he had selected. He never again made the same mistake, and the tour was highly remunerative.

For nearly a generation there was no subject which so interested the American people as the adventures of explorers. I met many of them, eulogized them in speeches at banquets given in their honor. The people everywhere were open-eyed, open-eared, and open-mouthed in their welcome and eagerness to hear them.

It is a commentary upon the fickleness of popular favor that the time was so short before these universal favorites dropped out of popular attention and recollection.

XXIV

SOCIETIES AND PUBLIC BANQUETS

The most unique experience in my life has been the dinners given to me by the Montauk Club of Brooklyn on my birthday. The Montauk is a social club of high standing, whose members are of professional and business life and different political and religious faiths.

Thirty years ago Mr. Charles A. Moore was president of the club. He was a prominent manufacturer and a gentleman of wide influence in political and social circles. Mr. McKinley offered him the position of secretary of the navy, which Mr. Moore declined. He came to me one day with a committee from the club, and said: "The Montauk wishes to celebrate your birthday. We know that it is on the 23d of April, and that you have two distinguished colleagues who also have the 23d as their birthday—Shakespeare and St. George. We do not care to include them, but desire only to celebrate yours."

The club has continued these celebrations for thirty years by an annual dinner. The ceremonial of the occasion is a reception, then dinner, and, after an introduction by the president, a speech by myself. To make a new speech every year which will be of interest to those present and those who read it, is not easy.

These festivities had a fortunate beginning. In thinking over what I should talk about at the first dinner, I decided to get some fun out of the municipality of Brooklyn by a picturesque description of its municipal conditions. It was charged in the newspapers that

SOCIETIES AND PUBLIC BANQUETS 375

there had been serious graft in some public improvements which had been condoned by the authorities and excused by an act of the legislature. It had also been charged that the Common Council had been giving away valuable franchises to their favorites. Of course, this presented a fine field of contrast between ancient and modern times. In ancient times grateful citizens erected statues to eminent men who had deserved well of their country in military or civic life, but Brooklyn had improved upon the ancient model through the grant of public utilities. The speech caused a riot after the dinner as to its propriety, many taking the ground that it was a criticism, and, therefore, inappropriate to the occasion. However, the affair illustrated a common experience of mine that unexpected results will sometimes flow from a bit of humor, if the humor has concealed in it a stick of dynamite.

The Brooklyn pulpit, which is the most progressive in the world, took the matter up and aroused public discussion on municipal affairs. The result was the formation of a committee of one hundred citizens to investigate municipal conditions. They found that while the mayor and some other officials were high-toned and admirable officers, yet the general administration of the city government had in the course of years become so bad that there should be a general reformation. The reform movement was successful; it spread over to New York and there again succeeded, and the movement for municipal reform became general in the country.

The next anniversary dinner attracted an audience larger than the capacity of the club, and every one of the thirty has been an eminent success. For many years the affair has received wide publicity in the United

States, and has sometimes been reported in foreign newspapers. I remember being in London with the late Lieutenant-Governor Woodruff, when we saw these head-lines at a news-stand on the Strand: "Speech by Chauncey Depew at his birthday dinner at the Montauk Club, Brooklyn." During this nearly third of a century the membership of the club has changed, sons have succeeded fathers and new members have been admitted, but the celebration seems to grow in interest.

During the last fourteen years the president of the club has been Mr. William H. English. He has done so much for the organization in every way that the members would like to have him as their executive officer for life. Mr. English is a splendid type of the American who is eminently successful in his chosen career, and yet has outside interest for the benefit of the public. Modest to a degree and avoiding publicity, he nevertheless is the motive power of many movements progressive and charitable.

Twenty-four years ago a company of public-spirited women in the city of Des Moines, Iowa, organized a club. They named it after me. For nearly a quarter of a century it has been an important factor in the civic life of Des Moines. It has with courage, intelligence, and independence done excellent work. At the time of its organization there were few if any such organizations in the country, and it may claim the position of pioneer in women's activity in public affairs.

Happily free from the internal difficulties and disputes which so often wreck voluntary associations, the Chauncey Depew Club is stronger than ever. It looks forward with confidence to a successful celebration of its quarter of a century.

SOCIETIES AND PUBLIC BANQUETS 377

I have never been able to visit the club, but have had with it frequent and most agreeable correspondence. It always remembers my birthday in the most gratifying way. I am grateful to its members for bestowing upon me one of the most pleasurable compliments of my life.

A public dinner is a fine form of testimonial. I have had many in my life, celebrating other things than my birthday. One of the most notable was given me by the citizens of Chicago in recognition of my efforts to make their great Columbian exhibition a success. Justice John M. Harlan presided, and distinguished men were present from different parts of the country and representing great interests. Probably the speech which excited the most comment was a radical attack of Andrew Carnegie on the government of Great Britain, in submitting to the authority of a king or a queen. Canada was represented by some of the high officials of that self-governing colony. The Canadians are more loyal to the English form of government than the English themselves. My peppery Scotch friend aroused a Canadian official, who returned his assault with vigor and interest.

It is a very valuable experience for an American to attend the annual banquet of the American Chamber of Commerce in Paris. The French Government recognizes the affair by having a company of their most picturesquely uniformed soldiers standing guard both inside and outside the hall. The highest officials of the French Government always attend and make speeches. The American Ambassador replies in a speech partly in English, and, if he is sufficiently equipped, partly in French. General Horace Porter and Henry White were equally happy both in their native language and in that of the

French. The French statesmen, however, were so fond of Myron T. Herrick that they apparently not only grasped his cordiality but understood perfectly his eloquence. The honor has several times been assigned to me of making the American speech in unadulterated American. The French may not have understood, but with their quick apprehension the applause or laughter of the Americans was instantly succeeded by equal manifestations on the part of the French.

Among the many things which we have inherited from our English ancestry are public dinners and after-dinner speeches. The public dinner is of importance in Great Britain and utilized for every occasion. It is to the government the platform where the ministers can lay frankly before the country matters which they could not develop in the House of Commons. Through the dinner speech they open the way and arouse public attention for measures which they intend to propose to Parliament, and in this way bring the pressure of public opinion to their support.

In the same way every guild and trade have their festive functions with serious purpose, and so have religious, philanthropic, economic, and sociological movements. We have gone quite far in this direction, but have not perfected the system as they have on the other side. I have been making after-dinner speeches for sixty years to all sorts and conditions of people, and on almost every conceivable subject. I have found these occasions of great value because under the good-fellowship of the occasion an unpopular truth can be sugarcoated with humor and received with applause, while in the processes of digestion the next day it is working with the audience and through the press in the way the pill

SOCIETIES AND PUBLIC BANQUETS

was intended. A popular audience will forgive almost anything with which they do not agree, if the humorous way in which it is put tickles their risibilities.

Mr. Gladstone was very fine at the lord mayor's dinner at Guild Hall, where the prime minister develops his policies. So it was with Lord Salisbury and Balfour, but the prince of after-dinner speakers in England is Lord Rosebery. He has the humor, the wit, and the artistic touch which fascinates and enraptures his audience.

I have met in our country all the men of my time who have won fame in this branch of public address. The most remarkable in effectiveness and inspiration was Henry Ward Beecher. A banquet was always a success if it could have among its speakers William M. Evarts, Joseph H. Choate, James S. Brady, Judge John R. Brady, General Horace Porter, or Robert G. Ingersoll.

After General Grant settled in New York he was frequently a guest at public dinners and always produced an impression by simple, direct, and effective oratory.

General Sherman, on the other hand, was an orator as well as a fighter. He never seemed to be prepared, but out of the occasion would give soldierly, graphic, and picturesque presentations of thought and description.

Not to have heard on these occasions Robert G. Ingersoll was to have missed being for the evening under the spell of a magician. I have been frequently asked if I could remember occasions of this kind which were of more than ordinary interest.

After-dinner oratory, while most attractive at the time, is evanescent, but some incidents are interesting in memory. At the time of Queen Victoria's jubilee I was present where a representative of Canada was called upon for a speech. With the exception of the Canadian and myself the hosts and guests were all English. My Canadian friend enlarged upon the wonders of his country. A statement of its marvels did not seem sufficient for him unless it was augmented by comparisons with other countries to the glory of Canada, and so he compared Canada with the United States. Canada had better and more enduring institutions, she had a more virile, intelligent, and progressive population, and she had protected herself, as the United States did not, against undesirable immigration, and in everything which constituted an up-to-date, progressive, healthy, and hopeful commonwealth she was far in advance of the United States.

I was called upon immediately afterwards and said I would agree with the distinguished gentleman from Canada that in one thing at least Canada was superior to the United States, and it was that she had far more land, but it was mostly ice. I regret to remember that my Canadian friend lost his temper.

One of the historical dinners of New York, which no one will forget who was there, was just after the close of the Civil War, or, as my dear old friend, Colonel Watterson, called it, "The War between the States." The principal guests were General Sherman and Henry W. Grady of Atlanta, Ga. General Sherman, in his speech, described the triumphant return of the Union Army to Washington, its review by the President, and then its officers and men returning to private life and resuming their activities and industries as citizens. It was a word-picture of wonderful and startling picturesqueness and power and stirred an audience, composed largely of veterans who had been participants both in the battles and in the parades, to the highest degree of enthusiasm. Mr. Grady followed. He was a young man with rare oratorical gifts. He described the return of the Confederate soldiers to their homes after the surrender at Appomattox. They had been four years fighting and marching. They were ragged and poor. They returned to homes and farms, many of which had been devastated. They had no capital, and rarely animals or farming utensils necessary to begin again. But with superb courage, not only on their own part but with the assistance of their wives, sisters, and daughters, they made the desert land flourish and resurrected the country.

This remarkable description of Grady, which I only outline, came as a counterpart to the triumphant epic of General Sherman. The effect was electric, and beyond almost any that have ever occurred in New York or anywhere, and Grady sprang into international fame.

Joseph H. Choate was a most dangerous fellow speaker to his associates who spoke before him. I had with him many encounters during fifty years, and many times enjoyed being the sufferer by his wit and humor. On one occasion Choate won the honors of the evening by an unexpected attack. There is a village in western New York which is named after me. The enterprising inhabitants, boring for what might be under the surface of their ground, discovered natural gas. According to American fashion, they immediately organized a company and issued a prospectus for the sale of the stock. The prospectus fell into the hands of Mr. Choate. With great glee he read it and then with emphasis the name of the company: "The Depew Natural Gas Company, Limited," and waving the prospectus at me shouted: "Why limited?"

There have been two occasions in Mr. Choate's after-dinner speeches much commented upon both in this country and abroad. As I was present on both evenings, it seems the facts ought to be accurately stated. The annual dinner of the "Friendly Sons of St. Patrick" occurred during one of the years when the Home Rule question was most acute in England and actively discussed here. At the same time our Irish fellow citizens, with their talent for public life, had captured all the offices in New York City. They had the mayor, the majority of the Board of Aldermen, and a large majority of the judges. When Mr. Choate spoke he took up the Home Rule question, and, without indicating his own views, said substantially: "We Yankees used to be able to govern ourselves, but you Irish have come here and taken the government away from us. You have our entire city administration in your hands, and you do with us as you like. We are deprived of Home Rule. Now what you are clamoring for both at home and abroad is Home Rule for Ireland. With such demonstrated ability in capturing the greatest city on the western continent, and one of the greatest in the world, why don't you go back to Ireland and make, as you would, Home Rule there a success?"

I was called a few minutes afterwards to a conference of the leading Irishmen present. I was an honorary member of that society, and they were in a high state of indignation. The more radical thought that Mr. Choate's speech should be resented at once. However, those who appreciated its humor averted hostile action, but Mr. Choate was never invited to an Irish banquet again.

The second historical occasion was when the Scotch

SOCIETIES AND PUBLIC BANQUETS

honored their patron saint, St. Andrew. The attendance was greater than ever before, and the interest more intense because the Earl of Aberdeen was present. The earl was at that time Governor-General of Canada, but to the Scotchmen he was much more than that, because he was the chief of the Clan Gordon. The earl came to the dinner in full Highland costume. Lady Aberdeen and the ladies of the vice-regal court were in the gallery. I sat next to the earl and Choate sat next to me. Choate said: "Chauncey, are Aberdeen's legs bare?" I looked under the table-cloth and discovered that they were naturally so because of his costume. I answered: "Choate, they are."

I thought nothing of it until Choate began his speech, in which he said: "I was not fully informed by the committee of the importance of the occasion. I did not know that the Earl of Aberdeen was to be here as a guest of honor. I was especially and unfortunately ignorant that he was coming in the full panoply of his great office as chief of Clan Gordon. If I had known that I would have left my trousers at home."

Aberdeen enjoyed it, the ladies in the gallery were amused, but the Scotch were mad, and Choate lost invitations to future Scotch dinners.

Few appreciate the lure of the metropolis. It attracts the successful to win greater success with its larger opportunities. It has resistless charm with the ambitious and the enterprising. New York, with its suburbs, which are really a part of itself, is the largest city in the world. It is the only true cosmopolitan one. It has more Irish than any city in Ireland, more Germans and Italians than any except the largest cities in Germany or Italy. It has more Southerners than are gathered in any place in any Southern State, and the same is true of Westerners and those from the Pacific coast and New England, except in Chicago, San Francisco, or Boston. There is also a large contingent from the West Indies, South America, and Canada.

The people who make up the guests at a great dinner are the survival of the fittest of these various settlers in New York. While thousands fail and go back home or drop by the way, these men have made their way by superior ability, foresight, and adaptability through the fierce competitions of the great city. They are unusually keen-witted and alert. For the evening of the banquet they leave behind their business and its cares and are bent on being entertained, amused, and instructed. They are a most catholic audience, broad-minded, hospitable, and friendly to ideas whether they are in accord with them or not, providing they are well presented. There is one thing they will not submit to, and that is being bored.

These functions are usually over by midnight, and rarely last so long; while out in the country and in other towns, it is no unusual thing to have a dinner with speeches run along until the early hours of the next morning. While public men, politicians, and aspiring orators seek their opportunities upon this platform in New York, few succeed and many fail. It is difficult for a stranger to grasp the situation and adapt himself at once to its atmosphere. I have narrated in preceding pages some remarkable successes, and will give a few instances of very able and distinguished men who lost touch of their audiences.

One of the ablest men in the Senate was Senator John T. Morgan, of Alabama. I was fond of him personally

SOCIETIES AND PUBLIC BANQUETS 385

and admired greatly his many and varied talents. He was a most industrious and admirable legislator, and a debater of rare influence. He was a master of correct and scholarly English, and one of the very few who never went to the reporters' room to correct his speeches. As they were always perfect, he let them stand as they were delivered.

Senator Morgan was a great card on a famous occasion among the many well-known men who were also to speak. Senator Elihu Root presided with his usual distinction. Senator Morgan had a prepared speech which he read. It was unusually long, but very good. On account of his reputation the audience was, for such an audience, wonderfully patient and frequent and enthusiastic in its applause. Mistaking his favorable reception, Senator Morgan, after he had finished the manuscript, started in for an extended talk. After the hour had grown to nearly two, the audience became impatient, and the senator, again mistaking its temper, thought they had become hostile and announced that at many times and many places he had been met with opposition, but that he could not be put down or silenced. Mr. Root did the best he could to keep the peace, but the audience, who were anxious to hear the other speakers, gave up hope and began to leave, with the result that midnight saw an empty hall with a presiding officer and an orator.

At another great political dinner I sat beside Governor Oglesby, of Illinois. He was famous as a war governor and as a speaker. There were six speakers on the daïs, of whom I was one. Happily, my turn came early. The governor said to me: "How much of the gospel can these tenderfeet stand?" "Well, Governor," I answered, "there are six speakers to-night, and the audience will not allow the maximum of time occupied to be more than thirty minutes. Any one who exceeds that will lose his crowd and, worse than that, he may be killed by the eloquent gentlemen who are bursting with impatience to get the floor, and who are to follow him."

"Why," said the governor, "I don't see how any one can get started in thirty minutes."

"Well," I cautioned, "please do not be too long."

When the midnight hour struck the hall was again practically empty, the governor in the full tide of his speech, which evidently would require about three hours, and the chairman declared the meeting adjourned.

Senator Foraker, of Ohio, who was one of the appointed speakers, told me the next morning that at the Fifth Avenue Hotel, where he was stopping, he was just getting into bed when the governor burst into his room and fairly shouted: "Foraker, no wonder New York is almost always wrong. You saw to-night that it would not listen to the truth. Now I want to tell you what I intended to say." He was shouting with impassioned eloquence, his voice rising until, through the open windows, it reached Madison Square Park, when the watchman burst in and said: "Sir, the guests in this hotel will not stand that any longer, but if you must finish your speech I will take you out in the park."

During Cleveland's administration one of the New York banquets became a national affair. The principal speaker was the secretary of the interior, Lucius Q. C. Lamar, who afterwards became United States senator and justice of the Supreme Court. Mr. Lamar was one of the ablest and most cultured men in public life, and a fine orator. I was called upon so late that it was impossible to follow any longer the serious discussions of the evening, and what the management and the audience wanted from me was some fun.

Lamar, with his Johnsonian periods and the lofty style of Edmund Burke, furnished an opportunity for a little pleasantry. He came to me, when I had finished, in great alarm and said: "My appearance here is not an ordinary one and does not permit humor. I am secretary of the interior, and the representative of the president and his administration. My speech is really the message of the president to the whole country, and I wish you would remedy any impression which the country might otherwise receive from your humor."

This I was very glad to do, but it was an instance of which I have met many, of a very distinguished and brilliant gentleman taking himself too seriously. At another rather solemn function of this kind I performed the same at the request of the management, but with another protest from the orator and his enmity.

In reminiscing, after he retired from the presidency, Mr. Cleveland spoke to me of his great respect and admiration for Mr. Lamar. Cleveland's speeches were always short. His talent was for compression and concentration, and he could not understand the necessity for an effort of great length. He told me that while Justice Lamar was secretary of the interior he came to him one day and said: "Mr. President, I have accepted an invitation to deliver an address in the South, and as your administration may be held responsible for what I say, I wish you would read it over and make any corrections or suggestions."

Mr. Cleveland said the speech was extraordinarily

long though very good, and when he returned it to Secretary Lamar he said to him: "That speech will take at least three hours to deliver. A Northern audience would never submit to over an hour. Don't you think you had better cut it down?" The secretary replied: "No, Mr. President; a Southern audience expects three hours, and would be better satisfied with five."

Justice Miller, one of the ablest of the judges of the Supreme Court at that time, was the principal speaker on another occasion. He was ponderous to a degree, and almost equalled in the emphasis of his utterances what was once said of Daniel Webster, that every word weighed twelve pounds. I followed him. The Attorney-General of the United States, who went back to Washington the next day with Justice Miller, told me that as soon as they had got on the train the justice commenced to complain that I had wholly misunderstood his speech, and that no exaggeration of interpretation would warrant what I said. The judge saw no humor in my little effort to relieve the situation, and took it as a reply of opposing counsel. He said that the justice took it up from another phase after leaving Philadelphia, and resumed his explanation from another angle as to what he meant after they reached Baltimore. When the train arrived at its destination and they separated in the Washington station, the justice turned to the attorney-general and said: "Damn Depew! Good-night."

Such are the perils of one who good-naturedly yields to the importunities of a committee of management who fear the failure with their audience of their entertainment.

The great dinners of New York are the Chamber of Commerce, which is a national function, as were also for a long time, during the presidency of Mr. Choate, those of the New England Society. The annual banquets of the Irish, Scotch, English, Welsh, Holland, St. Nicholas, and the French, are also most interesting, and sometimes by reason of the presence of a national or international figure, assume great importance. The dinner which the Pilgrims Society tenders to the British ambassador gives him an opportunity, without the formalities and conventions of his office, of speaking his mind both to the United States and to his own people.

The annual banquets of the State societies are now assuming greater importance. Each State has thousands of men who have been or still are citizens, but who live in New York. Those dinners attract the leading politicians of their several States. It is a platform for the ambitious to be president and sometimes succeeds.

Garfield made a great impression at one of these State dinners, so did Foraker, and at the last dinner of the Ohio Society the star was Senator Warren G. Harding. On one occasion, when McKinley and Garfield were present, in the course of my speech I made a remark which has since been adopted as a sort of motto by the Buckeye State. Ohio, I think, has passed Virginia as a mother of presidents. It is remarkable that the candidates of both great parties are now of that State. I said in the closing of my speech, alluding to the distinguished guests and their prospects: "Some men have greatness thrust upon them, some are born great, and some are born in Ohio."

One of the greatest effects produced by a speech was by Henry Ward Beecher at an annual dinner of the Friendly Sons of St. Patrick. At the time, the Home Rule question was more than ordinarily acute and

Fenianism was rabid. While Mr. Beecher had great influence upon his audience, his audience had equal influence upon him. As he enlarged upon the wrongs of Ireland the responses became more enthusiastic and finally positively savage. This stirred the orator up till he gave the wildest approval to direct action and revolution, with corresponding cheers from the diners, standing and cheering. Mr. Beecher was explaining that speech for about a year afterwards. I was a speaker on the same platform.

Mr. Beecher always arrived late, and everybody thought it was to get the applause as he came in, but he explained to me that it was due to his method of preparation. He said his mind would not work freely until three hours after he had eaten. Many speakers have told me the same thing. He said when he had a speech to make at night, whether it was at a dinner or elsewhere, that he took his dinner in the middle of the day, and then a glass of milk and crackers at five o'clock, with nothing afterwards. Then in the evening his mind was perfectly clear and under absolute control.

The Lotos Club has been for fifty years to New York what the Savage Club is to London. It attracts as its guests the most eminent men of letters who visit this country. Its entertainments are always successful. For twenty-nine years it had for its president Mr. Frank R. Lawrence, a gentleman with a genius for introducing distinguished strangers with most felicitous speeches, and a committee who selected with wonderful judgment the other speakers of the evening. A successor to Mr. Lawrence, and of equal merit, has been found in Chester S. Lord, now president of the Lotos Club. Mr. Lord was for more than a third of a century managing editor of the *New York Sun,* and is now chancellor of the University of the State of New York.

I remember one occasion where the most tactful man who ever appeared before his audience slipped his trolley, and that was Bishop Potter. The bishop was a remarkably fine preacher and an unusually attractive public speaker and past master of all the social amenities of life. The guest of the evening was the famous Canon Kingsley, author of "Hypatia" and other works at that time universally popular. The canon had the largest and reddest nose one ever saw. The bishop, among the pleasantries of his introduction, alluded to this headlight of religion and literature. The canon fell from grace and never forgave the bishop.

On Lotos nights I have heard at their best Lord Houghton, statesman and poet, Mark Twain, Stanley the explorer, and I consider it one of the distinctions as well as pleasures of my life to have been a speaker at the Lotos on more occasions than any one else during the last half century.

In Mr. Joseph Pulitzer's early struggles with his paper, the *New York World,* the editorial columns frequently had very severe attacks on Mr. William H. Vanderbilt and the New York Central Railroad. They were part, of course, of attacks upon monopoly. I was frequently included in these criticisms.

The Lotos Club gave a famous dinner to George Augustus Sala, the English writer and journalist. I found myself seated beside Mr. Pulitzer, whom I had never met. When I was called upon to speak I introduced, in what I had to say about the distinguished guest, this bit of audacity. I said substantially, in addition to Mr. Sala: "We have with us to-night a great journalist who comes to the metropolis from the wild and woolly West. After he had purchased the *World* he came to me and said, 'Chauncey Depew, I have a scheme, which I am sure will benefit both of us. Everybody is envious of the prestige of the New York Central and the wealth of Mr. Vanderbilt. You are known as his principal adviser. Now, if in my general hostility to monopoly I include Mr. Vanderbilt and the New York Central as principal offenders, I must include you, because you are the champion in your official relationship of the corporation and of its policies and activities. I do not want you to have any feeling against me because of this. The policy will secure for the *World* everybody who is not a stockholder in the New York Central, or does not possess millions of money. When Mr. Vanderbilt finds that you are attacked, he is a gentleman and broad-minded enough to compensate you and will grant to you both significant promotion and a large increase in salary.'" Then I added: "Well, gentlemen, I have only to say that Mr. Pulitzer's experiment has been eminently successful. He has made his newspaper a recognized power and a notable organ of public opinion; its fortunes are made and so are his, and, in regard to myself, all he predicted has come true, both in promotion and in enlargement of income." When I sat down Mr. Pulitzer grasped me by the hand and said: "Chauncey Depew, you are a mighty good fellow. I have been misinformed about you. You will have friendly treatment hereafter in any newspaper which I control."

The Gridiron Club of Washington, because of both its ability and genius and especially its national position, furnishes a wonderful platform for statesmen. Its genius in creating caricatures and fake pageants of current political situations at the capital and its public men is most remarkable. The president always attends, and most of the Cabinet and justices of the Supreme Court. The ambassadors and representatives of the leading governments represented in Washington are guests, and so are the best-known senators and representatives of the time. The motto of the club is "Reporters are never present. Ladies always present." Though the association is made up entirely of reporters, the secrecy is so well kept that the speakers are unusually frank.

There was a famous contest one night there, however, between President Roosevelt and Senator Foraker, who at the time were intensely antagonistic, which can never be forgotten by those present. There was a delightful interplay between William J. Bryan and President Roosevelt, when Bryan charged the president with stealing all his policies and ideas.

If the speaker grasped the peculiarities of his audience and its temperament, his task was at once the most difficult and the most delightful, and my friend, Mr. Arthur Dunn, has performed most useful service in embalming a portion of Gridiron history in his volume, "Gridiron Nights."

Pierpont Morgan, the greatest of American bankers, was much more than a banker. He had a wonderful collection in his library and elsewhere of rare books and works of art. He was always delightful on the social side. He was very much pleased when he was elected president of the New England Society. The annual dinner that year was a remarkably brilliant affair. It was the largest in the history of the organization. The principal speaker was William Everett, son of the famous Edward Everett and himself a scholar of great acquirements and culture. His speech was another evidence of a very superior man mistaking his audience. He was principal of the Adams Academy, that great preparatory institution for Harvard University, and he had greatly enlarged its scope and usefulness.

Mr. Everett evidently thought that the guests of the New England Society of New York would be composed of men of letters, educators, and Harvard graduates. Instead of that, the audience before him were mainly bankers and successful business men whose Puritan characteristics had enabled them to win great success in the competitions in the great metropolis in every branch of business. They were out for a good time and little else.

Mr. Everett produced a ponderous mass of manuscript and began reading on the history of New England education and the influence upon it of the Cambridge School. He had more than an hour of material and lost his audience in fifteen minutes. No efforts of the chairman could bring them to attention, and finally the educator lost that control of himself which he was always teaching to the boys and threw his manuscript at the heads of the reporters. From their reports in their various newspapers the next day, they did not seem to have absorbed the speech by this original method.

Choate and I were both to speak, and Choate came first. As usual, he threw a brick at me. He mentioned that a reporter had come to him and said: "Mr. Choate, I have Depew's speech carefully prepared, with the applause and laughter already in. I want yours." Of course, no reporter had been to either of us. Mr. Choate had in his speech an unusual thing for him, a long piece of poetry. When my turn came to reply I said: "The reporter came to me, as Mr. Choate has said, and made the remark: 'I already have Choate's speech.

It has in it a good deal of poetry.' I asked the reporter: 'From what author is the poetry taken?' He answered: 'I do not know the author, but the poetry is so bad I think Choate has written it himself.'"

Mr. Choate told me a delightful story of his last interview with Mr. Evarts before he sailed for Europe to take up his ambassadorship at the Court of St. James. "I called," he said, "on Mr. Evarts to bid him good-by. He had been confined to his room by a fatal illness for a long time. 'Choate,' he said, 'I am delighted with your appointment. You eminently deserve it, and you are pre-eminently fit for the place. You have won the greatest distinction in our profession, and have harvested enough of its rewards to enable you to meet the financial responsibilities of this post without anxiety. You will have a most brilliant and useful career in diplomacy, but I fear I will never see you again.'"

Mr. Choate said: "Mr. Evarts, we have had a delightful partnership of over forty years, and when I retire from diplomacy and resume the practice of the law I am sure you and I will go on together again for many years in the same happy old way."

Evarts replied: "No, Choate, I fear that cannot be. When I think what a care I am to all my people, lying so helpless here, and that I can do nothing any more to repay their kindness, or to help in the world, I feel like the boy who wrote from school to his mother a letter of twenty pages, and then added after the end: 'P. S. Dear mother, please excuse my longevity.'"

Where one has a reputation as a speaker and is also known to oblige friends and to be hardly able to resist importunities, the demands upon him are very great. They are also sometimes original and unique.

At one time, the day before Christmas, a representative of the *New York World* came to see me and said: "We are going to give a dinner to-night to the tramps who gather between ten and eleven o'clock at the Vienna Restaurant, opposite the St. Denis Hotel, to receive the bread which the restaurant distributes at that hour." This line was there every night standing in the cold waiting their turn. I went down to the hotel, and a young man and young lady connected with the newspaper crossed the street and picked out from the line a hundred guests.

It was a remarkable assemblage. The dinner provided was a beautiful and an excellent one for Christmas. As I heard their stories, there was among them a representative of almost every department of American life. Some were temporarily and others permanently down and out. Every one of the learned professions was represented and many lines of business. The most of them were in this condition, because they had come to New York to make their way, and had struggled until their funds were exhausted, and then they were ashamed to return home and confess their failure.

I presided at this remarkable banquet and made not only one speech but several. By encouraging the guests we had several excellent addresses from preachers without pulpits, lawyers without clients, doctors without patients, engineers without jobs, teachers without schools, and travellers without funds. One man arose and said: "Chauncey Depew, the *World* has given us such an excellent dinner, and you have given us such a merry Christmas Eve, we would like to shake hands with you as we go out."

I had long learned the art of shaking hands with the

public. Many a candidate has had his hands crushed and been permanently hurt by the vise-like grip of an ardent admirer or a vicious opponent. I remember General Grant complaining of this, of how he suffered, and I told him of my discovery of grasping the hand first and dropping it quickly.

The people about me were looking at these men as they came along, to see if there was any possible danger. Toward the end of the procession one man said to me: "Chauncey Depew, I don't belong to this crowd. I am well enough off and can take care of myself. I am an anarchist. My business is to stir up unrest and discontent, and that brings me every night to mingle with the crowd waiting for their dole of bread from Fleischmann's bakery. You do more than any one else in the whole country to create good feeling and dispel unrest, and you have done a lot of it to-night. I made up my mind to kill you right here, but you are such an infernal good fellow that I have not the heart to do it, so here's my hand."

On one occasion I received an invitation to address a sociological society which was to meet at the house of one of the most famous entertainers in New York. My host said that Edward Atkinson, the well-known New England writer, philosopher, and sociologist, would address the meeting. When I arrived at the house I found Atkinson in despair. The audience were young ladies in full evening dress and young men in white vests, white neckties, and swallow-tails. There was also a band present. We were informed that this society had endeavored to mingle instruction with pleasure, and it really was a dancing club, but they had conceived the idea of having something serious and instructive before the ball.

Mr. Atkinson said to me: "What won me to come here is that in Boston we have a society of the same name. It is composed of very serious people who are engaged in settlement and sociological work. They are doing their best to improve the conditions of the young women and young men who are in clerical and other employment. I have delivered several addresses before that society, and before the audiences which they gather, on how to live comfortably and get married on the smallest possible margin. Now, for instance, for my lecture here to-night I have on a ready-made suit of clothes, for which I paid yesterday five dollars. In that large boiler there is a stove which I have invented. In the oven of the stove is beef and various vegetables, and to heat it is a kerosene lamp with a clockwork attached. A young man or a young woman, or a young married couple go to the market and buy the cheap cuts of beef, and then, according to my instructions, they put it in the stove with the vegetables, light the lamp, set the clockwork and go to their work. When they return at five, six, or seven o'clock they find a very excellent and very cheap dinner all ready to be served. Now, of what use is my five-dollar suit of clothes and my fifty-cent dinner for this crowd of butterflies?"

However, Mr. Atkinson and I made up our minds to talk to them as if they needed it or would need it some day or other, and they were polite enough to ask questions and pretend to enjoy it. I understand that afterwards at the midnight supper there was more champagne and more hilarity than at previous gatherings of this sociological club.

During one of our presidential campaigns some young men came up from the Bowery to see me. They said:

"We have a very hard time down in our district. The crowd is a tough one but intelligent, and we think would be receptive of the truth if they could hear it put to them in an attractive form. We will engage a large theatre attached to a Bowery beer saloon if you will come down and address the meeting. The novelty of your appearance will fill the theatre."

I knew there was considerable risk, and yet it was a great opportunity. I believe that in meeting a crowd of that sort one should appear as they expect him to look when addressing the best of audiences. These people are very proud, and they resent any attempt on your part to be what they know you are not, but that you are coming down to their level by assuming a character which you presume to be theirs. So I dressed with unusual care, and when I went on the platform a short-sleeved, short-haired genius in the theatre shouted: "Chauncey thinks he is in Carnegie Hall."

The famous Tim Sullivan, who was several times a state senator and congressman, and a mighty good fellow, was the leader of the Bowery and controlled its political actions. He came to see me and said: "I hope you will withdraw from that appointment. I do not want you to come down there. In the first place, I cannot protect you, and I don't think it is safe. In the second place, you are so well known and popular among our people that I am afraid you will produce an impression, and if you get away with it that will hurt our machine."

In the course of my speech a man arose whom I knew very well as a district leader, and who was frequently in my office, seeking positions for his constituents and other favors. That night he was in his shirt-sleeves among the boys. With the old volunteer fireman's swagger and the peculiar patois of that part of New York, he said: "Chauncey Depew, you have no business here. You are the president of the New York Central Railroad, ain't you, hey? You are a rich man, ain't you, hey? We are poor boys. You don't know us and can't teach us anything. You had better get out while you can."

My reply was this: "My friend, I want a little talk with you. I began life very much as you did. Nobody helped me. I was a country boy and my capital was this head," and I slapped it, "these legs," and I slapped them, "these hands," and I slapped them, "and by using them as best I could I have become just what you say I am and have got where you will never arrive."

A shirt-sleeved citizen jumped up from the audience and shouted: "Go ahead, Chauncey, you're a peach." That characterization of a peach went into the newspapers and was attached to me wherever I appeared for many years afterwards, not only in this country but abroad. It even found a place in the slang column of the great dictionaries of the English language. The result of the meeting, however, was a free discussion in the Bowery, and for the first time in its history that particular district was carried by the Republicans.

After their triumph in the election I gave a dinner in the Union League Club to the captains of the election districts. There were about a hundred of them. The district captains were all in their usual business suits, and were as sharp, keen, intelligent, and up-to-date young men as one could wish to meet. The club members whom I had invited to meet my guests were, of course, in conventional evening dress. The novelty of the occasion was so enjoyed by them that they indulged

SOCIETIES AND PUBLIC BANQUETS 401

with more than usual liberality in the fluids and fizz and became very hilarious. Not one of the district captains touched a drop of wine.

While the club members were a little frightened at the idea of these East-siders coming, my guests understood and met every convention of the occasion before, during, and after dinner, as if it was an accustomed social function with them. The half dozen who made speeches showed a grasp of the political questions of the hour and an ability to put their views before an audience which was an exhibition of a high order of intelligence and self-culture.

In selecting a few out-of-the-way occasions which were also most interesting and instructive, I recall one with a society which prided itself upon its absence of narrowness and its freedom of thought and discussion. The speakers were most critical of all that is generally accepted and believed. Professor John Fiske, the historian, was the most famous man present, and very critical of the Bible. My good mother had brought me up on the Bible and instilled in me the deepest reverence for the good book. The criticism of the professor stirred me to a rejoinder. I, of course, was in no way equal to meeting him, with his vast erudition and scholarly accomplishments. I could only give what the Bible critic would regard as valueless, a sledge-hammer expression of faith. Somebody took the speech down. Doctor John Hall, the famous preacher and for many years pastor of the Fifth Avenue Presbyterian Church, told me that the Bible and the church societies in England had put the speech into a leaflet, and were distributing many millions of them in the British Isles.

It is singular what vogue and circulation a story of the

hour will receive. Usually these decorations of a speech die with the occasion. There was fierce rivalry when it was decided to celebrate the four hundredth anniversary of the landing of Columbus in America, between New York and Chicago, as to which should have the exhibition. Of course the Western orators were not modest in the claims which they made for the City by the Lakes. To dampen their ardor I embroidered the following story, which took wonderfully when told in my speech.

It was at the Eagle Hotel in Peekskill, at which it was said George Washington stopped many times as a guest during the Revolutionary War, where in respect to his memory they preserved the traditions of the Revolutionary period. At that time the bill of fare was not printed, but the waiter announced to the guest what would be served, if asked for. A Chicago citizen was dining at the hotel. He ordered each of the many items announced to him by the waiter. When he came to the deserts the waiter said: "We have mince-pie, apple-pie, pumpkin-pie, and custard-pie." The Chicago man ordered mince-pie, apple-pie, and pumpkin-pie. The disgusted waiter remarked: "What is the matter with the custard?" Alongside me sat a very well-known English gentleman of high rank, who had come to this country on a sort of missionary and evangelistic errand. Of course, he was as solemn as the task he had undertaken, which was to convert American sinners. He turned suddenly to me and, in a loud voice, asked: "What was the matter with the custard-pie?" The story travelled for years, was used for many purposes, was often murdered in the narration, but managed to survive, and was told to me as an original joke by one of the men I met at the convention last June in Chicago.

SOCIETIES AND PUBLIC BANQUETS 403

After Chicago received from Congress the appointment I did all I could to help the legislation and appropriations necessary. The result was that when I visited the city as an orator at the opening of the exhibition I was voted the freedom of the city, was given a great reception, and among other things reviewed the school children who paraded in my honor.

The Yale alumni of New York City had for many years an organization. In the early days the members met very infrequently at a dinner. This was a formal affair, and generally drew a large gathering, both of the local alumni and from the college and the country. These meetings were held at Delmonico's, then located in Fourteenth Street. The last was so phenomenally dull that there were no repetitions.

The speakers were called by classes, and the oldest in graduation had the platform. The result was disastrous. These old men all spoke too long, and it was an endless stream of platitudes and reminiscences of forgotten days until nearly morning. Then an inspiration of the chairman led him to say: "I think it might be well to have a word from the younger graduates."

There was a unanimous call for a well-known humorist named Styles. His humor was aided by a startling appearance of abundant red hair, an aggressive red mustache, and eyes which seemed to push his glasses off his nose. Many of the speakers, owing to the imperfection of the dental art in those days, indicated their false teeth by their trouble in keeping them in place, and the whistling it gave to their utterances. One venerable orator in his excitement dropped his into his tumbler in the midst of his address.

Styles said to this tired audience: "At this early hour

in the morning I will not attempt to speak, but I will tell a story. Down at Barnegat, N. J., where I live, our neighbors are very fond of apple-jack. One of them while in town had his jug filled, and on the way home saw a friend leaning over the gate and looking so thirsty that he stopped and handed over his jug with an offer of its hospitality. After sampling it the neighbor continued the gurgling as the jug rose higher and higher, until there was not a drop left in it. The indignant owner said: 'You infernal hog, why did you drink up all my apple-jack?' His friend answered: 'I beg your pardon, Job, but I could not bite off the tap, because I have lost all my teeth.'" The aptness of the story was the success of the evening.

Some years afterwards there was a meeting of the alumni to form a live association. Among those who participated in the organization were William Walter Phelps, afterwards member of Congress and minister to Austria; Judge Henry E. Howland; John Proctor Clarke, now chief justice of the Appellate Division; James R. Sheffield (several years later) now president of the Union League Club; and Isaac Bromley, one of the editors of the *New York Tribune,* one of the wittiest writers of his time, and many others who have since won dintinction. They elected me president, and I continued such by successive elections for ten years.

The association met once a month and had a serious paper read, speeches, a simple supper, and a social evening. These monthly gatherings became a feature and were widely reported in the press. We could rely upon one or more of the faculty, and there was always to be had an alumnus of national reputation from abroad. We had a formal annual dinner, which was more largely

SOCIETIES AND PUBLIC BANQUETS 405

attended than almost any function of the kind in the city, and, because of the variety and excellence of the speaking, always very enjoyable.

The Harvard and Princeton alumni also had an association at that time, with annual dinners, and it was customary for the officers of each of these organizations to be guests of the one which gave the dinner. The presidents of the colleges represented always came. Yale could rely upon President Dwight, Harvard upon President Eliot, and Princeton upon President McCosh.

Of course, the interchanges between the representatives of the different colleges were as exciting and aggressive as their football and baseball contests are to-day. I recall one occasion of more than usual interest. It was the Princeton dinner, and the outstanding figure of the occasion was that most successful and impressive of college executives, President McCosh. He spoke with a broad Scotch accent and was in every sense a literalist. Late in the evening Mr. Beaman, a very brilliant lawyer and partner of Evarts and Choate, who was president of the Harvard Alumni Association, said to me: "These proceedings are fearfully prosaic and highbrow. When you are called, you attack President McCosh, and I will defend him." So in the course of my remarks, which were highly complimentary to Princeton and its rapid growth under President McCosh, I spoke of its remarkable success in receiving gifts and legacies, which were then pouring into its treasury every few months, and were far beyond anything which came either to Yale or Harvard, though both were in great need. Then I hinted that possibly this flow of riches was due to the fact that President McCosh had such an hypnotic influence over the graduates of Princeton and their fathers, mothers, and wives that none of them felt there was a chance of a heavenly future unless Princeton was among the heirs.

Mr. Beaman was very indignant and with the continuing approval and applause of the venerable doctor made a furious attack upon me. His defense of the president was infinitely worse than my attack. He alleged that I had intimated that the doctor kept tab on sick alumni of wealth and their families, and at the critical moment there would be a sympathetic call from the doctor, and, while at the bedside he administered comfort and consolation, yet he made it plain to the patient that he could not hope for the opening of the pearly gates or the welcome of St. Peter unless Princeton was remembered. Then Beaman, in a fine burst of oratory, ascribed this wonderful prosperity not to any personal effort or appeal, but because the sons of Princeton felt such reverence and gratitude for their president that they were only too glad of an opportunity to contribute to the welfare of the institution.

The moment Beaman sat down the doctor arose, and with great intensity expressed his thanks and gratitude to the eloquent president of the Harvard alumni, and then shouted: "I never, never, never solicited a gift for Princeton from a dying man. I never, never, never sat by the bedside of a dying woman and held up the terrors of hell and the promises of heaven, according to the disposition she made of her estate. I never, never looked with unsympathetic and eager anticipation whenever any of our wealthy alumni appeared in ill health."

The doctor, however, retaliated subsequently. He invited me to deliver a lecture before the college, and entertained me most delightfully at his house. It was

SOCIETIES AND PUBLIC BANQUETS

a paid admission, and when I left in the morning he said: "I want to express to you on behalf of our college our thanks. We raised last evening through your lecture enough to fit our ball team for its coming contest with Yale." In that contest Princeton was triumphant.

The Yale Alumni Association subsequently evolved into the Yale Club of New York, which has in every way been phenomenally prosperous. It is a factor of national importance in supporting Yale and keeping alive everywhere appreciation and enthusiasm for and practice of Yale spirit.

My class of 1856 at Yale numbered ninety-seven on graduation. Only six of us survive. In these pages I have had a continuous class meeting. Very few, if any, of my associates in the New York Legislature of 1862 and 1863 are alive, and none of the State officers who served with me in the succeeding years. There is no one left in the service who was there when I became connected with the New York Central Railroad, and no executive officer in any railroad in the United States who held that position when I was elected and is still active.

It is the habit of age to dwell on the degeneracy of the times and lament the good old days and their superiority, but Yale is infinitely greater and broader than when I graduated sixty-five years ago. The New York Legislature and State executives are governing an empire compared with the problems which we had to solve fifty-nine years ago.

I believe in the necessity of leadership, and while recognizing a higher general average in public life, regret that the world crisis through which we have passed and which is not yet completed, has produced no Washington, Lincoln, or Roosevelt. I rejoice that President Harding, under the pressure of his unequalled responsibilities, is developing the highest qualities of leadership. It is an exquisite delight to visualize each administration from 1856 and to have had considerable intimacy with the leaders in government and the moulders of public opinion during sixty-five unusually laborious years.

Many who have given their reminiscences have kept close continuing diaries. From these voluminous records they have selected according to their judgment. As I have before said, I have no data and must rely on my memory. This faculty is not logical, its operations are not by years or periods, but its films unroll as they are moved by association of ideas and events.

It has been a most pleasurable task to bring back into my life these worthies of the past and to live over again events of greater or lesser importance. Sometimes an anecdote illumines a character more than a biography, and a personal incident helps an understanding of a period more than its formal history.

Life has had for me immeasurable charms. I recognize at all times there has been granted to me the loving care and guidance of God. My sorrows have been alleviated and lost their acuteness from a firm belief in closer reunion in eternity. My misfortunes, disappointments, and losses have been met and overcome by abundant proof of my mother's faith and teaching that they were the discipline of Providence for my own good, and if met in that spirit and with redoubled effort to redeem the apparent tragedy they would prove to be blessings. Such has been the case.

While new friends are not the same as old ones, yet I have found cheer and inspiration in the close communion with the young of succeeding generations. They have made and are making this a mighty good world for me.

INDEX

INDEX

Aberdeen, Earl of, 383
Adams, Charles Francis, 91, 191
Alden, 278, 279
Aldrich, Senator Nelson W., 180, 190
Alger, General Russell A., 219
Andrew, Governor, 333, 334
Andrews, Rufus C., 58, 59
Appleton, Colonel, 218, 219
Arnold, Matthew, 369-371
Arthur [Chief, Locomotive Brotherhood], 245
Arthur, Chester A., 101; Chapter IX, 116-123
Asquith, Mrs. Margot Tennent, 263
Astor, Mrs. John Jacob, 359
Athenæum Club, 307, 308
Atkinson, Edward, 397, 398

Bacon, Reverend Doctor, 16
Bacon, Senator, 175
Bailey, Senator Joseph W., 183
Balfour, Arthur J., 196
Barlow, General Francis C., 40
Barnum, P. T., 364, 365
Beaman, C. C., 405, 406
Beecher, Henry Ward, 313, 323-327, 379, 389, 390
Bell, Professor, 354, 355
Bennett, James Gordon, 345, 346
Beresford, Admiral Lord Charles, 279, 280
Beveridge, Senator Albert J., 183
Bigelow, John, 216
Bissell, C. M., 253, 254
Black, Governor Frank S., 160, 161, 218, 219
Blaine, James G., 85, 100, 121, 130, 134, 139; Chapter XII, 141-146; 266, 267, 285, 286
Bliss, William, 235
Booth, Edwin, 358, 359
Brady, Judge John T., 70
Brewer, Justice David J., 5
Brewer, Doctor James, 11

Bromley, Isaac, 404
Brotherhood of Locomotive Engineers, 245-248
Brown, Justice Henry Billings, 5
Brown, John Mason, 6
Brown, W. C., 250
Browning, Robert, 193-195
Bruce, General, 335-337
Bryan, William Jennings, 152, 153
Buckley, Doctor, 215, 216
Buffalo Evening News, 344
Burchard, Reverend Doctor, 144, 145
Burlingame, Anson, 43-45
Burroughs, John, 253
Burt, Silas W., 101
Butler, Edward H., 344
Butterfield, John, 53

Caldwell, D. W., 238
Callaway, Samuel R., 250
Callicot, T. C., 24-26
Carnegie, Andrew, 377
Carter, Senator, 180, 181, 187, 188
Cassatt, A. J., 237, 238
Cassini, Ambassador, 197, 198
Catherine of Russia, 197
Century Club, 372
Chamberlain, Joseph, 261, 262
Chase, Salmon P., 65-67, 106
Choate, Joseph H., 106, 200-202, 381-383, 394, 395
Churchill, Lord and Lady Randolph, 268, 269
Civil Service Association, 117
Clark, Erastus, 83
Clarke, Horace F., 330, 331
Clarke, Justice John Proctor, 404
Clarkson, James S., 135
Clay, Senator Clement C., 61
Clay, Henry, 139, 141
Clemens, Samuel, see Twain, Mark
Cleveland, Grover, Chapter X, 124-128; 285, 387
Coleridge, Lord Chief Justice, 206, 207

INDEX

Conkling, Senator Roscoe, 35; Chapter V, 75–86; 99, 100, 103, 111, 112, 120, 122, 123
Cook, Charles, 28
Coolidge, Vice-President Calvin, 177, 342
Cork, Lady, 291, 292
Cornell, Governor Alonzo B., 101, 218
Corwin, Thomas, 321, 322
Crane, Senator W. M., 183
Curtin, Governor Andrew G., 31, 32
Curtis, George William, 17, 70, 79–81, 318, 319
Czolgosz, Leon, 156

Daly, Augustin, 363, 368, 369
Daly, Judge Charles P., 70
Dana, Charles A., 344, 345
d'Aumale, Duke, 304–306
Davenport, Fanny, 364
Davies, Professor, 47
Davis, Senator Jeff., 184, 185
Davis, Jefferson, 62
Dawson, George, 119
Depew Club, 376, 377
Depew, Mrs. [mother of Chauncey M. Depew], 10, 11
Dickens, Charles, 11, 12
Dickinson, Daniel S., 60, 61, 333–335
Disraeli, Benjamin, 274, 303
Dix, John A., 95, 96
Dunn, Arthur, 393
Dwight, President Timothy, 8

Edward VII, 276, 278, 282–284, 287–290, 292, 293
Elkins, Stephen B., 138
English, William H., 376
Evarts, William M., Chapter VII, 99–106; 395
Everett, William, 393, 394

Farragut, Admiral, 63, 64
Farrar, Canon, 306, 307
Fenton, Governor Reuben E., 34, 35, 77, 84
Fink, Commissioner Albert, 234
Fisher, Lord John, 281
Fiske, Professor John, 401
Fitzgerald, General Louis, 218, 219
Flower, Roswell P., 220–224

Foraker, Senator Joseph B., 149, 183, 386, 389
Forney, John W., 32
Foster, John W., 139
Frye, Senator, 178–180

Ganson, John, 59
Garfield, James A., Chapter VIII, 107–115; 121, 317, 341, 389
Garrett, John W., 231, 232, 234, 239
Garrison, William Lloyd, 313
Gibbs, Frederick, 158, 159
Gillett, Speaker Frederick H., 342
Gladstone, 256–261, 263–266, 274, 299, 379
Gladstone, Mrs., 260
Gould, Jay, 350
Grady, Henry W., 380, 381
Grant, General Frederick D., 71, 72
Grant, General Ulysses S., 49–51; Chapter IV, 67–74; 75–77, 95, 99, 111, 277, 278, 379
Graves, 247
Greeley, Horace, 12, 23, 62, 63; Chapter VI, 87–98; 356, 357
Gridiron Club, 181, 182, 392, 393
Griscom, Clement A., 178, 179
Griswold, John A., 88
Grow, Galusha A., 34

Hadley, Professor, 7
Hale, Senator Eugene, 185
Hall, Doctor John, 401
Hancock, General, 107, 108
Hanna, Senator Mark, 147, 149, 150, 157, 168, 184
Harding, President Warren G., 177, 340–342, 389, 408
Harlem Railroad, 227, 229
Harrison, Benjamin, Chapter XI, 129–140
Hastings, Hugh J., 328, 329
Hay, John, 196, 197
Hayes, Rutherford B., Chapter VII, 99–106; 117, 125
Herrick, Ambassador Myron T., 311, 378
Hewitt, Abram S., 216, 217, 299–301
Hill, Governor David B., 219, 220
Hiscock, Senator Frank, 134
Hoar, Senator George F., 122, 181

INDEX

Hobart, Vice-President, 156
Homburg, 282, 283
Hopkins, Johns, 239
Hoppin, William J., 191, 192
Howard, Bronson, 366
Howland, Judge Henry E., 404
Hubbard, Gardner, 354
Hudson River Railroad, 226, 227, 229, 230
Hughes, Secretary Charles E., 339
Hughitt, Marvin, 254
Hurlburt, William H., 244
Husted, General James W., 137

Ingalls, Senator John J., 219
Ingalls, Melville E., 235, 236
Ingersoll, Colonel Robert G., 100, 309, 319-321, 379
Irving, Sir Henry, 301-303
Irving, Washington, 361
Ismay, J. Bruce, 276

James, General Thomas L., 84
Japan, 45
Jefferson, Joseph, 360
Jerome, Leonard, 268
Jerome, William, 268
Johnson [Secretary of State Committee], 119
Johnson, President Andrew, 46-50, 60, 61
Jones, George, 67, 68

Kernan, Senator Francis, 93
King, John, 239
Kingsley, Canon, 391
Knights of Labor, 246-248

Labouchère, Henry, 260, 261
Lamar, Lucius Q. C., 386-388
Larned, Professor, 7
Lawrence [of State Committee], 80, 81
Lawrence, Frank R., 390
Ledyard, Henry B., 235
Leighton, Sir Frederick, 303, 304
Leo XIII, 295-297
Liliuokalani, Queen, 279
Lincoln, Abraham, 27, 28; Chapter III, 52-66; 108, 114, 316, 317, 327
Lincoln, Robert T., 260, 261
Livingstone, David, 372

Lodge, Senator Henry Cabot, 183
Logan, General John A., 206
Lord, Chester S., 390
Lotus Club, 372, 390, 391
Lowden, Governor, 341
Lowell, James Russell, 191, 204, 205, 262, 263
Lucy, Sir Henry, 308, 309

McCosh, President James, 405
McCulloch, Secretary Hugh, 47, 48
McKinley, William, 137; Chapter XIII, 147-157; 164
MacVeagh, Attorney-General Wayne, 5, 6, 31, 120, 322, 323
Manchester, Duke of, 285, 286
Mansfield, Richard, 361-363
Mayer, Charles F., 239
Merritt, General Edwin A., 101
Merry del Val, Cardinal, 296
Miller, Justice, 388
Miller, Warner, 131
Montauk Club, 374-376
Moore, Charles H., 374
Morgan, Senator Edwin D., 20, 25
Morgan, Senator John T., 384, 385
Morgan, Pierpont, 241, 393
Morton, Governor Levi P., 147, 218, 220
Murphy, Thomas, 69

New York Central Railroad, Chapter XVIII, 225-255
New York Herald, 345, 346
New York Sun, 344
New York Times, 67, 68
New York Tribune, 93
New York World, 244, 391, 392, 396
Newell, John, 235
Newman, William H., 250
Nye, Senator James W., 73, 336, 337

Odell, Governor, 65
Oglesby, Governor, 385, 386
Olmstead, Professor, 8
Orton, William, 355

Peekskill Academy, 3, 4
Peekskill-on-the-Hudson, 3, 4, 225, 326, 402
Phelps, Edward J., 192, 193, 195

INDEX

Phelps, Mrs. Edward J., 195
Phelps, William Walter, 404
Philippe, Louis, 304, 305
Phillips, Wendell, 313-315
Platt, Senator Thomas C., 85, 112, 113, 129, 131, 134, 135, 160
Porter, General Horace, 377
Potter, Bishop, 391
Potter, William, 298
Priest, Major Enos, 253
Princeton University, 405-407
Proctor, Senator Redfield, 148, 271, 272
Pulitzer, Joseph, 244, 391, 392

Quay, Matthew, 107, 135

Ralph, Julian, 346, 347
Randolph, John, 318
Raymond, Henry J., 20-23, 331
Reed, John, 81
Rehan, Ada, 364, 369
Reid, Ambassador Whitelaw, 198-200
Richmond, Dean, 22, 35-37
Roberts, George B., 237, 238
Robertson, Senator William H., 60, 61, 112, 113
Robinson, Governor Lucius, 218
Roosevelt, Theodore, 156; Chapter XIV, 158-174; 176, 199
Root, Senator Elihu, 117, 156, 385
Rosebery, Lord, 257, 258, 267, 268, 286, 379
Rothschild, Baron Alfred, 269-271
Rothschild, Ferdinand, 195
Rutter, James H., 242

Sackville-West, Lord, 284, 285
Sage, Mr. and Mrs. Russell, 348-350
Salisbury, Lord, 298
Saratoga Conference, 231-234
Schell, Augustus, 353
Schurz, Carl, 91
Scott, Colonel Thomas A., 231, 232, 244
Scott, Sir Walter, 361
Selden, Henry R., 92
Seward, Secretary William H., 42, 43, 56, 57, 60, 61, 331, 332
Seymour, Governor Horatio, 17, 23, 27-29, 35, 36, 38, 41, 42, 64
Shafer, Senator, 36

Shah of Persia, 194, 195
Sheffield, James R., 404
Sheridan, General Philip, 30, 31, 71
Sherman, General, 50, 51, 63, 64, 379, 380
Sherman, James S., 175-177
Sherman, Secretary John, 101
Slocum, General Henry W., 40
Smith, Alfred H., 250
Spencer, Earl, 266
Spooner, Senator John C., 183
Spurgeon, Charles, 306, 307
Stanley, Sir Henry, 372, 373
Stanton, Edwin M., 53-55
Storrs, Emory, 120, 202-208
Sullivan, Tim, 399, 400
Sutherland, Duke of, 194, 195

Taft, Chief Justice William Howard, 174, 176, 177, 339
Terry, Ellen, 358
Thackeray, William Makepeace, 371, 372
Thatcher, Professor, 8
Thomas, E. B., 239
Thompson, Frank, 237
Thompson, Sir Henry, 272, 273
Thompson, Senator Jacob, 61
Thurston, John M., 167
Tilden, Governor Samuel J., 105, 209, 218
Tillinghast, 37, 38
Tillman, Senator Benjamin, 181-183
Tilton, Theodore, 326
Toucey, John M., 251, 252
Trunk Line Association, 241
Twain, Mark, 72, 291-295
Tweed, William M., 209
Twichell, Doctor Joseph, 291

Union League Club, 400, 401

Vallandigham, Clement L., 28, 29, 64
Van Buren, John, 41
Vance, Zebulon, 126
Vanderbilt, Commodore, 14, 37, 38, 91, 92, 97, 227-232, 234, 239
Vanderbilt, William H., 229, 240-244
Victor Emmanuel III, 298
Victoria, Queen, 273-279
Voorhees, F. W., 251

INDEX

Wadsworth, General James W., 23
Wagner, Senator Webster, 120
Waite, Chief Justice Morrison R., 106
Washburne, Congressman Elihu B., 54, 55, 63
Washington, George, 305, 402
Webb, H. Walter, 251
Webster, Daniel, 21, 22, 328–331
Weed, Thurlow, 19, 20, 23
Welles, Gideon, 56
Wellington, Duke of, 309
Wells, Edward, 14
West Shore Railroad, 242, 243
White, Andrew D., 5, 6, 78

White, Henry, 377
Whitman, Governor Charles S., 340, 341
William II, 173, 174, 276, 277
Wilson, Senator Henry, 332, 333
Wilson, President Woodrow, 158, 189
Wood, General Leonard, 341
Woolsey, President Theodore D., 6
Wyndham, 365, 366

Yale Alumni Association, 403, 404, 407
Yale University, 4–9, 313
Young, John Russell, 88

E664.D4 D39
Depew, Chauncey M. (c.1
100105 000
My memories of eighty years, b

3 9310 00026496 8
GOSHEN COLLEGE-GOOD LIBRARY